RESET

RESET

Moving Korean Culture Forward

Sun Segura

ISBN: 1539936562
ISBN 13: 9781539936565
Library of Congress Control Number: 2016921559
CreateSpace Independent Publishing Platform
North Charleston, South Carolina

Table of Contents

Author's Note

- I include myself in the "we" in this book even though I have been living in America for two thirds of my life. I write this book as an insider and outsider as my DNA, upbringing, and foundation is solidly Korean.
- South Korea is referred to as Korea. (In South Korea, we refer to ourselves as Koreans and call our country Korea.)
- The symbol * is used to indicate contributors who wish to remain anonymous.

Introduction

September 2008. My husband Carlos and I were descending into Seoul, my birthplace. I was forty-five years old and had lived in Chicago since I was eighteen. I hadn't been back to Korea in many years. We were ambivalent about this trip to present the design work our company did for one of the South Korean multinational conglomerates. We work with clients from all over the globe and especially in the age of the Internet, we normally never travel to present in person. Our studio was very busy at that time, and it seemed wasteful to fly fourteen hours for one meeting. But it was one of the requirements of the contract, and I admit, I was curious. I had been hearing from friends how much Korea had changed in the last decade.

Since we had to go, we decided to extend the trip and take time to get reacquainted with the city. I'm so glad we did. From the moment I got off the plane at the airport, I noticed the difference. That feeling of being in a Third World country was gone. I was in a modern, fast-paced and sophisticated city, a city of energy and liveliness, a city full of promises. When we got on the bus to go to the hotel, the driver stood up in front of the passengers and bowed. Bowing is how Koreans greet one another, but I never thought it was anything other than that. But after being away for so long, looking at everything that used to be so familiar to me, I was seeing everything with a new set of eyes—Western eyes. It was cool and refreshing! I was ready to embrace anything that came across my way and discover the new Korea.

In January 2008, I met my German friend Anja when she was teaching at the University of Miami, a city where we have spent the last eight winters. We became good friends quickly, and when I told her about my trip to Seoul, she said, "You have to meet my friend Jisook when you go to Seoul!" Anja and Jisook met at the University of Southern California as visiting scholars, and they shared an office. Jisook and I had connected via email before we left for Seoul. Upon our arrival, Jisook took us around to the different neighborhoods in Seoul. At the end of the visit, she said with a big smile, "I think we will be good friends." Those warm, welcoming words made my Seoul stay even more pleasant and complete. I have to thank her forever for those few days she spent introducing us to the new Seoul. There was a big new city that I didn't even know existed! And the old part of Seoul that I knew well, where I had spent my young teenage years, was different, too. Whereas before it felt uninteresting and had no charm, now it seemed very romantic and inviting. There were many great restaurants both Korean and international and traditional teahouses with amazing teas. I still think about the teahouse called Wednesday in Insadong and wish I could have a cup of jujube tea right now. It has become my favorite tea but I can't get it in the U.S. Whenever I think of Seoul, I reminisce about the deep flavor and rich taste of the tea that's now associated with the city of my birth. I see many packaged jujube teas at the Korean grocery stores in Chicago, but they are nothing like the ones I had in Seoul.

I was so happy to see many of the old traditional houses had modernized their interiors while maintaining the same structure and exterior designs. It was fun to see many of those houses being used as restaurants, tea houses, stores or galleries. These old structures are what make Korea charming and interesting for outsiders. I haven't been to Singapore yet, but when I ask friends who have been there what it's like, they all say, "They have no culture left. There's nothing interesting to see. Anything old is gone to build new." What a shame.

The young people were so much taller than when I was young—and very fashionable! People dress a little more formally in Korea than in the U.S. The use of technology was also way more advanced and woven into daily life. (This was 2008, remember, before everyone in America was looking at his/her smartphone all day long.)

Korea is having a moment. Its pop culture is now known around the world, the epicenter of a global cultural phenomenon. In 2013, South Korea's cultural exports brought five billion into the country. The "Gangnam Style" music video broke the counters on YouTube after two billion plus hits. If you'd told me when I was sixteen that Korea would become "cool," I would have thought you were delusional.

When I got back to Chicago, I was so excited about my home country. I couldn't believe the transformation. Then I started to wonder about what happens to people internally when there is such an incredible external transformation in such a short period. How do people keep up?

That visit in 2008 was the experience that started me on the path to writing this book. It has taken many years to bring to fruition, mainly because I had to do my daily work and write whenever I had extra time. I have been thinking, talking, and asking about it constantly as I meet people, watch TV, and see the changes in the world. My life has been hugely affected by the design world and working with creative people who are always interested in trends, innovation, and how technology extends our love of beauty and function in surprising ways. As an American, I believe in personal growth, self-invention, transformation, getting along with different kinds of people, and the pursuit of happiness. But I was raised Korean and have many of the same values as my parents: hard work, education, and respect for elders. The successes of my home country fill me with emotion, and my main concern is how to communicate this emotion in the right words, to put out in the world the connection I feel inside.

I left Seoul for Chicago in December of 1980 when I was eighteen years old. I knew very little about the world. I vividly remember the feeling of adventure—the idea of a new life awaiting me. It didn't much matter that the journey was from Korea to America—I would have been excited to go anywhere.

My family came here because my father went bankrupt. My half-brother Jon, who was a martial arts teacher, had settled in Chicago after working in Germany for three years. He'd married and started a family and wanted my mother near him to help raise the children. As long as my father had a business in Korea, there was no chance of this, but when circumstances changed, Chicago seemed like the obvious place to go.

I knew nothing about Chicago other than it was a major U.S. city—the third most populous, in fact. But I liked how the name "Chicago" sounded. I liked it better than "New York." "Chicago" had a softer sound: more inviting and friendlier. I knew the city was on the shores of Lake Michigan—one of the Great Lakes—that it snowed a lot and has four seasons, just like Korea. Later, I learned about its history of gangsters, slaughterhouses, jazz, blues, comedy, trade and transportation. O'Hare International Airport is one of the busiest in the world.

It took nearly a year for the paperwork to be processed, and while I was waiting, I took some English classes and a portrait class. Why a portrait class? I saw a bunch of newspaper ads saying, "Portrait classes for people who are immigrating to the U.S." or something like that, so I assumed this was something I should learn! I had plenty of extra time since I no longer had to kill myself to study for the university entrance exam like all the other students my age. So, I signed up. Looking back, I smile as I recall just how easy it was to get money out of a person who had no clue about what was awaiting her on the other side of the world!

When I arrived in America, Mom and I stayed with Jon in his Wisconsin house for a month. I didn't know my half brother at all. He is twenty-plus years older than I am and has lived abroad since I was born. I had only seen him two or three times when he came to Seoul to visit my mother. I was very shy whenever we were in the same room. I remember him asking my mother if I was smart.

The first time I saw Chicago, it was in the late evening. I was amazed by the bright lights on Lake Shore Drive and the neighborhood streets. In Seoul, where we learned to conserve and recycle, leaving the lights on at night wasn't ever done. This dazzling brightness spoke of a kind of fairytale abundance that made me feel like anything could happen. I still feel that way, although now I'm thinking of more than my own life and one American city.

After a year or so, I transferred to another junior college to earn credits that could be transferred to a state university. After one year of studying music theory, I started wondering how I was going to make a living with a music degree. I played classical piano for ten years when I was growing up, but I never thought of myself as concert pianist material. I didn't have that kind of talent. So, after a few months of deep thinking on what to major in at school, I decided to study interior design. The entire five years in school, I worked as a waitress in the Lincoln Park neighborhood. I don't think I was a very good waitress because I didn't smile very much. In Korea, smiling at customers is not expected. Koreans are polite to customers but not friendly in the American style. It took me a long time to learn how I was coming across to people. This happens to a lot of Koreans who have to deal with the public for their business. It takes time to understand another culture, even if you are living in it.

I studied hard and worked hard, married a wonderful man, and started and managed two successful companies with my husband, Carlos. I have become an American in most respects, but I feel fortunate to have been able to begin this American life with a Korean foundation. Most of all I am grateful to have had the experience of being a stranger—of learning firsthand how custom and culture can be misinterpreted.

My early adulthood was a very busy time. For many years, I didn't pay much attention to what was happening in Korea. But now, at the midpoint of my life, I find myself thinking of Korea every day. It's also clear that the world is getting smaller all the time. Countries and cultures are influencing each other at a rate we have never seen before. Maybe I was spoiled by that amazing experience of seeing Seoul so transformed, but I am keenly aware of how much more open, curious and aware we Koreans could be—and how much we have to offer the world. I have experienced both East and West, as well as having had the opportunity to make many dear friends from all over the world. (This is one of the beauties of living in America—you meet people from everywhere.) I feel like I know a few things about how cultures can merge harmoniously and create something interesting and exciting.

This book explores certain social topics that I believe are preventing Koreans from moving forward as world citizens and achieving more happiness as individuals. It is about my experiences as an American and a Korean; what I have discovered living in a multiracial, diverse, still young culture; what I want to share with people in Korea. The world is changing very rapidly. I feel we need to adopt some of the Western values I have come to cherish now, not next month or next year, and definitely we shouldn't wait for the next generation. We accept and follow new American trends every day without thinking, without evaluating them on their merits. The values I propose in this book are not as easy to adopt as following fashion or music trends. But the work of thinking and feeling they require offers more lasting rewards.

There is plenty of room for debate on many of the topics I cover in this book. I have learned that when, instead of reacting emotionally either in favor of your traditional ways or in favor of what is shiny and new, you reflect and when you make a conscious choice, your confidence increases. That kind of confidence will be of enormous benefit to Koreans on the world stage.

In the U.S., there are enough Koreans now that most urban people have interacted with them and have opinions about who Koreans are. They are not always very accurate or fair, but this is a reality we have to consider. And lately, Korean culture—food and movies as well as music—have become more popular among non-Asian Americans. Attitudes toward Koreans are open-ended and full of questions, especially among young people. The time is ripe for us all to pause and think about each other, honestly and with open minds. I want to examine what it means to be a global citizen, without rigid geographical boundaries, while evolving as individuals and maintaining a sense of home, neighborhood and community.

What excites me is the possibility that the Korean people's contribution to global society can go far beyond economic success and pop culture, beyond outward changes and toward inner ones. By inner changes, I mean how we think and act intellectually and emotionally. Some of the baggage that has been generated from thousands of years of poverty doesn't fit into the modern, Western society that we want to be part of. But Western society has its baggage, too. Rather than just copying Western cultures blindly, we have the opportunity to consider and adopt only the behaviors and ways of thinking that we truly admire. We can abandon some of the outdated modes of thought that have become embedded in our daily lives while holding on to what is valuable and unique about our culture. Koreans have persevered and triumphed over many hardships and challenges throughout our history. We have learned the eternal human lessons in our own way and created economic and political miracles. We have also created cultural phenomenona with K-pop, Korean cinema, fashion and our innovations in cosmetics, medicine…the list goes on. Now we have an opportunity to update this, to choose from a variety of cultures and philosophies, as a society and as individuals making personal and professional decisions. As the East becomes more Western (not just modern in appearance)—and the West more Eastern—why not embrace the moment and take the best from both sides?

Is it okay to critique another culture? One which may have been your own originally, but one in which you haven't lived for decades? I'm still thinking about that—it's not an easy question. I may miss the mark at times, but my hope is that I will find the right tone to say what I want to say and to inspire and connect with my readers. My goal is to open up possibilities.

Why This Book

When I was starting to write this book, I sent one of the initial draft chapters to a Korean friend in Seoul. She sounded a little bit concerned and told me that Korean people might say, "She doesn't even live here. What does she know?" I responded, "That's why I wrote this book. Because I don't live in Korea." When you live in the woods, it's impossible to see the forest. You can only see it when you are outside of the woods.

The words of my Seoul friend affected me strongly. I want to communicate in the best and most effective manner. I have no interest in lecturing and certainly no desire to insult people. It would be easier to be a passive observer and wait for certain things to change in Korea, however long it takes. But it seems that I can't help wanting to share my journey of lessons learned: how I have come to adopt new values during the last thirty-six years living in the West.

I absolutely love those times when someone says something—and aha!—all of a sudden, thoughts and views I had carried for as long as I remember change. It's like a door opening into a country that I never even knew was there. It's a spark, a new connection in the brain that is valuable not only for the insight it brings but because it reminds you that the world is full of so much you don't yet know. We're all aware of this, but we tend to forget it when we are caught up in our jobs and family life.

Those aha moments don't come often or regularly but have happened to me a few times. I used to see the world as black and white, right or wrong, but the more aha moments I have, the more I understand the limits of my perception. You open your mind at each of those moments, and each time it's a little easier. Your existing beliefs can dramatically shift when you get a chance to see things from a different angle. Be on the lookout for these moments because you never know when, where or from whom they will come.

It is my sincere hope that this book will give you a few aha moments. I can't think of a better gift. I'm not a social psychologist or social scientist. I don't pretend to know more than you do. I only want to share my personal experiences and the experiences and views of people whom I respect. I'm always interested in seeking and learning about myself and others. The process can be challenging and surprising, but I know it has enriched me. I'm still learning and practicing. The things I have learned, I want to learn again with you.

When someone talks about things that have nothing to do with making money, or that question the supreme importance of money, many Koreans respond, "Your belly must be full to say such things." That is true. People don't get to reflect or have time for other thoughts when their bellies are not full. I believe that our time for worrying about our bellies being full is behind us. It's okay for us to talk about our states of mind, whether we are happy at home, school and work, and much more.

Before writing this book, I read a lot of books written by foreigners who lived in Korea for ten-plus years and wrote about their experiences. One of the books was by Marteen Meijer. It's called *What's so good about Korea, Marteen?* The irony is that roughly sixty percent of the book's content is what's <u>not</u> so good about Koreans. The common thread in the books I read, other than descriptions of Korean tradition and culture—often very complimentary—was the recognition of Korea's shortcomings in a global world. These are not writers who are arrogant or critical, thinking everything Western is better than everything Korean. These are people who care about our country, who want Koreans to be happy, and Korea to be better known in the world. Many have a vision of Korea advancing much further than where we are now, making strides not only in business, but in art, culture, and social justice as well. They believe in us as a society, and as a people. Korean Americans, Korean Europeans—Korean wherever we live—however busy we are with our own lives, are also deeply, passionately cheering for Korea to move forward with a more progressive and worldly mindset.

How can it happen? We need to learn, to listen, to be open, to see what's causing the issues we are facing. Hearing different perspectives changes your thoughts and feelings, which changes your behavior. But first, you have to want to see.

Dave Hazzan, a writer and journalist living in Korea, tells me, "We should speak up for changes in our attitudes. We can propose solutions, propose ideas. We can't force it. It's up to Koreans. How do we want to proceed? Things are changing. We need to talk about the importance of character, of being a good person, having compassion."

We think we are good people. We have compassion. We know the importance of character. We have huge hearts. So, what is he talking about? Is he saying we are not good? Is he advocating that our traditional way of thinking and living be disrupted? Or do we Koreans want to disrupt our ways of thinking, to leave parts of the past behind—the parts that aren't working—and forge a new culture?

"[My husband] wanted [our children] to come to a more globalized place, so that their minds become more globalized, larger," Lee said through a translator. Lee said her children are here not only to learn English but also to gain a special edge when they go back home. Lee's Korean-American friend, Diana Park, explained that having lived in America carries significant status.[1]

We send our children overseas at enormous sacrifice so they can have a Western education, see the world, and develop a global mindset.[2] But when the global mindset is introduced in our backyard, we dislike or ignore it. That doesn't make a lot of sense. If our children become Westernized, and we don't, there will be a communication gap, and the existing generation gap will become even bigger when they return. Let's try narrowing that gap. We don't want to be left behind.

There is much about the West that is not ideal. Some things are simply tragic or incomprehensible. But this book is not about those things. This book explores the ideas and values I find meaningful. Some of them have been around in the West for hundreds or thousands of years and are well known to many Koreans; some of them are brand new. They won't—and shouldn't—supplant Korean culture as a whole, but can fit into those places where we are discarding outdated customs and ideas. I hope they will help you frame your world a little differently than you have up until now.

Korea has been absorbing Western influence—particularly American influence—rapidly over the last few decades. Everyone knows that and has seen it in his or her daily life, from teenagers to grandmothers. But the West is not only the English language, the music and movies, and the technology. The West is a way of life: social, political, philosophical, and psychological. There is so much more we can learn from each other. This book is about shifting the Korean mindset a little bit towards the best of Western ideas and attitudes. It is about how we treat others—as parents, children, bosses, employees, wives, husbands, friends, citizens— and how we treat ourselves.

From the time I started to write this book, I saw and heard many talks going on in Korea about the importance of learning different perspectives. *Achim Madang, 15 Minutes to Change the World* and other Korean TV shows have been weaving new messages into old stories. Many people such as Changyeun Hwang, a priest, and BeopRyun, a monk, speak on many of the topics in this book. I was very happy to see this evidence of Koreans' openness to new ways of thinking. If you already are familiar with these topics, I hope I'm offering you a little bit more, or that you can use these stories and examples as a reminder. We all need frequent reminders when we are trying to change something. Habit is very powerful. We need and look for more discussion and more reminders every day.

While this book is primarily written for Koreans living in Korea, the topics are universal, particularly to many of the Asian countries that share similar thoughts and values based on the teachings of Confucius. I think that anyone with an Asian background, living in an Asian country, or just interested in Asian peoples and cultures can learn something from this book. The meeting of East and West that has happened over the last fifty years is momentous. There are many streams that feed into the river, from Korea to India to China and Japan, Thailand, Tibet, Vietnam, and elsewhere. Americans have different relations with all these countries, and we all have different relations with each other. But that there are stark differences between East and West—and that these differences are beginning to erode with the rise of global culture—cannot be denied.

Koreans are naturally indirect in their communication even though we can be very upfront and even over-the-top straight shooters as well. Whether we are direct or indirect depends on the situation and to whom we are talking. This book is probably more direct than indirect, even though I was advised to be indirect. To be frank, I've forgotten how to speak indirectly. I hope you will forgive me if I sound too direct at any point. You know how when we speak in a family discussion, we often get more emotional and speak openly? I consider this book a family discussion.

You may say again, "You don't live here. You are an outsider." It's true that I don't live in Seoul anymore. But when you live abroad, you are more Korean in some ways than when you live in Korea. Your identity as a Korean becomes stronger. I know the DNA of Koreans. I'm fundamentally Korean before anything else.

I believe the need for frank conversation is urgent. To move forward, we have to study the facts in the most honest way possible. Some of these facts may sound harsh, and you may disagree or deny what I'm saying, but before you slam the book closed or swipe the screen of your tablet, I hope the open part of yourself keeps flipping pages. James Baldwin, a famous, black American writer (1924-1987) once wrote, "Not everything that is faced can be changed, but nothing can be changed until it is faced."

This book is part autobiographical and part inspirational. It is intended as a call to action. I include the voices and opinions of people I interviewed in Seoul and America, people whose quotes, writing or TED talks that have inspired me. I also include common American proverbs that I consider a reflection of positive Western values. Many of the Korean characters that I use in my examples may not describe you but are probably someone you know well. They might be your uncle, your neighbor or your boss. After reading this book, I hope you start observing our Korean society more closely. Compare it to what you know of other cultures, what you have learned from this book, and what you feel in your heart is the best way for people to think and act. Societies change. Imagine that ours is changing for the better—fast. Don't you want to be a part of that change?

Social psychologist Serge Moscovici's minority influence theory—the idea that a minority can change the beliefs or behavior of the majority—proposed that even with small numbers participating, if there are commitment and consistency over time, formerly radical, disruptive or just unfamiliar ideas can spread throughout a society and become the new normal. If you think about it, it's obvious that everything starts small—from life itself to social change. It can start with one aha moment. It can start with you.

I want to end with a story that has always moved me. It's from Elif Shafak, a fiction writer, very popular in her native Turkey. Shafak has lived in cities throughout the world, both as a child and an adult, and writes about global issues, identity politics, Sufism and Ottoman culture as well as contemporary Istanbul.

Shafak was born in France but raised mostly in Turkey by a well-educated, Westernized mother and a less educated, less rational but more spiritual grandmother. Her grandmother read coffee grounds to read the future and had techniques to ward off the evil eye. Many people visited her to get rid of blemishes like severe acne on their faces or warts on their hands. She cured them by taking a red apple and stabbing it with rose thorns, then encircling the thorns with dark ink. Shafak never saw anyone go home unhealed. She asked her grandmother how she did this. "Was it the power of prayer?" In response, her grandmother said, "Yes, praying is effective, but also be aware of the power of circles."

Shafak continued, "From her, I learned, amongst many other things, one very precious lesson—that if you want to destroy something in this life, be it an acne, a blemish or the human soul, all you need to do is to surround it with thick walls. It will dry up inside. Now we all live in some kind of a social and cultural circle. We all do. We're born into a certain family, nation, class. But if we have no connection whatsoever with the worlds beyond the one we take for granted, then we too run the risk of drying up inside. Our imaginations might shrink, our hearts might dwindle, and our humanness might wither if we stay for too long inside our cultural cocoons. Our friends, neighbors, colleagues, family—if all the people in our inner circle resemble us, it means we are surrounded with our mirror image."[3]

1

Redefining Koreans

FREEDOM IS NOT FREE

A few years ago, I was in Washington, D.C., for my niece Julie's wedding. I decided to check out the city briefly before heading back to Chicago. The Lincoln Memorial was grand and majestic, as I had imagined. However, being Korean, the memorial I still remember vividly is the Korean War Memorial. Nineteen 7-foot-tall statutes of troopers, sculpted from unpolished stainless steel with haunting facial expressions, stand in a rice field, symbolized by juniper bushes and granite strips.

The inscription reads:

OUR NATION HONORS
HER UNIFORMED SONS AND DAUGHTERS
WHO ANSWERED THEIR COUNTRY'S CALL
TO DEFEND A COUNTRY THEY DID NOT KNOW
AND A PEOPLE THEY HAD NEVER MET

A second focal point, where the mural wall meets the water of a circular reflecting pool, bears the words *FREEDOM IS NOT FREE.*

As I was standing in front of this Korean War Memorial and reading the inscription, an eerie feeling seeped through my throat and heart—a deep appreciation and sadness for the 36,914 American soldiers who lost their lives and the over 103,000 who were wounded for South Korea's freedom. Over 1,000,000 Korean civilians and 217,000 soldiers were also killed in this devastating conflict. [4]

FROM NOBODIES TO MIRACLE MAKERS

The sacrifice of so many lives allowed South Koreans to climb out of poverty and build an economy that surprised everyone. Korea has been described as a phoenix rising from the ashes. Koreans are called miracle makers. We have created the 11th largest economy in the world in one generation. This achievement in such a short period is nothing more than a wonder to outsiders and Koreans living overseas. Korean K-pop, dramas, and movies—collectively called Hallyu (Korean Wave)—have gained significant popularity throughout Asia and parts of the Western world. Despite these accomplishments, in the Western mind, there is still a huge gap between what Korea is today and what people think Korea is.

In M*A*S*H*, the popular American TV show about a mobile army surgical hospital during the Korean War, which ran from September 1972 to February 1983, all the Koreans are seen in dirty rags, with dirty faces, looking like beggars.[5] When you have watched that depiction of Koreans for over a decade, and you haven't been paying much attention to the growth of South Korea, it can be difficult to see Korean people in a different light. People may understand that Korea is better off now, but they assume that it can't be by much. Then, a few times a year, North Korea is in the news. Typically, North Korea is firing missiles into the sea for military drills or nuclear tests. The lasting image is the military march and synchronized dance of thousands of people worshiping and celebrating their "supreme leader." These two images make many Westerners want to stay away from South Korea altogether. They see it as a Third World country (dog-eating is a big part of the Third World image) and a dangerous country. My friend Jisook Hong, executive director at Healience in Seoul, said, "When I was living in L.A., I went to Koreatown, and it was not that great. It was a little dirty, and the area was not well planned. So, when I saw that, I felt a little frustrated that American people would think Korea is like that. In reality, that's not Korea at all."

Even someone who knows a lot more about Korea and Koreans than the average person in the U.S.—my husband—says, "I still have a sense of sadness for the Koreans, having learned what they have gone through, the wars and all the hardships they have endured. Even today, when I think of what North Koreans are going through, I find it just incomprehensible that human beings can do that to other humans. That is so attached to my aura of what Korea is. Which, by the way, is what I suspect most people feel today. People see Korea as nothing more than a conflicted nation. Despite the fact that there are South and North, people don't see the South and North as cleanly divided. I feel like most people think that Korea, as a nation, is still not as advanced as it could be, and because of that, it isn't thought of as a place to visit. There are also safety factors. Every time you see the news about Korea, it's usually about North Korea, and even though the conscious mind knows North and South Korea are not the same, the subconscious mind simply hears Korea and after a while that sticks. If all you hear are bad things about Korea—nuclear testing and such—who wants to go to Korea? I'm a pessimist. Until the conflict with the North is resolved, things will not get better as far as the perception."

In the eyes of the world, for the longest time, Korea was regarded as backward, with no real hope of becoming a developed country. Korea is still called an emerging market, even though Korea has already emerged. The world has been reluctant to pay attention to such a small and insignificant country.

In January 2012, Jim O'Neill, former chairman of Goldman Sachs, was interviewed by Charlie Rose, an American television talk show host and journalist, in connection with the publication of his new book *The Growth Map.* O'Neill discussed a trip he had taken to Korea in November 2010.

"It was the first time I'd actually been to Korea for a number of years. And I hadn't at all appreciated how much Korea was adapting and changing… Why do we call South Korea an emerging economy anymore? I get into it a bit in there, and I have all these indicators I look at about development and productivity. And Korea scores better than every G-7 country, except Canada. And yet we call it an emerging economy."

Rose asked, "Why is that?"

O'Neill responded, "I think it's because of the…laziness of business culture and history."

In most cases, when you talk with Westerners who haven't been to or don't know much about Korea, it's hard to interest them in the idea of visiting Korea—even just as something to imagine or think about. That's how little Korea interests the majority of Westerners. The person who can't afford an international vacation may still dream of seeing Paris or the Greek Isles or going on a safari in Kenya or trekking in the Himalayas—but they won't think about Korea. There are just too many negative images and not enough positive or intriguing ones. Things are changing. But the question is: how much time is it going to take for Westerners, in general, to think of Korea as a destination?

My friend Shirley went to Seoul with me in 2012. She was going to Shanghai around the same time I was planning to visit Seoul to do some interviews for this book. So, we decided that I'd go to Shanghai with her, and she'd come to Seoul with me. She had never been to Korea, and I'd never been to Shanghai, and the best way to travel to a foreign country is with somebody who speaks the language. When she told her parents about her plans, they were surprised and asked her, "Why are you going to Seoul among all the places you can go in the world?"

Right after coming back from Seoul in 2008, I was so excited to share with my friends how fun and exciting the trip had been. Mary is a friend from Denmark who is now living in her home country again. We used to go to Korean BBQ restaurants in Chicago quite a bit, and this was her only exposure to Korean places. These restaurants had real sad décor and the restrooms were even sadder. After talking enthusiastically for an hour about my experience in Seoul, I asked Mary, "So, do you want to go to Korea now?" She replied, "So… is Korea clean?"

My dog Kino's veterinarian, Dr. Cohen, told me that he went to Asia about ten years ago. He went everywhere in Asia—China, Japan, Vietnam, Thailand—except Korea. It just wasn't on his radar. Even now he tells me that he thinks of Korea as a country where a lot of people just sit at their desks and work. That's his image of modern Korea.

Melissa Kim, VP of Marketing for a U.S. company in Seoul, said, "People in Asia who have been exposed to Korean culture through TV shows or music would love to visit Korea. Because of the popularity of Korean entertainment content across Asia, Korea is a hot destination for many in Asia, which has changed the image of the nation quite significantly. Westerners who have had no exposure to Korea whatsoever don't know what to expect of Korea. There's no brand image when it comes to Korea."

At a dinner party at friend's house a couple of years ago, one of the guests mentioned, "Korea has no identity. People know hardly anything about Korea. We go to China, Japan, Thailand—but what's in Korea? What's there to see?" It sounds absurd when we have such a strong identity: a distinct culture, traditions, food, 5000 years of history, technology, art, and music, film, etc... People are surrounded by and use Korean products everyday—cars, electronics, and house appliances. Yet the country that makes this range of products is still unknown to most Westerners.

We haven't presented Korea to the world in a way that's memorable. Psy, the Korean singer/producer, deserves much credit for introducing the new Korea to the West through the song 'Gangnam Style', Youtube's most watched video since November 2012. But one song, no matter how popular, is not enough to replace an ingrained image. When traveling in the West, many Koreans realize that South Korea is not as well known as they thought.

I could share many more stories of people expressing negative or no interest in Korea. While doing research for this book, I came across a short article in *The Korea Times* by Lee Ji-young (2008). In the article, she says that when she was traveling overseas, she was a little offended that most people didn't know anything about Korea, and she blamed the United States' educational system for not teaching their students.

I'm not sure how many Koreans presume that the world should know a lot about Korea when Korea has not, until recently, put much effort into branding itself for tourists. Why should they know? We are all busy with our lives, and we don't pay much attention to what happens in other countries, beyond whatever we hear on the news, unless we have a personal or work relationship to the country. So, let's not cling to the idea that everybody should know about us even though our first instinct may be that they should. Enjoo Um, an office worker in Seoul, was on a train in Germany when a couple of people asked her if she was a North Korean. "I was very shocked. A lot of people use Samsung products, but they don't know it's a Korean brand. Purposely the company doesn't market themselves as a Korean brand. When I heard that, I felt a little uneasy."

SEEING IS BELIEVING

Even I wasn't interested in visiting Korea, and I'm Korean. I assumed it was still the same country that I left in 1980. I heard a few times from friends that Korea had changed, but I still had no real desire to visit. I was too wrapped up in my life in Chicago.

Carlos, my husband, has been converted to an evangelist for the new Korea. After his visit in 2008, he shared his thoughts. "First, I knew about Korea via media, mostly about North Korea. Originally, I thought it was a Third World country. I have always been intrigued by Asian culture, mostly Japanese culture. The Japanese have always been in the forefront. Japan was the country that made everything for America. Sony and many of the great companies who ran the world came out of Japan.

"South Korea's global reputation is getting better. It is kind of a hidden jewel in regard to destination. The average person doesn't think about going to Korea for a vacation. Koreans are just not in the public eye, despite the fact that some of the biggest companies are from Korea.

People think Kia is a division of General Motors. Koreans are doers, not braggers. They need to develop the global positioning of South Korea. It's just a matter of time before Korea takes over the global stage and starts to own its presence.

"My first-time visit in 1990 was a Third World-type experience. It wasn't bad, but it was what I expected. But on the second visit, in 2008, Seoul was a modern metropolis. It was inspiring. It was like going to Germany, especially the Gangnam Area. But the important thing was the people. Every place and restaurant we went, the people and service were fantastic. The behavior seemed so authentic and welcoming. Definitely, you can measure the growth between 1990 and 2008."

Industrial success does not make for an appealing reason to visit. People don't want to go to China because of its economic power. That might make it interesting to business people looking for ideas or connections, but to others, it's the history and culture that are the draw. Korea is a small country and has not had a global impact historically or through literature, art, or religion.

Terri O'Dea wrote a blog post in 2014 about how she cried and felt bad for herself when she received the news that her husband would be stationed with the Army in Seoul. "There wasn't a single part of me that had ever wanted to visit that place."

After living in Seoul for one year, Terri described Seoul as "My happy place. I mentioned that before I left, I had no desire to see Seoul at all. How foolish I had been! It is a lovely city with friendly people (who don't seem to mind crying children either!) The food is unusual, tasty, and cheap. The public transportation was easy to navigate, and I became confident that no matter how far I ventured from our apartment, I would be able to get us home before dark. I read *The Lonely Planet* guide to Seoul and did every walking tour it listed, finding treasures lurking in hole-in-the-wall places which always seemed to be guarded by a nondescript door. Tea shops, boutiques, and restaurants—it was so thrilling to duck inside a door I had never been through before."

She added, "The most important lesson I learned from Seoul is to never turn down or fear an opportunity to go to a new place. The value and inspiration that it will add to your life simply cannot be measured or predicted." [6]

My friend, Jisook, said about Korea's image in the world, "We haven't made a true effort, as a country, in this area until now. We weren't thinking that far ahead because we were too busy developing the Korean economy.

"We have Korean philosophies, deeper meanings behind each historical monument, that a lot of Koreans don't even know. We need to dig up our treasures, cherish and share them with the world in a way that people can understand and appreciate. We need to create more narratives about the great things in Korea and start managing our image."

YOUNG K-POP LOVERS

If you are thirty or forty-plus years old and not interested in K-pop, the image of South Korea will pretty much be what I have described. But a large part of the younger generation around the world is crazy about Korea.

I have been an avid tennis player for a few years now. One day last winter in Miami, I entered the tennis court to do a clinic session at the Flamingo Park Tennis Center in South Beach. One of the instructors, whom I hadn't seen before, asked me, "Are you Korean?" When I said yes, he gave me a 90-degree bow, saying "Ahn Young Ha Se Yo!" I was a little taken aback, obviously because of the deep bow in front of so many people, but mostly because of his enthusiasm for all things Korean. He had a pleasant and genuine demeanor. I wanted to know more about his love of Korea, especially K-pop, so we set up a time to talk the following week.

Brad Batstone, twenty-five years old, and a tennis professional, took a Chinese history class when he was studying in college. "I went to the University of Miami. I took a class in Chinese history, and there were times when some of the lectures would spill over into Japan or Korea."

I asked him, "What made you take the Chinese class?"

Brad said, "I've always been a history and language person. Asia intrigued me because I knew very little. I decided to take just one class. But the real reason I learned about Korea and fell in love with it was because of a TV show in 2014 about food. It was called *K-POP Tasty Road*. It was a rainy day. A tennis professional can't do much when it rains, so I was in the house flipping channels, just trying to find something. I was bored with the usual stuff. After flipping and flipping, I found a show featuring two gorgeous young people, a guy and a girl. They were taking you around Seoul and showing you all the best restaurants and places where celebrities eat and how they sneak in and out of the restaurants. It was amazingly cool. They were funny and spoke many languages perfectly. They were charismatic, and the music in the background was amazing. I'd find myself using my phone identifying all the songs. Then after that show, another one came on—a romantic type of thing. It was really entertaining. The next one offered live performances of the bands whose songs I'd heard. I saw them dance, and I was sold.

"That's what introduced me to the dramas, to the movies, and ever since then, I have loved everything Korean. Because, honestly, they take it to the next level. The dancing is more intense. The emotions are pure. There is just something different about them that I can't explain."

He is also learning Korean on his own. "There is a fabulous website. I'm not sure if I'm supposed to give any plugs but it's howtostudykorean.com. The site is for people who know English and want to learn Korean. But it's also available in a Spanish version and even in a Russian version. He explains everything. Sometimes it's too much information, but he teaches you everything."

Bianca Matheson, twenty-four years old, is an English teacher in Seoul now. "In 2010, I started a dance group called GPK and at the same time I also made a page on Facebook called Florida K-pop Fans. I made it so we could get more people who are interested in K-pop to come together. At the time, there weren't many avenues for communicating with the other K-pop fans. So I started the group and then we had our first fan meet a few months afterward. Ever since then it's just been growing."

I asked Bianca the same question. "When was the first time you became interested in K-pop?"

She said, "My friend showed me a video of Lollipop by BigBang and 2NE1. I think I was seventeen. First, I thought…okay, this is cool. I didn't think too much about it then. Slowly I started researching more, and the song start getting stuck in my head, and I kept researching, and then eventually I started dancing to K-pop, researching more and more, then just completely loving it."

11

I asked, "So at your age, I would think you like Taylor Swift in America?"

"She is okay. I like her but not as much as K-pop. I think she just has the image and the music only. She doesn't have the dancing. You kind of know what to expect. She doesn't have the group, and every song is very similar. Whereas in K-pop, it's a whole group, so every member has a different personality and different style and K-pop groups are always changing their styles. They will do something sexy, and they'll do something cute, and they'll do something HipHop. You never know what to expect."

I chatted with some other K-pop fans in the same fan group. They were truly diverse in background: white, black, Latino, straight and gay. All in love with Korea.

Andrea Concepcion, twenty-six years old, was introduced to K-drama in 2007 when she was in college. "One of my friends got me into watching Asian dramas via mysoju.com. Initially, I thought Korean dramas were a little too dramatic. In 2010, I went to China as part of a traveling writing course. While in China, I heard a lot about Korean influences in China and also about K-pop bands like Girl's Generation and BigBang. The things I liked were not just the music. It's about fashion, lyrics…there are more layers to it. Now I'm careful how I talk to people about Korea. Initially, people didn't understand. But after Psy, people understand a little bit better. I feel like an international ambassador. While I'm telling people, I also want people to get into it, too. It used to be one in ten people who knew something about Korea. Now it's more like six out of ten."

Rachel Thornton, twenty years old, said, "Asian countries are attractive. It's so different from America. I think America is boring compared to Asian countries. Asia is so rich in culture that I love it so much. I started listening to K-pop, then moved to indie music, soft electronic and other Korean music. My favorite now is Casker. I'm also learning the Korean language. It seems much easier than other Asian languages.

"Most of my friends are very closed-minded. Before, when I would talk about Korea, people thought about North Korea. Also, they would make fun of me, but now they've kind of changed. They are not as closed-minded. Now when I talk about Korea, they are interested."

I asked: What would you tell older people (thirty-plus years) about Korea? Rachel said, "They may not listen to the music of Korea but will be interested in the culture, the food, and travel experiences in South Korea. There is a lot of ignorance and generalization. A few years ago, they would give me a look and say, 'Oh, she is Asian obsessed.' Now there are so many more international fans."

Beth Rivera, twenty years old, went to Seoul and Jeju Island. She said, "People are very respectful and nice. Korea feels so much safer than America. I love Korea because the people are so different. When I told people I listen to K-pop, before Psy, people would ask why, but after Psy, they say, 'Ah, okay.' Now, people are more understanding and tolerant. I want to tell people there that there is a whole other world out there."

Gigi, forty-nine years old, and Miranda, fourteen years old (mother and daughter K-pop fans) are planning to go to Seoul this year. They were overjoyed when they were telling me this. Gigi said, "Korean interest has brought us together. Korea has united us in a strange way. What we have here is amazing."

They all fell in love with Korean culture the same way. It started with a friend showing them one K-pop video. Then they moved on to liking Korean food, dramas, even learning the language. Although many of their friends and families give them puzzled looks for liking Korean things, they just can't hide their love of K-pop, K food, K everything.

It felt strange, after hearing from so many people who were skeptical about Korea and had an old image of Korea, that these young people were the complete opposite. They were very excited. Korean culture is their passion, and they can't get enough of it.

To her friends who don't know much about Korea, Bianca would explain, "Korea is an awesome country. It has a rich culture. It has such an interesting perspective. I would tell them that they should learn more about it. They are missing out. I feel like Korea has almost the best in everything. Korean food is probably one of the best. I think K-pop is among the best pop. Even other Korean music is great. Seoul itself is an amazing city and just has so many things to offer. It's just a shame that people don't know more about it. So I'll just say more people should explore."

Bianca ended our talk by saying, "I just love Korea so much. Honestly. I just hope that they can overcome their obstacles like people living with so much pressure or the high rate of suicide…I think the turning point for Korea will be taking the hard-work spirit, taking that competitiveness and using it to keep progressing but not so harshly that people break. Korea can be one of the top countries and be sustainable. Right now, it is not sustainable. It's good to be competitive, but it reaches a certain point where it can destroy. You have to keep a balance."

A DEVELOPED COUNTRY REQUIRES DEVELOPED MINDS

"'If I'm happy here, that's enough. Why do I have to care about being a global citizen?'

This would be what the Korean general public would say," said Jooyun Kim, a professor of industrial design at Hongik University. I agree with him that most Koreans probably feel that way. I can completely understand that statement. Why would we care when we are busy and struggling with our daily lives and have so much to do already?

I asked Melissa Kim what qualities she thinks Koreans lack today. "Understanding global perspectives and interests. Koreans are very much focused on Korea. Also, common sense and common etiquette. Korean children are not taught general manners these days."

Now that we have accomplished the unimaginable task of developing a miracle economy from ashes, the world is starting to pay attention to us. They are watching where we are headed. Many people in the world are showing curiosity and interest. Some young Westerners are even crazy about us. Instead of being the influenced, we are becoming the influencer. When you reach a certain level of success and gain a name for yourself, you get scrutinized as celebrities do. The world wants to get to know Koreans better. People from all over want to come and check us out. Let's show them we are world-class citizens—not narrow, backward-minded people. Let's not think or talk or behave as if foreigners are aliens. Remember, we are all the same inside. We all want acceptance, respect, and to have good manners shown to us.

If you are still not convinced as to why we should care, think about how much revenue tourism brings into the country. Tourism is one of the fastest growing economic sectors in the world. The tourism revenue equals or even surpasses that of oil exports, food products, mobile phones or automobiles. The 2015 Tourism Competitiveness Index shows the rankings of all the countries of the world; for Asia, they are as follows: Japan #9, Singapore #11, Hong Kong #13, China #17, South Korea #29. *Lonely Planet* named Singapore its top country destination for 2015. Singapore has over 15 million tourists visiting yearly. It's known for its street food. Tourism is a key contributor to Singapore's economy. [7]

We already have quite a few tourists in Korea, mostly from Asia now, but I picture Seoul, Busan, and other historical cities' every major street being filled with tourists from all over the world—from the East and the West—like Tokyo, Hong Kong, Beijing, Barcelona, Paris, London, Rome, Moscow, Sydney, New York, Los Angeles, and Chicago. I imagine Seoul as a truly international city. And I see places like JeJu Island and Mt. Seoraksan attracting the people who would love and appreciate the beauty of nature in Korea.

KOREAN CONTRADICTIONS

The Koreans are not easy to understand. There are many contradictions and obstacles to understanding. The Koreans are forthright and obscure at the same time. This kind of communication failure manifests a lot in business.

The Koreans have a way of upsetting you and getting into your heart at the same time. [8]

I never thought of Koreans as a people of contradictions, but that explains a lot about how we are.

We are warm/cold; generous/selfish and greedy; overly accommodating/insensitive and inconsiderate; think manners and respect are of the utmost importance / rude, disrespectful; humble/arrogant; intelligent/ignorant; direct/indirect; courageous/cowardly; adaptable/stubborn; aggressive/passive; extremely judgmental/very forgiving; want fair treatment and equal justice/corrupt; xenophobic/love of all Western things; superiority complex/inferiority complex; nationalistic and fiercely patriotic /I hate Korea. (Eighty percent of young people want to leave Korea.)

We are the worst critics of ourselves, but if someone mentions anything even slightly negative about Korea, we get offended and defend its reputation with every argument we can make. In his book *The Koreans*, Michael Breen goes on to say, "They can be unrestrained in their passions, quick to cry and to laugh. One of the nicest aspects of Koreans is that they are not raised to feel that displays of emotion are a weakness. They push themselves to study and succeed. At the same time, they can be embarrassingly earthy and blunt." He considers Koreans' willingness to display emotion as one of the nicest aspects of our people, but highly emotional individuals get into more trouble than not, especially in work environments and in personal relationships.

NO FILTER

Words are very important. A few kind words can lift a person's spirit; unkind words can wound the spirit for a long time. Words can be more hurtful than physical pain. In America, a person who says whatever comes to his/her mind is said to be a person with no filter.

My friend Rebecca once told me that she likes me because I'm direct and straightforward. She can always count on getting an honest opinion from me if she wants one. You might guess by her comment that this personal trait isn't too common in American culture. In general, when you are talking among friends, coworkers or in social settings (as opposed to partisan battles or online comments), people don't say anything that will hurt the other person's feelings. You only say things that are positive, pleasant, encouraging, or well wishing. If you have to say something negative to a person, there is a common rule that you say something positive first to lessen the blow of the necessary criticism. For example, "We love that you are creative, Tom, but you are one lazy person." Or, more likely, the criticism is softened as well. "We love that you are creative, Tom, but you could work a little harder." Most Americans know how to interpret a statement like this—Tom knows that his supervisor or co-worker is upset that he is not getting enough work done.

What I have learned since I moved to America is that there is a fine line between being honest or direct with your opinions and being too honest, not considering a listener's feelings. The line is between honesty and rudeness, unpleasantness or even offensiveness.

In college, I was meeting a classmate for lunch after summer break. I hadn't seen her for a couple of months, and the first thing that came out of my mouth was, "Wow, you gained weight!" I still remember her reaction. She was taken aback by my outburst and was annoyed, even a little upset. Probably she felt bad about gaining weight, then I announced it publicly, drawing attention to what was a sensitive issue. My directness is part of my personality but also part of my Korean identity. Being honest is great, and we all should be as honest as we can—especially with ourselves. But if your honest feeling or thought is expressed too directly or carelessly, without consideration for the other person, it can hurt someone, as well as expose your ignorance. When you speak without filtering your thoughts, words can easily come out as insensitive and inappropriate, and even make you sound like an uneducated person. We all have things we are ignorant of. If you have never been to a certain country, there's no way you can know what it's like there, and nobody expects you to know. But if you are careful to only give an opinion when it is either clearly a matter of personal preference (blue is my favorite color; I love spicy food; I prefer winter to summer) or it is something you have thought seriously about or experienced, you will avoid sounding ignorant.

When I was in college, I was still learning the nuances of American manners and behavior. You learn the hard way when you are confronted with the result of your careless comments or thoughts. No matter how much you feel that you are right or think it's just a casual comment, sometimes, it's better to bite your tongue. Over the years, I had to learn to tame my directness and keep myself in check. I'm happy to report that I like my current level of directness, though I'm still learning to be honest in more diplomatic ways. I wish more American people would speak more openly. Sometimes I feel that the high-alert political correctness climate in America forces people to keep their true thoughts to themselves and just be fake-pleasant all the time. This is especially true for people in the public eye. This means that much of what we see and hear from well-known people is not what they really think, only what they pretend to think. It is a complex subject, as you can imagine, and this book is not about America, so I won't go any further. I am not advocating that Koreans become just like Americans in this respect. Surely there is a happy medium between the Korean way and the American way.

Koreans have many admirable characteristics like being hard working, tenacious, and vigorous, to mention a few. At the same time, we have some aspects of our character that we need to reflect upon. One of them is making rude remarks to people you don't know well or to complete strangers. Most Koreans don't do this, but there are just enough Korean people who are doing it and making bad impressions without realizing it. Please don't confuse being direct with people you already know with making rude remarks to a complete stranger. Typically, these rude remarks come from middle-aged or older people. Does this mean that this type of rudeness will end with the older generation? I hope so. Some of the examples are so infuriating to the listener that it makes newspaper headlines, as with the drunk person on the bus I wrote about in a later chapter who disrespected the Indian university professor and his Korean female friend. Also, I will never forget the comment/ accusation/lecture made by the antique cart vendor on Insadong street: "What are you doing going around with such a person?" (The person was my foreign husband.) If you are a foreigner and hear disrespectful words, you might hold onto a negative feeling about the people and the place for your whole life. It's like having a bitter taste in your mouth that won't go away.

The problem is not only that Koreans make remarks like this in public, but that so many of us believe in the rigid categories we put people in. Dave Hazzan, a Canadian journalist and writer in Korea, says, "I dislike attitudes, the so-and-so are thieves, the so-and-so are evil, stereotyping people from other nations. It just sounds ignorant." Anyone who has traveled and met people from many countries knows that we are all human under the skin. Certainly, cultural practices vary and this can lead to misunderstanding and offense, but remember: unless you think you are just the same as every other Korean person, how is it possible that all Americans, Chinese, Russians, Japanese, etc, are the same?

OFFICE TALK

A job interview is another place where many rude remarks are made because the interviewer holds the upper hand. He thinks he can ask any personal questions or make unwelcome comments.

While Jeric Park*, a professor/designer/consultant in Seoul, was working in Chicago, one of the major Korean corporations called him several times, asking him to come to Seoul for an interview, so he did. Jeric presented his work in Korean. Korean is his first language; he is fluent, and he was presenting to Koreans. However, at the end of Jeric's presentation, one of the interviewers commented, "Are you considering coming back to Korea because you don't speak good English?" Jeric was pretty much rendered speechless by this question. The interviewer thought Jeric's Korean was so good that he assumed his English couldn't be very good. He was presumptuous about Jeric's English fluency without ever hearing him speak English. Mostly, though, what does Jeric's English fluency have to do with Jeric's design skills?

Simply because you have the upper hand—you are hiring someone, or you are a boss or a client—doesn't give you the right to say whatever you feel like, to make personal or insulting comments. Some examples, especially aimed at young women are: "Behave like a woman!" "You are ugly." "You are fat." "Why don't you dress better, like Ms. Kim!" "Hey! (Ya!)" "Why don't you come with us to eat? I think the food will taste better if you come."

This kind of talk has been going on for so long that many people do it habitually and accept it without anyone asking, "Is this a civilized way to talk to one another?" It's demeaning and disrespectful to the listener. The person who is saying it appears like a "jackass" (stupid person), as they say in the West. I'm sure that those people who speak this way without thinking are used to it and assume everyone else is, too.

My friend, Shin Yoon, worked as a computer engineer for Hitachi in Japan for eight years during the late 80s and early 90s. I remember her telling me that whenever she went to Seoul for work, she wasn't sure how to behave around the men in the Korean company because of their unprofessionalism towards her. She simply hated going to Seoul.

The person's intention might be innocent enough. Maybe it's prompted by curiosity, maybe what he's saying seems funny to him, but in fact it's rude, it's obnoxious, and if it has a sexual connotation, it's just cheap. Any talk that shames another person is wrong and should be stopped. If you hear anyone being shamed at work, even if the shame is not directed at you, you and your coworkers may choose to speak up. Doing this requires courage and is not always the best choice as your job may be on the line. But here is another positive sign that the work environment is changing in Korea. Many companies have policies on certain behaviors in place already. The important thing is to create needed policies and then enforce them. Once people trust that the policy is taken seriously, they will be more conscious of professionalism at the workplace, and there will be less risk in speaking up. The older men and others in senior positions especially need to know that they can't talk this way to younger people, or to whoever is in the weaker position. We as individuals need to be more aware of what being professional means.

PRESUMPTION

Several Western K-drama fans I have talked with say that Koreans appear to have pure emotions. Brad Batstone elaborated, "We mean how genuine Korean People can be. I once heard it said, "With Koreans, you never have to wonder whether they like you or not, they will let you know right away. I have even heard Koreans compared to Italians because both can be very vibrant and emotional people."

I welcome that comment because it implies that we express and convey our emotions in more honest or unfiltered ways (although that could be good or bad depending on the situation). The only issue is that we can easily cross the line and impose our raw emotions on another person by making rude remarks or asking inappropriate questions. This comes from being overly presumptuous. Not knowing people at all or having very limited information about them, we imagine and talk as if we know other people's situations and lives as we do our own. We don't know how to draw a boundary between what's our business and what's another's.

These seem to be the reasons that some foreign authors describe us as almost childlike. (Maarten Meijer, author of *What's So Good about Korea, Maarten?*) Children say things without filtering their thoughts. It is very cute and funny when a child does it, but when an adult does it, it is a display of ignorance or bad manners. We can have healthier and more respectful relationships when we keep our thoughts to ourselves and try to mind our own business no matter how curious we may be. We should be careful not to take an automatic position of moral superiority towards anyone. I won't ask you to censor your thoughts, but perhaps you can censor what comes out of your mouth. Expressing opinions carelessly to people, intruding on their privacy or dignity, can cost you your reputation.

> *There is a probably no more homogeneous a country on earth. You feel that you are forever the guest, never the family member. Guess I'm not supposed to give advice, but Korea is one of those countries that people always seem to be lecturing about how to behave and manage themselves. Close up, Koreans seem to always be making mistakes.*
>
> — MICHAEL BREEN.[9]

BAD MANAGERS

Treat others the same way you want them to treat you

- LUKE 6:31 NEW AMERICAN STANDARD BIBLE

You can tell the person's character by how he or she treats other people.

There is a Korean restaurant called Cho Sun Ok in Chicago. It's been around for decades, attracting many Koreans and locals with their authentic, consistently good Korean food. I tried my first Cha Dol Bae Gi grill here. People line up for it seven days a week. Cha Dol Bae Gi is a dish of thin, unseasoned slices of beef cooked in a stone pot. You dip the meat in the sesame oil, salt, and black pepper sauce, then eat it with seasoned green onions or pickled onions. Yum! It's one of the Chicago landmark places for Carlos and me. I have been going there for more than thirty years now. I love going to Cho Sun Ok even though it's a little stressful to eat there because it's such a small space and always crowded. Every time we go, Carlos mentions that he can't stand the owner. The funny thing is I didn't even notice until Carlos mentioned how much it bothered him. While the waitresses are running around like chickens with their heads cut off, the owner sits on a stool and does absolutely nothing, no matter how busy the place gets. I also order a lot of carry-out from the place. One day the waitress made a mistake and gave my food to someone else. The owner started yelling at her, using very foul language. I just couldn't believe how he was talking to his employee, who was about fifty years old. He used the word "Nyun" repeatedly, the lowest term for a woman. I felt so bad for her but also felt bad that he was doing it in front of the customers.

The content of your character is your choice.
Day by day, what you choose, what you think
and what you do is who you become.

— HERACLITUS

Recently I was at a party talking with a businessman who used to go to Seoul quite a bit. I asked him if he could share any experiences from his time in Seoul. One of the things he remembers was that he was at a business lunch in Seoul with some colleagues. He couldn't recall the exact details, but the waitress made a mistake. In a minute, the restaurant manager slapped her in front of everyone. He was in such shock that he couldn't believe what he had just seen.

We all make mistakes. I have made them. You have made them. How these restaurant owners and managers reacted to the waitress's mistakes was shocking to the people who saw it happen. I cannot describe their behavior as anything other than cruel, barbaric, and humiliating for the recipients. Maybe that was the old way of dealing with people, but if you want loyal and dignified employees, you will want to take a different approach. Managing people is an important part of any business. Dealing with employee mistakes can be frustrating and maddening, but verbal and physical abuses are not the solution. Whether it's a restaurant, office, or any other workplace, publicly shaming your employees is not professional. It just makes you appear vile and unqualified to be a manager.

Praise in public; criticize in private.

—VINCE LOMBARDI, AMERICAN FOOTBALL COACH

WE ARE HOW WE ACT

Watch your thoughts, for they become words. Watch your words, for they become actions. Watch your actions, for they become habits. Watch your habits, for they become your character. And watch your character, for it becomes your destiny.[10]

In the movie *Uncle John,* a slow-burn thriller and low-key romantic com-edy, there is a scene where the character, Ben, is sitting on one end of the bench, and a Korean female is sitting on the other end of the bench. She is talking in Korean on her cell phone. It sounds like she is yelling but in an agonized way. She is loud and animated, with vivid facial expressions, and pretty much looks like a caricature. Obviously, the director thought this scene had some entertainment value and decided to dedicate the twenty seconds, though it had nothing to do with the story line. I have to say that I didn't like the portrait because most Koreans don't talk that way.

It's quite interesting to hear how outsiders look at us. Ron Ezsak, a soft-ware industry veteran for more than thirty years, traveled throughout Asia working with many different companies during the eighties and nineties.

"There are cultural similarities among Korea, Japan, China, and other Asian countries. A similarity of faith at a social level, reverence and respect for elderly family members. There are attributes that are shared throughout the region. But there are far more distinctive kinds of things as well.

"What happened in Korea—having the peninsula torn in half, con-flict and all of that, and the constant threat of the psychopath that the artery pours in towards Seoul—is unusual in Asia. The students bubble up every five to six years in Seoul. Korea is very different. There is a tension in South Korea that makes people work harder and play harder and be more aggressive as individuals. I think they possess that ability. I see similar attributes in Israelis. The threat of conflict and the longing to reconnect. I think it makes a difference. It's a different time but the same kind of mistreatment and the same kind of occupation. They have similar experiences. Korea's poverty and struggles are not that long ago. It's still very much affecting the living generation."

Ron's observation on Korean people makes me think about the Korean traits that could use some conscious changes. While Koreans have many wonderful qualities that I love, we also have some aspects of ourselves that have become rigid. We would benefit from breaking out of old patterns. I asked some of the Korean Americans I have interviewed what are some of the things that they wish Koreans would do differently. To begin with, we seem to feel pride in being Koreans. Most of us have reached a place where we are comfortable with who we are. We acknowledge and carry the innate strength and struggles that reside within us through our parents.

"Koreans have a tremendous sense of personal responsibility. I think the average person feels the weight of their decisions and understands that they need to work hard because of that. Because there are plenty of cultures where it isn't nearly as strong. I think ambition is another thing that is a double-edged sword. By and large, I think it is good. People are willing to work toward things. They have the ability to sacrifice what they want now for a greater good later on.

> The main thing I wish Koreans would change is sizing everybody up. As soon as you meet someone, the first thing you're trying to figure out is are you above me or below me because of age, status, job, etc... Do I have to use the honorific or regular talk? That I don't like. I think maybe there is some good to it, but it is mostly harmful."

> – THOMAS KIM, CHICAGO, IL

"The great Korean trait is respect for the elderly. I don't follow it to the letter when it comes to me (I don't demand others call me 언니, 누나, 선배, addressing older sister,

27

older brother, school senior in close age range), but I do respect that principle towards others. Another one is camaraderie. I know every culture has this quality. However, I think Koreans go to extremes most of the time... They think they already know you because you are Korean...It's hard to explain. The bad part is when all of the above go to extremes, get exploited and taken advantage of…"

– Miriam Kim, Los Angeles, CA

"We are invasive in other people's business. We prefer to find negative stuff than positive. We are more likely to see the glass half empty than half full. It's easier to find fault than to praise. The hyper-competitiveness. We don't have to be so extreme and driven. We are too severe on ourselves. We are always in a hurry, have no patience. We discriminate based on educational backgrounds and jobs. We get angry easily."

– Edward Lee, Chicago, IL

"Koreans don't question things. There's a general culture of…well, it's like a hive mind, you know. Something's happening, we all gotta do it. My neighbor just bought this glass set. It is very nice. Everybody lives in an apartment building, so you know what your neighbor has. A week later everybody has it. You don't question if it's good or bad. Whether it actually suits your space or not. People don't question things."

– Alfredo Park, Toronto Canada

Peter Kim was recruited to work at one of the major Korean companies. I asked him, "What's one thing you would tell Koreans that you think they don't know about themselves?" Peter answered, "I think the most important thing that Koreans need to know about themselves is that they don't have to do what is expected of them. They should take the opportunity to do something different than what they are expected to do, and they should be transparent. Koreans are the most untransparent people. They don't let their inner lives show through. I think it is a very community, peer-pressure thing. They should be open and transparent about bad things as well as positive things, like 'This is what I like to do. This makes me happy,' rather than having so many rules."

A slightly different take on the Korean character—something positive—comes from Carlos, "One of the things I like [about Koreans] is they have this kind of sarcastic sense of humor that on the surface appears like they are arguing, but they're kind of making fun of each other in a comedic way. Even when we watch movies, fighting or cop talks or whatever, I see how they smack each other like how you smack me. Now I know where that comes from. It's like a funny way to deal with a situation, and I really like that." By the way, I stopped hitting people a long time ago because a couple of my American friends got offended.

OUR WORTH

"I had this conversation with a lot of people in Korea," Ron said, "Koreans are apologetic. Korea feels that it has got to catch up. One of the reasons Korea has become so successful globally in a number of industries is because they have that kind of insecurity. I think Koreans feel like they have to compete harder."

When people visit a new place, the sign of how much they loved it is when they say, "I want to live there!" This is what Carlos and I said after returning from Seoul in 2008. Barcelona, New York, Paris, London, Chicago, Rome—these are beautiful and exciting cities, but Seoul has its own charm, energy, and attractions. I can see why many Korean Americans and Europeans and other foreigners want to settle down in Korea. Seoul is becoming an international and dynamic city.

When Peter Kim started working in Seoul, many people said to him, "You came from America to work in Korea? Why?"

It seems like that's a question every Korean is asking any Western foreigner who wants to live in Korea. When you can live in America or Europe, why would you want to live in Korea? Why do you want to learn Korean? We never thought of our country as a place foreigners would find so fascinating, attractive, and cool that they would want to live there. Korea is interesting to a lot of people, and more people will be interested as word spreads. Seoul is an advanced modern city now, with a ton of history and culture. A lot of people are interested in experiencing different cultures. We can stop the self-deprecating talk about Korea. We are not an emerging country anymore. We are an industrial powerhouse and a cultural phenomenon.

Yet Peter's impressions of Koreans were: "I have to say they don't have low self-esteem. They have extremely high self-confidence nowadays. It's interesting that you have so many Korean Americans, and you have so many non-Koreans, Indians, Chinese and Hispanic Americans working in Korea. They come to teach English, and they want to live in Korea. I know so many Americans who go back to Korea. I would say that Koreans do think highly of themselves. The Hallyu, the Korean cultural wave, is a big part of it."

Korea is changing very fast, and it makes sense that people don't understand yet what our place is in the world, how the world sees us, or how we should view ourselves. There's no one answer, of course, but it is always beneficial to look at things from another angle, to get out of the boxes we—and our upbringing—have constructed around us. Listening to all of these people talk and reflecting on my own experiences, I have come to believe that the best way to have an accurate perception of your country is to live outside of the country for a few years, then go back. You will appreciate it a lot more. You will have a fresh perspective. Instead of asking people, "Why do you want to live in Korea?" you will say, "Welcome, we are glad to have you living here. Hope you enjoy Korea and make lots of happy memories living here!"

2

Looks

JOB = PRETTY FACE

When I first heard about plastic surgery being popular in Korea, I didn't think too much about it. Personally, I think it's okay to get minor fixes like double eyelid surgery if that makes you feel better about how you look. I probably would have done it myself if I didn't have the double eyelid already. Basically, the surgery changes your eyes from looking kind of sleepy to a little bit more awake. As girls, we have stared at ourselves in the mirror, looking at the imperfect parts of our faces or bodies, wishing we could fix them. We want to look beautiful. Who doesn't? Does that mean we should run to a plastic surgeon and go under the knife? Reshape our noses? Shave down our cheekbones and jawbones to look like someone else? How far will you go to look more beautiful? How far could your daughter or sister or wife or friend go before it made you uncomfortable? And what if the ideal of beauty you have at nineteen is not the one you have when you are forty? Is there a word for missing your original face?

South Korea has the highest per capita rate of plastic surgery in the world. (The US comes in sixth.)[11] Is the desire to take control of this aspect of our identity a result of our increased prosperity? Our interest in global culture, pop culture, our love of all things Western? All of these are factors and are not necessarily indicative of a problem. With money and greater awareness of choices, of course, people start wanting more options. So the double eyelid surgery—quick and mostly safe—and the facelift for the woman or man over forty, nips and tucks: these are perhaps inevitable.

I heard that young women were getting surgeries to get a job because better-looking people have a much higher probability of being hired for some jobs. It's a requirement in Korea to attach a photograph to a job application, which isn't the case in the U.S. Of course, good looks help one get ahead in any country, but Korea seems to be the only country where people get plastic surgery just so they can get a job—a regular job, not one in the field of entertainment or modeling. I don't mean to imply that looks count MOST in Korea—you do need to meet the qualifications—but when it's a choice between qualified applicants, the prettiest one usually gets the job.

It has even become common for Korean parents to pay for the surgeries as a college, or even high school, graduation gift. Your relatives may suggest changing your face when they talk to you about how to get a good job or succeed at the one you have. Patricia Marx, writing about Korea in *The New Yorker,* says remarks like this are not considered any more insulting than saying, "You'd get a lot more for the apartment if you redid the kitchen.'"[12] Perhaps the person saying it doesn't consider it more insulting. But the person hearing it? The teenager or young adult? I'm not so sure. Just because you are used to your elders speaking in a certain way doesn't mean it doesn't affect you.

I shared the article with my American friend, Meredith. She commented, "Wow, this is so shocking! I would freak out if someone told me I needed to change my face! I mean, we are who we are…I suppose it's one thing if you're not happy with how you look and want to change it, but if you're content, then to have someone tell you that you should change would just be so upsetting!" This would be a typical response if you told a Western woman that she needed to fix some part of her face.

"Plastic surgery is so common in South Korea that if you *don't* do it, you are considered the weird one," Jane Kim says. Your friends are doing it. Everyone else applying for the job has! (Not really, but it seems that way.) This is beginning to sound very sad. From the outside, it looks like a dangerous obsession.

Bianca Matheson, an English teacher from Miami, Florida, and a K-pop fan in Seoul, has a pretty face already. She talked about how powerful the influence of advertising can be "I knew about the beauty culture [in Korea] of course, the importance of beauty. But you really feel that in Seoul when you are in the subway. Because there are so many advertisements everywhere for plastic surgery… I was thinking 'Should I get a plastic surgery?' I would have never thought that in America. I was thinking, 'Wow, this is very influential!' I can only imagine Korean people living here—the pressure that they feel."

Mia Park, yoga instructor/actress/drummer in Chicago, says, "I think it's gone out of control. I think it's detrimental to the cultural consciousness. I think it's training Korean people to be embarrassed by their natural beauty, and it's making them [have] lower cultural self-esteem."

BE YOURSELF, THE WHOLE SELF!
Society won't accept you unless you have a perfect V-bone facial structure, right size nose and bigger eyes? You are not good enough as you are unless you have an ideal- looking face? I doubt that this is the best way to build young women's self-esteem and confidence.

I think parents and schools ought to be stressing the importance of character rather than fanning the fires of image obsession in Korean culture. You can't have it both ways. You can't expect people to value skill, good behavior, hard work and inner beauty if you put too much emphasis on looks. It's silly to pretend looks don't matter at all, but the proper balance is important. Maybe no society gets that balance exactly right, but I fear we are in danger of losing those qualities that have allowed us to survive and prosper. And on the individual level—how sad for a young woman entering the workforce. You may get a job with that pretty face, but once you're hired, you still have to perform.

And what about the more talented and qualified people who weren't hired because they were not as pretty as other applicants? They aren't the only ones missing out. Wouldn't that be a big loss for the company?

Beauty is important. Humans want beautiful things. We long to live in beautiful houses and surround ourselves with beautiful objects. We travel far to experience places of striking or exotic beauty, and of course, we want to make ourselves look as attractive as we can, with clothing, grooming, makeup, and jewelry. All cultures do this and have done so throughout history, even though standards of beauty vary.

I'm in the design business, so I'm even more aware of beauty. But when I think of a large number of people from one society embracing plastic surgery to make themselves beautiful to the degree we Koreans do, it feels unsettling.

(It is reported that a third of all Korean plastic surgery patients are unhappy with the results of surgery, and up to seventeen percent experience at least one negative side effect. Many die on the operating table, partly because the huge popularity of the surgery has resulted in many untrained medical personnel wielding the knife.)[13] Knowing how many people are going to such lengths, risking serious complications, even death, to make themselves beautiful, it seems like we are putting our confidence in the wrong places.

A new study seems to confirm the idea that, at least at younger ages, plastic surgery patients are a more troubled group—and that surgery didn't help. This study is important because it followed more than 1,500 teenage girls for thirteen years, and the researchers didn't know who would actually have surgery during that time. The seventy-eight girls who did have surgery were more likely to be anxious or depressed and had a greater increase in those symptoms over the study period than non-patients. Viren Swami, an expert on body image and a psychologist at the University of Westminster, London, said, "And their findings seem quite clear: those who chose to have cosmetic surgery tended to have a history of poorer mental health to begin with, but having cosmetic surgery did not result in a positive outcome."[14]

AM I UGLY?

Meaghan Ramsey of the Dove (global brand for soap and cleansing products) Self Esteem Project, gave a TED talk titled "Why Thinking You're Ugly is Bad For You."[15] She is mostly talking about girls, but she mentions that the fears that girls have—and how they affect their participation in life—continues into adulthood. "Seventeen percent of women would not show up to a job interview on a day when they weren't feeling self-confident about the way that they look."

She is talking about girls and women around the world. Men face the same pressures, to a somewhat lesser extent. When kids grow up focusing on their looks as the gateway to a successful career, they neglect other things. There's only so much room in our brains! Think of all the time you have spent in your life worrying about how you look. I'm not talking about how much time you've spent shopping, grooming, going to the hair salon, putting on make-up, doing whatever you do to present yourself at your best, but rather how much time you've spent worrying. Imagine what you could have done with that time. Imagine how much better you'd feel if the thought that you were "ugly," "not pretty enough," "fat," or whatever else you tell yourself had never even occurred to you.

> *I'm not pretty, and I'll never be pretty, but it doesn't matter.*
> *I have something much better. I have style.*

> – IRIS APFEL.

I adore the boldness, attitude, and confidence of Iris Apfel, interior designer, businesswoman, fashion icon. She consulted on restoration projects, including work at the White House, for nine presidents from 1950 to 1992. I wish all girls could absorb even a little bit of Iris Apfel into themselves. She is eccentric, chic, daring, and witty. In the documentary *Iris*, I was more than entertained by her style and by how active and energetic she is at ninety-four. But what is really captivating is her wisdom and outlook on life. I find it refreshing and enchanting.

Here are some of Iris Apfel's words. "Fashion you can buy, but style you possess. The key to style is learning who you are, which takes years. There's no how-to road map to style. It's about self-expression and, above all, attitude."

"I never felt pretty; I don't feel pretty now; I'm not a pretty person. I don't like pretty, so I don't feel bad. And I think it worked out well, because… when you're somebody like me, in order to get around and be attractive, you have to develop something, you have to learn something, and have to do something, so you become a bit more interesting. And when you get older, you get by on that. Anyway, I don't happen to like pretty. Most of the world is not with me, but I don't care."

Ramsey talks about the image-obsessed culture and how we can help our teenagers overcome image-related pressures and build their self-esteem so they will have the mental energy to focus on their skills and talents. I agree that we need to start judging people by what they do, not what they look like. How can we start complimenting people based on their effort and their actions and not their appearance?

UNREAL REALITY SHOWS

This is a challenge for parents and educators because the influence of popular culture is so huge. The media is not interested in quality TV shows, films, or online sites, only in ratings, ticket sales or social "likes." Most people don't think about the negative influence of having someone like the U.S. reality star Kim Kardashian as a role model for young women. Low-quality TV shows are flooding the airwaves. Simply put, that's just worrisome. Americans have been bombarded with Kardashian photos and useless detailed stories about them on a daily basis for some years now. Kim became famous for a sex tape and then a reality show, which made the rest of her family famous. She has no talent. She does nothing interesting and yet is richer and more famous than so many talented actors, musicians, and other amazingly gifted people. We have to acknowledge the fact that Kim Kardashian is the epitome of how shameless self-promotion can bring you fame and fortune. Many millions of people put her there.

I tried to watch her show one day so I could understand what I was missing. Twenty minutes into it, I had to turn it off. I could feel my brain going numb. The people who watch this type of show don't realize that their minds are shrinking. At the end of a hard day, it's fine to watch something light and entertaining to relax our brains, but this type of show actually undermines our intelligence. It dumbs us down.

During my research for writing this book, I read some thoughts on the Korean TV show *Gossip of Beauties* (Minyudleae Suda). The show aired for eighteen months, starting in October 2006. It is no coincidence that the show was mentioned in more than one of the books I read that were written by foreigners. It tells me how many non-Koreans felt the same thing watching the show that I did. They were disheartened and questioned the motives of the producers. Their observation about the show was, "Is this the best Koreans can do to portray and share foreigners' experience living in Korea?" The show featured female foreigners, about whom many Koreans are curious, but as the name says clearly, the main qualification was the women had to be young and pretty.

When I see something that is focused around cute and pretty people, I can't help but feel like it's a fake. The reality of the world is that we have beautiful people and not so beautiful people, possessing their own uniqueness. How about featuring a diversity of people so we can learn from all life experiences, not just pretty people's experiences? What if an average-looking foreigner has better and more interesting stories? Of course, that person would be disqualified from the show because she is not pretty enough. I understand it all comes down to entertainment and ratings. But when we create shows that are more mindful, intelligent and inclusive, that present a variety of men and women, old and young, from diverse backgrounds and with different life experiences, that will allow a better understanding of what foreigners are really like. If we want to create opportunities for average Koreans to get to know foreigners via

TV shows, to offer Koreans authentic and broad exposure to the world's people, it would be more effective to focus on qualifications such as the depth and diversity of people's experience rather than on their looks. Then we would have a show that's real, fun and intelligent.

You can watch or talk with pretty people for only so long. For me, it gets boring very fast unless the person has a worthwhile story to tell. In general, I'm much more impressed by people who have intelligence, courage, creativity, a sense of humor, or a passion for something than by those who have a lot of money or good looks. The first kind of person is simply more interesting.

In America, there is a name for some blonde people who are beautiful but not so intelligent. They are called "dumb blondes"—a phrase used more to refer to women than men. Of course, not every blonde person is dumb, but there are plenty of good-looking people who are not-so-good-looking inside their heads. Take Paris Hilton, for example. She is the great-granddaughter of Conrad Hilton, the founder of Hilton Hotels. She also became known for a sex tape and is famous for being famous, a celebrity not through talent or work, but through inherited wealth and lifestyle. I mention her because when you look up "blonde stereotype" on Wikipedia, you see her photo. Please don't get mad at me, my dear, smart, blonde friends! I'm just trying to make a point here.

Time after time, I hear that many Korean companies hire the better-looking Caucasian candidate even though she or he may be less qualified than other candidates. Unless you're a model, your looks don't do your job. Your talents and experience do. We should consider creating a system where hiring practices focus on the candidates' past and present work, references, skills and any other proof of their capabilities rather than looks. Don't let the work suffer because of the poor judgment of the hiring person!

BE YOUR OWN BEST FRIEND
Dr. Phil, the popular talk show host who used to be a regular guest on *The Oprah Winfrey Show* many years ago, writes about the importance of self-esteem in his book *Life Law:*

"Self-esteem plays a vital role in our growth. It fuels our growth. Feedback reinforces personal growth. Personal growth nourishes self-esteem. And in turn, more self-esteem generates more growth." At the red carpet event celebrating the story, Matt Lauer on the *Today Show* asked a few of those named the 100 Most Influential People in the World 2014 by *Time* magazine, "What advice would you have given to your younger self?" Most of them answered things like, "Don't be afraid to be yourself." "I wish I had had more confidence growing up." "You should be your own best friend."

Dozens of studies show that when your self-esteem is lower, you are more vulnerable to stress and anxiety; failures and rejections hurt more, and it takes longer to recover from them. You already know this, of course. What you don't know is what to do about it. You think, like those girls in the study, that if you change your face or body, your self-esteem will go up. If only it were that easy! Patricia Marx quotes from, Eunkook Suh, a psychology professor at Seoul's Yonsei University, who said, "In Korea, we don't care what you think about yourself. Other people's evaluations of you matter more."[16]

This statement is the opposite of what people believe in the West. I don't mean Westerners don't care what others think of them. They do, deeply. It's a core human trait. We'd all be sociopaths if we didn't care what others thought. And some Westerners care to a degree or in ways that are harmful to them, which is why the women Meaghan Ramsey mentions don't go to their job interviews. But at least society and pop culture are telling them repeatedly that this is not healthy—there is a chance for the message to sink in.

I'm not taking what Professor Suh said literally. He probably meant that appearance is simply that much more important. If I took what he said literally, I'd worry whether our Korean society could climb out from under such a mountain of psychological issues!

Professor Suh described an experiment he did in which he gave students, both at Yonsei University and at the University of California at Irvine (where he once taught), a photograph and a written description of the same person. Which format, he asked the students, gives you a better understanding of this person? The Koreans chose the photograph, and the Americans chose the description.[17]

Is it true that we live our lives to make other people—not ourselves—happy? Doesn't that sound like a recipe for unhappiness? If you are a confident and secure person, it won't matter as much to you what other people think. Of course, you listen. Maybe they're right; maybe you have something to learn. Is what you're doing or saying offensive? Maybe you should rethink it. But you don't base your important choices in life—your career, your marriage, your interests, what you do with your leisure time—on what others want.

I understand that it's easy for outsiders to comment on things without considering the cultural reality of people's daily lives. And as someone who has lived in the West for decades, I may qualify as an outsider. But sometimes, there are things we don't realize just because we never questioned what's all around us. If we can step back and look at what is being said by those outside—without feeling criticized—it can be very illuminating. All cultures, like all individuals, have blind spots. The important thing is to consider other ideas and be willing to change if some other way may help us and future generations live better lives.

We Koreans often attribute our mindset and behavior to Confucianism. Most of Confucius' teachings are still relevant and valued. But as people and society evolve and become influenced by other cultures and new thinkers around the world, it's worth examining some of our current norms and asking ourselves, "Is this working for us?" "Are we happy?" If not, maybe it's time to reevaluate and open our minds to new perspectives.

In the West, slavish conformity would indicate a person with psychological problems, someone with a very low opinion of himself, willing to erase what makes him unique to be accepted. You may want others to like you, love you, and respect you. But first, you have to feel those things about yourself. You have to become someone that you like. After all, you are the one who has to live with yourself, today and for the rest of your life.

THROUGH MY MOTHER'S EYES

I used to visit my mom often at the senior citizen apartment where she lived. There were a few other Korean ladies who lived in the same building. One day I parked my car in the parking lot and was walking toward the entrance door. One of the Korean ladies stopped me and asked, in an accusatory and lecturing tone, "Why do you dress so *sachihage* (fancy)?" I answered her, "*Halmuni* (grandmother, a general name for any elderly female), I'm not wearing anything fancy. This is how young people dress nowadays." I smiled at her and walked away politely. I still laugh about the encounter. No wonder my mom made a big fuss and disapproved of how I looked when she saw me wearing a sleeveless top or a skirt slightly above the knee.

Mom was consumed with worry about how I might appear to her neighbors in the building, no matter how often I mentioned to her, "Mom, please don't tell me how to dress." Trust me, I dressed like any average young woman you would see on the streets of Chicago. But to my mom, every strand of hair on my face was a concern. When we went to a Korean travel agency to buy tickets to Seoul in 1996, she saw a life-size cutout of a Korean airline stewardess and really liked her uniform. She suggested that I should dress like an airline stewardess.

Clearly, the older and younger generations think and behave very differently. The younger generation is much more open and accepting of the new, in matters of style and substance. But that has its own downside as well, which will be covered in another chapter.

I moved my mom to a nursing home in February 2015. As much as she detested the idea of going to a nursing home—and told me so for years—it ended up being a very good decision for both of us. The nursing home has a Korean floor, which means all the residents are Koreans with a Korean person in charge and several Korean staff. Residents eat Korean food every day and can visit each other's room and keep each other company.

When my mom moved in, I wanted her to have friends right away, so she would feel comfortable in the new environment. I saw a friendly-looking lady who was passing by mom's room, and I invited her to come in. She was much younger than my mom, maybe fifteen-twenty years younger. I said, "My mom just moved here. I hope you can be friends with her." She said, "Sure," then proceeded to tell me, "My son is a successful lawyer. I have my own money, and I drive a car." Some Korean people must have asked her why she lives in a nursing home when she has a son who can take care of her. The way she introduced herself to us was to state that she has money and a successful son, well known in the Korean community in Chicago. She went on and on. Honestly, I wasn't interested in why she was there or if she had money or not. I just wanted her to be friends with my mom.

I hadn't met an old Korean person for a long time. I wasn't used to hearing how much money a person has in the first five minutes after meeting. In Western culture, it's considered obnoxious to tell people how much money you have except in certain contexts. I understand that this lady said what she did, at least in part, to justify her residence in a nursing home. Traditionally, in Korea, most families don't send parents to nursing homes. We take care of them until the end. That is changing. Nowadays, each family has a different set-up, depending on financial circumstances. But she didn't want me to think poorly of her and her family, even though my own mother was in the same nursing home. She wasn't able to see the situation for what it was. She also wanted to put a high value on herself by listing what she had (money, a successful son). She wanted to make sure I knew where to place her in some imaginary chart of important people. What would have made her seem important to me was if she was kind and welcoming to my mother.

~ RESET PERSPECTIVE ~

In your twenties and thirties, you worry about what other people think about you.
In your forties and fifties, you stop worrying about what other people think of you.

In your sixties and seventies, you realize no one was ever thinking about you in the first place.

It takes a lot of time and energy to try to please other people. First your family, relatives and friends, then other students at school and teachers, then colleagues and bosses at work, people who use the same gym or yoga studio or playground where you take your kids, the strangers you see on the street, your parents' old and new friends and acquaintances…. This list is getting very long! Just imagine if you didn't worry about pleasing more than a handful of people—and those only when it made sense. Once you are an adult, you need to take into account what your work supervisor thinks, what your spouse or romantic partner thinks, your close friends…YOURSELF. You are the most important person to please, because aside from that small group who depend on you, people aren't thinking about you nearly as much as you imagine.

Other people are busy thinking about themselves. Aren't you more worried about whatever is a problem in your life than about how someone else looks? Sure, maybe you notice that the new woman at work forgot to touch up her roots or has gained a bit of weight. But if she does her job well and is friendly and courteous to you, do you really care? Are you going to treat her differently?

I'm not saying that other people don't judge you; they do. And some people will notice every little thing you do "wrong" and maybe gossip about it. So what? You should do your best not to be friends with, marry or work for someone who is overly judgmental. As for the rest of the world—let them think what they want. What I've found is that if you work on not judging other people and not judging yourself, if you come from a place of compassion, always reminding yourself that there is probably a very good reason why that person (who may be you) didn't do things perfectly, you will stop caring so much what others think of you. If someone loves to talk about other people constantly, that person has an unhealthy habit.

If you take time to think about the people who have meant the most to you, the ones you remember years later, the ones you always wanted to see if you had a chance, you will realize that maybe some of them are beautiful or always perfectly "put together," but most aren't. Chances are, the members of your "favorite people" list include a wide range of attractiveness—and if the list is long enough (and if you don't happen to work in the modeling profession or come from an exceptionally good-looking family), your list will not be too different from a random sample of people. The uniqueness in each one of us makes us human and special. Honestly, I find the thought of coming out of plastic surgery with the same nose, eyes, or mouth as someone next to me quite creepy. Are we headed for a mass production of sameness like those robots in the movie, *I, Robot*? Are our souls intact, or are we on the brink of losing them?

We notice how people look. We find beauty appealing. It is very difficult to resist not only social but career pressures; I would never blame anyone for making difficult choices to get a good job. But the actions of individuals also affect society and corporations. Often an individual act of resistance inspires many others to think differently. Only you can decide when and how you will ignore what "everyone" is saying or doing. The first step is to think it through and decide what you want for yourself. Don't turn it into something that controls you. If someone tells you, "You are not pretty enough and you need a surgery," that person has a maturity issue. Maybe there's nothing you can do about what they think, but you don't have to buy into it. I'll surely value your individuality, your original face much higher than a face that has same nose, eyes, mouth, and cheekbones everyone else has. Let's work on being "cool" inside and leave the outside alone.

3

Roots & Wings

There are two things we should give our children: one is roots and the other is wings.

--HENRY WARD BEECHER (1813-1887)

ROOTS

I LOVE YOU, MOM, BUT......

Mother love is the ultimate love. There is nothing you can compare it to. A mother's love is fierce, courageous, determined, and bottomless.

I feel my mother's love and presence every day. I know she worries about me twenty-four/seven. Even though she is old and sick and can barely move her own body, she worries about me. It's kind of crazy. It's almost too much love to handle. I begged her to stop worrying about me and worry about herself, but that's just not possible for her.

Living through the war and all of life's challenges, like other mothers of her generation, her main and the most important goal was to take care of my physical well-being, making sure I was eating right and looking healthy. The umbilical cord might have been cut when we came out

48

of our mothers' wombs, but mothers feel that we are attached to them forever; they feel uneasy when we are out of their sight and go out in the world alone without them. It appears to me that this uneasy feeling is much stronger for Korean mothers.

The reality is that we need more than our mothers' love and protection to live our lives. Much more. We need to have the confidence to face the world without our mothers. We need healthy self-esteem to know who we are and who we want to be. We need emotional resilience to deal with life's ups and downs. We need to be independent thinkers so we can make the best decisions for ourselves and our loved ones rather than constantly following or being influenced by others around us. We need to build our character, so we are respected by others and know how to respect others. We need to be encouraged to chart our own course to reach our potential without feeling like our hands are tied by our mothers' assumptions and fears. We need the moral courage to own up to our mistakes and do the right thing even when we are faced with serious consequences. We need the security of knowing that we are loved by our parents, regardless of whether we succeed or fail.

WHAT IF...

My mother may have wanted these things for me; I don't know. I realize it's hard to figure out how to raise a daughter when you yourself were raised to accept limitations and tradition, and when you are buffeted by strong emotions. However what I know about independence, taking healthy risks and accountability I learned after I was on my own. My mom was an incredibly hard worker with a strong personality. I hardly ever saw her just resting. I have no doubt that I have learned many things just by being around her. She embodied many of the qualities I mentioned above—courage, resilience—but she didn't know how to teach or share them with me. She did as most other Korean parents did back then: she controlled and instilled obligation in her children. She made sure I was fed well and looked good, but she understood very little or nothing about how to nurture the emotional needs of a child; she wasn't aware that children needed any such thing. She was repeating how her parents raised her. I know she did her absolute best, and I'm grateful. There are parents who don't care, who abandon their children. My mom cared, and she tried very hard. Yet I carry some resentment about the nurturing I didn't get. I don't like admitting it, but it's important because this story is not only about me. It's about the women of my generation—and especially the younger generations.

Like any child would, I feel guilty analyzing and critiquing my mom's parenting style. I didn't have to live her life. I had more opportunities and more access to other societies' ways of doing things. I've also never been a mom myself. But I know that we can't change things unless we face them; we can't understand how we want to do things differently until we articulate what was wrong with what our mothers did. My story is not just my story. There are many women around the world and especially in Korea who want to cast aside worn-out traditions and use the best of modern knowledge and understanding to remake parenting culture.

As an adult, I have wondered how I might have been different if I had been criticized less, compared to others less often (it didn't happen routinely, but whenever it did, it hurt deeply). Who would I be today if I had been more supported, if I had been encouraged to become my own person? That such a thing was desirable would have been a radical concept in the Korea of my childhood. Maybe even now it seems radical to many people, but I have thought a lot about it.

I think I would have had much higher self-esteem and achieved confidence in myself much sooner.

HOW ARE MODERN MOMS RAISING THEIR CHILDREN?

I had a chance to view one of the Korean Educational Broadcasting System's documentaries on the difference between Korean mothers and American mothers.[18] A word puzzle was presented to several children and their mothers. Each mother was instructed not to help her child even if the child didn't know the answers. Interestingly, American mothers and Korean mothers behaved very differently. All the American mothers followed the instructions and didn't help their children, even though they saw them struggle. They just tried to encourage the child, saying, "It's okay; take your time and think." The Korean mothers, on the contrary, tried to give direct hints or solve the problem themselves—especially when the researcher stepped out for a moment.

After the test, the mothers were interviewed about the experience and why they did what they did. The Korean mothers said that they wanted to help with the answers so the child could pass the test. They felt bad and frustrated watching their children struggle. The American mothers were not so frustrated. They just watched the child until the end without getting involved. They said things like, "If I give him the answer every time, he won't learn how to figure things out by himself. I always encourage him to solve problems on his own." "I was really happy when she did it herself." "I tried hard not to help her so she could do it herself."

The test results were twofold. The Korean children got higher scores on finding the correct answers—62.1 percent—but the Korean moms scored 82.4 percent on negative support and negative expressions. When the child didn't get the answers correctly, the Korean mothers' reactions were negative. "Why didn't you get that right the first time?" "You almost got it right, wow, it's so frustrating."

Researchers call this over-parenting, over-involved style "helicopter parenting." We think the only way of helping our children is to be like a horse wearing blinders, looking straight ahead, focusing on one narrow slice of reality—tests, grades—ignoring everything else going on. My child must pass the test with the highest score. It sounds positive. But let's think of it in another way. This parenting style can do long-term damage to the child, and we wouldn't even realize it.

Children need to have a certain amount of autonomy. They need experiences of using their own unique brains to solve problems, so they can build a sense of self and develop confidence. Once they have been given certain cognitive tools and examples of how to approach problems, let them sort it out. Let them use their inner resources so they will become familiar with the process of trial and error, remembering what worked last time. The process of thinking and searching for solutions is a skill that must be practiced. Learning when to stop thinking and go to an authority for help—a book, parent or teacher—is also a skill that must be practiced. There are no shortcuts.

Researchers tried to find something positive about helicopter parenting—surely it must offer some advantage?—but they couldn't find any.[19]

THE DANGERS OF HELICOPTER PARENTING

Many parents live their lives through their children. Their children's achievements become their own. Of course, we want to be proud of our children and do everything we can do for them. We do it because we love and worry about them. That's what parents are supposed to do, right? But many studies are telling us that we are doing it wrong—that our methods are harmful to our children. The children who grow up with parents who overprotect, over-direct, and are over-involved stay in the parents' shadow. They are not able to shine on their own. They are in need of constant guidance and remain unsure of their decisions even after they grow up. Some may say that it's good for a mother and grown child to have a close relationship, that there's nothing wrong with a son or daughter seeking a parent's advice on things. Maybe it makes the parents feel better—more important, more necessary. But it's not so good if you want your sons and daughters to go out in the world and blaze their own paths of personal and professional growth and have healthy relationships with others.

Some findings on over-parented children are:

They have low self-esteem and low self-efficacy. Kyung H. Lee*, a professor at Hongik University in Seoul, observed that students who were overparented are not as motivated, independent or resourceful as the ones who weren't. They have become so used to being told what to do and when to do it that they become paralyzed when they are on their own. They are fearful of making mistakes. They don't understand the process of exploring new territory or how to take that bold step that will lead them to find answers for a school project or in life. The first part of any new project, creative, scholarly, or business, always involves striking out in a seemingly random way, looking for ideas, checking out resources, casting out a net for anything that will provide a way in or a first step. Everyone does it to begin something. But if you've never learned to do that, if someone always told you exactly where to find information, what to do first, whom to ask...then being on your own is deeply confusing. That confusion can lead to panic, anger at adults who didn't prepare you or are expecting too much from you now and resentment and envy towards other students who have more confidence. Do we want this for our children? I don't think so.

Children raised this way, who don't manage to break from their parents, become adults with an exaggerated sense of entitlement and narcissism.[20] They see themselves as the center of the universe and are very afraid of having that illusion shattered. But because it's an illusion, their coping skills are much weaker. Conflict, struggle, rejection and failure are much harder for them to navigate. If you're anxious about your child's future, think about this: not having coping skills can be disastrous. Julie Lythcott-Haims' *How to Raise an Adult* and Jessica Lahey's *The Gift of Failure* are two good books on this subject.[21]

A ship in port is safe, but that is not what ships are built for.

– Grace Hopper.

So what's a parent to do? How do parents give freedom and support in the right balance? How can parents prepare kids for the rough sailing in the sea called Life?

Here are a few tips from education experts:

Stop controlling and start coaching. Coaches help kids develop skills to play the game. The coach's focus is on bringing out the best in the kid so that he will succeed in both expected and unexpected circumstances. The kids play the game, not the coach. The coach is on the sidelines. It's easier to understand how this works when you're talking about a game that happens a few hours, days or weeks after coaching, and when the rules are strict. The coach who runs out on the field will be fired. The kid who freezes because he doesn't know how to react to a surprising play will lose. But life is not much different; it's just more complicated and takes place over many years. If you want your child to succeed, you have to let go of your need to control.[22] You have to teach the skills—strengthen the muscles—and then trust that he will take it from there. You can't play the game for him. If you feel anxious about his chances, that's your problem. It can be very difficult and painful. There's no worry like a parent's worry. But it's your job to manage your anxiety, so you don't transfer it to your child. Children of anxious parents are more likely to be anxious themselves.

Remember that perfection is not the goal. Constant parental involvement undermines a child's confidence and ability to learn on his own. Give him room to think for himself. No one is perfect, and the most talented and brilliant people are bad in some things, or at some ages. Einstein didn't start to speak until he was four years old. Many very creative people—artists, scientists, mathematicians—tend to become lost in their thoughts and forget obligations, are late, or dress oddly. This doesn't mean your tardy child is a genius. Most of us are not geniuses, and that's fine. The point is that by focusing on what your child is not doing well, you may be ignoring what he does do well—what could become a life's passion. You could also be reacting to a passing phase or slower development in such a catastrophic way that what you fear—that he will never learn—actually comes true.

Psychologists talk about the necessity of learning to "emotionally regulate" oneself. This means being able to handle painful but very ordinary emotions. As adults, we have to do this every day, dealing with the normal stresses of life, but it's not innate; we learn it from our parents, at school, from other kids. But mostly from our parents. Don't jump into solving problems for them. If your daughter gets a low mark on a test or book report, she may be sad or depressed, but once she is done grieving her failure, with your compassion and your expression of confidence in her, she will pull herself together and try again the next day. That's how children build resilience.

Many mothers face high anxiety when they think that their children will reflect badly on them, that people will talk behind their backs. "What was she thinking…Did you see what that child was wearing? How he behaved? She must be a terrible mother…" Of course, it's painful if people gossip about you (and they will, no matter what you do). But it's not a sufficient reason to be critical of your child—to hurt her now and harm her emotional development. Do you think that your fear of looking "bad" in the eyes of other mothers, whom you may not even like, is more important than the well-being of your child? Let go. Let your daughter be her own strange, imperfect self—her own wonderful self.

Focusing on your children so much is not only bad for them, it's bad for you, too. One study showed that parents who judge their self-worth by their children's accomplishments report sadness and diminished contentment with life in general. [23]

More on the process, less on the results. Give positive feedback on things she has control over, like hard work or perseverance, rather than things she has no control over, like being smart in a particular area or having physical limitations. The most important thing is trying and improving with practice over time, not earning the best score or winning. Those things are the byproduct of having a good process.

If you focus less on results and more on process and techniques, you will learn faster and become more successful.[24] We like to focus on results because results are easier to measure, and we know people judge on results. And it feels great to get good results, obviously. However, especially when you are young with a developing mind and brain, process is much more important. A process-driven outcome will take your child much further and get him more excited about learning.

Many of the most useful inventions and innovations are the results of accidental discoveries while experimenting. Joe Tan, an industrial product designer, says, "The process itself is a source of great joy—searching for solutions, solving problems, learning, creating, asking, uncovering, realizing, manifesting and sharing the result. It's all a part of the experience.

"I give my parents a lot of credit. They created an environment that not only allowed us—but also encouraged us—to explore new things and pick up new hobbies without judgment or bias on their part. They were always really supportive and provided whatever means they had available towards the pursuit of these things. They never made us feel that we weren't good at something. Instead, they set us free and had the patience and presence of mind to give us the time to nurture our interests instead of giving up on them. Through exploration and repetition, we naturally hone our skills. And it's always more fun when you make progress. Now that my wife and I are raising a son of our own, I realize just how important it is to give the gift of freedom and encouragement to our children. Just by doing something with enthusiasm and curiosity, you can inspire someone else to do it with you."

THE POWER OF IMITATION

Children emulate their parents. This is the fundamental structure of human civilization. A recent book, *The Secret of Our Success: How Culture is Driving Human Evolution,*[25] explains how humans have come so far because of their ability for social learning. Children have an inborn tendency to copy older, more successful people without having to think about it. We do this far more than do animals, whose survival depends much more on instinct. This means that we are at the mercy of those who are our role models, particularly our parents. A young child is wired to watch, listen, repeat. It's very basic—they don't see your intentions or fears, just what you say and do.

If a child fails at something or there is something negative about your child—or, to be more precise, you think there is something negative—discouraging talks or blaming comments can start to pour out of your mouth: "What an idiot!" Bite your tongue! Your child was just told that he is an idiot. Will that shame him into trying harder? Or will it make him curl up inside, feeling like there's no point in trying since he is an idiot? Maybe your child will take the first path—work to prove you wrong. Even if this is the case, he will have doubts; he will be angry, and he will be at risk when he faces the normal setbacks of life. Instead of hearing your voice encouraging him in a time of crisis, he will hear "What an idiot!"

When we talk and compare ourselves to others that falls into this category, as well. Our first response is to believe what people say. We learn to be more discerning as we get older, but the emotional effect remains strong. Many parents berate themselves or their children without thinking of the long-term effect this has on their children. You shouldn't let anyone talk to you or your child that way—including yourself.

PUSH AND PULL AMBITIONS

In one of my interviews with Thomas Kim, entrepreneur and early stage investor, we talked about the two types of ambition. Many of our Korean parents push their children to become doctors, lawyers, government officials or accountants. These are the most respected professions and offer financial security. This is a "push" ambition, where the pressure coming from other people is what motivates the child. It is based on external drives. Sometimes this ambition is instilled through fear or obligation. "Your father went to Seoul University and you should, too."

The downside is that if you become a doctor or lawyer only because your parents wanted it when your real desires and talents lie elsewhere, you are in for an unhappy and stressful life.

"Pull" ambition comes from dreams that are pulling you forward. It's a longing you have, an internal drive. It keeps you going through good times and bad; it is a natural expression of who you are and what you value. In the best cases, it fits your talents and strengths and leads to success, but even when it doesn't—when the dream exceeds your ability—it puts you in a positive relation to life, wanting to contribute because of genuine interest and passion. Dreams often have to be modified. Society is not set up to make all of us perfectly fulfilled. But strong "pull" is the best predictor of continued effort and engagement with life. Don't we want our children to have "pull" ambition, to be motivated and working towards something that they have a passion for and are enthusiastically interested in learning? That's when personal satisfaction and self-validation levels will be at their highest. Parents can try to instill "pull" ambition by encouraging their children's interests, helping them to find their passions, stick with them and excel. The best way to ensure your child has this kind of ambition, however, is to have it yourself. Let your child see that you are pursuing something you love, even if you aren't able to make a career of it. Share your dreams.

When a child is pushed, the child learns to turn off his internal desires. Then, when and if an opportunity comes to explore that desire—without an external push—his motivation is either too weak or is nowhere to be found.

One kind of ambition is highly negative, especially if the child is not up to the task or shows no interest in the type of work he is being pushed to do. The other one is positive and compelling on a profound level. Which kind of ambition would you want your child to have?

WINGS

MOTHERS IN LAW: LIVE AND LET LIVE!

Initially, I wasn't planning to write about this, but when I started interviewing people, I realized that so many families are living with conflicts are torn apart because of a thousand years of mother-in-law/daughter-in-law traditional adversarial relations. Mothers think that no woman is good enough for their sons. They may have such high expectations of their daughters-in-law that it's difficult to have normal family relationships, not to mention happy ones. Our Korean mothers dedicate their lives to their children, and many of them develop a special possessiveness about their sons. When you become a full-time mom, you put 100 percent of your energy into your child(ren), which can get a little obsessive. Your children become your main purpose in life. If a woman is unhappy in her marriage, if she feels neglected by a husband who is working all the time or out drinking with colleagues, her focus on her children may intensify. And that obsessive emotion doesn't just stop when the kids grow up and get married.

I have met many full-time mothers who feel lonely and unfulfilled after their children grow up, especially the ones who compromised their career to raise children. Many young mothers feel isolated, invisible, and depressed while raising children even though they love being with their children. [26] This is one of the reasons that it's good to spread your energy outside of your children by pursuing a career or finding ways to stimulate your intellectual capacities. Continuing and exploring one's personal growth is important to each of us whether through a career and/or other creative outlets. But whether you work outside the home or not, you can have problems with your in-laws: particularly your mother-in-law or daughter-in-law.

My mother and my sister-in-law had one of those awful relationships. They had many disagreements when they were living in the same house. Finally, my mom moved out, and I came to the U.S. There were no more arguments since they only saw each other once every two or three years. When my mom first told me about her relationship with her daughter-in-law after my arrival in Chicago, I decided that I wasn't going to take a side. I didn't know my sister-in-law, but I know my mother isn't the easiest person to get along with. In any case, I was glad that it was in the past and I didn't have to witness any of it. I could tell how intense the relationship was, however, by the way my mother talked about some of the incidents. What a shame that they don't have any good memories of each other. It's the same for all the Korean mothers-in-law and daughters-in-law who live, or lived, with conflicts.

A lot of the conflicts center on the kitchen. Whenever families get together, there is an enormous amount of work to be done in the kitchen, preparing the food and cleaning the dishes. It is expected that the daughters-in-law will help their mothers-in-law while the men are sitting around chatting or drinking. However much or little of the kitchen work is done by the daughter-in-law or the mother-in-law, there are complaints. Some daughters-in-law describe themselves as "slaves" while mothers-in-law say their daughters-in-law are not doing their parts.

There are many modern, open-minded mothers-in-law in Korea, but it seems that we still have a lot more traditional mothers-in-law. Hyemi Jung, a graduate student living abroad in San Francisco, shares her story.

"Many Korean mothers' ambition and greed for their sons are strong. Mothers think of sons as their possessions. Because the parents sacrificed themselves for their sons, when the son gets married, they believe he and his wife also should pay back to them. There are many good mothers-in-law, too, but there are still many traditional mothers-in-law who think this way.

"My mother-in-law didn't acknowledge the fact that her son and I created a separate family unit. She thinks she owns her son; therefore she couldn't accept any decisions that were made between my husband and me. Both my mother and father-in-law thought it was our responsibility to take care of them and my sister-in-law and her husband. They always talked as if this was our duty and the purpose of our marriage. They would say 'How come you only did this much for us? How come you did so little for your sister-in-law?'

"When we decided to study overseas, the parents got very upset and said to my husband, 'How could you make a such a decision without asking us! You are our son, and you need our permission to do things like this!' They basically didn't allow us to have our own lives and make our decisions. The in-laws felt that it was our duty to make them happy before considering our own happiness. Because they sacrificed their lives for their son. It was payback time now."

I asked, "How did your husband handle the situation?" Jung responded, "He really wanted independence from his parents in the beginning, so he tried to fight them. But as time passed and things got worse, he felt that he should think of his parents first. They had the obey-your parents'-orders and follow-your-parents'-wishes relationship, like most Korean family relationships.

"Whenever I went to my mother-in-law's house, I felt like I was a domestic helper. Always working in the kitchen. I didn't even feel comfortable sitting down for a bit. I felt like I was there as a housemaid. I sensed that my mother-in-law didn't want her own daughter to work in the kitchen. Since I got that feeling from her, I'd just say, 'I'll do it my-self.' I cannot change my mother-in-law's thoughts. We cannot change the old generation. If I tried to fight or tried to make them understand, I became the crazy person. I got accused of receiving bad education from my parents. You have to obey your parents regardless. My parents were different. My parents respected my decisions since I was little. If there were things I wanted to do, my parents always said, 'Go ahead and try it!' That's how I grew up. So it was very hard when I got married and was introduced to my husband's family. It was a very different family environment. My mother-in-law talked about and treated me very dis-respectfully. She spoke to me politely in front of other family members, but when she talked to me alone or on the phone, she was very rude and talked without any consideration. So we went to America. Then the rela-tionship with my husband soured because I refused to take my mother-in-law's phone calls after a while. I couldn't endure it. He took it as I was disrespecting his mother because I was ignoring her calls. That was the cause of our bad relationship. We are not together at the moment."

Miriam Kim, who grew up in Argentina and is happily married to a Korean husband, now lives in Los Angeles. She loves her mother-in-law, but she is also familiar with the sad experience of her best friend Carmen, who grew up with her in Argentina. "Carmen and her family moved to the U.S. when she was fifteen years old," Miriam told me. "She went to the University of California Los Angeles (UCLA) and met Jack, who is Korean. They became college sweethearts and wanted to get married. Even though Carmen came from a good family with money, Jack's parents never approved of Carmen, saying that she was not good enough for their son. There was always tension and hatred between the families. Despite all these unhealthy feelings, Jack proposed to Carmen and gave her a ring. And the ring became the cause of their eventual breakup.

"Carmen is the kind of person who never talks about her problems. On the outside, she is always smiling. She was raised differently than me. I never cared what people think. I'm very opinionated. If I have to argue, I will argue to the end, but she is not like that. She will swallow everything. Her mother is very traditional, very conservative. That's how she was raised, too, even though she was born in Argentina.

"Carmen, having good taste and some knowledge of diamonds, wanted to upgrade the ring with a diamond with better clarity and change the gold band to a platinum band, which was the trend at that time. She was willing to pay for it herself. When Jack's parents heard this, they became furious at Carmen. Their attitude was 'How dare she!' To them, it was a matter of pride and, ultimately, disrespect. Eventually, Jack and Carmen called off the wedding even though they loved each other immensely. She was heartbroken. A few years went by. Jack moved to Chicago for work, but they kept in touch and still loved each other. Then they decided to get married. They were determined to stand up for themselves this time—no matter what. Carmen suffered emotional distress for many years. They finally got married and had two children. Sadly, they found out that Carmen had stomach cancer during her third pregnancy. She passed away shortly after."

It's still an open question among scientists if there is a direct relationship between stress, the immune system and cancer.[27] Whatever the answer may be, nobody can deny the tragic sequence presented in Miriam's story about her friend Carmen. Its sad ending reminds us of Romeo and Juliet's love story.

Korean children are raised with many rules and obligations. There are many, many "you can'ts" and "you shoulds." If you do anything that "you can't do" or "we don't do," you are looked upon as a bad, rude, inconsiderate, shameful, even crazy person. Of course there are also rules in the West for children when it comes to proper manners and how to behave, but there are not so many obligations. Living in this strict environment of so many "you can'ts" and "you shoulds," anyone can easily become the problem daughter-in-law.

In the mothers-in-law's defense, they are just being cautious, looking out for their sons' best interests. Since they have more experience in life, they think their advice is important and necessary. They are intrusive, but they think they are helping; they are stubborn because they think they are right. It doesn't occur to many mothers-in-law that constant conflict with a child's spouse is always stressful and that unless the spouse is doing something seriously wrong (dangerous), interfering will only increase unhappiness.

WESTERN MOTHERS-IN-LAW

Western mothers are devoted to their sons, too, but they are, in general, far less involved in their adult sons' day-to-day lives. They tend to be much more careful about expressing complaints about their daughters-in-law. I'm not saying every Western mother-in-law and daughter-in-law have a great relationship (it is a universal conflict) but compared to Asians, they do. The major difference is Western families set boundaries with people. There is a limit on how intrusive you are allowed to be in each other's lives. Angela Pettit, a mother of two from Milwaukee, Wisconsin, says this about Western in-law relationships, "There are bad relationships, for sure, but in general it's not a big topic, as relationships are usually rather loose." In regard to her own in-laws, "I wouldn't call our relationship warm and fuzzy. I do need to be careful with what I say. But overall, we enjoy each other's company and get along."

I would have to say that it's much better to have a loose relationship than to have a conflicted relationship and have the marriage suffer.

My niece Julie who lives in Seattle, Washington, seems to have things figured out for herself. "How is your relationship with your mother-in-law?" I asked her. She responded, "I've seen horrible mother-in-law relationships. I think my mother-in-law is in the middle of the road. Yes, there is a difficulty there, but I hear so many stories. Constant criticism! The number one thing I hear is either the husband will side with his wife or with his mother, and that has to be consistent. Husbands who are either wishy-washy about that or side with their moms are horrible for the wives. But if the husband is with the wife like Wes [Julie's husband]—he will always side with me even if I'm wrong. He always defends me and sides with me. He will not say anything negative about me to his mom."

I said, "Whoa, what a husband Wes is! How did that happen?"

"When we got engaged we did the pre-marriage counseling. That was the advice the pastor gave. Also, it was coming from me. I was already aware that it could be an issue, so I told him that we are only getting married if you and I are always together on this."

Julie and Wesley have two children: Hayley, eleven years old, and Elijah, six. I asked, "When you become a mother-in-law yourself, if you don't approve of your daughter-in-law, how will you handle it?" There were a few seconds of silence. "Elijah is very close to me, like extremely close. I always joke with Wes that I only get him until he is married. Once he's married, I'm never going to see him," she said jokingly. "I think that's healthier. Well, Hayley will be around all the time even after she gets married. I think she will always be calling me. We will be hanging out. It's a very different relationship, but with him, I'm already praying that I'll like my future daughter-in-law. I'm of the opinion that I don't have any say in who he eventually picks. I get to parent him and try to influence him to make the right decisions until he's in college; from then on, whomever he takes, I don't have any right to criticize or even give any real input unless he asks for my advice. I'm already preparing myself that I have to let go. It'll be much healthier even if he is still close to me. It doesn't matter if I like his wife. There is that tension there because I anticipate he and I'll be close. I think that has to change."

We all hear about how close Italian mothers and sons are. Italian mothers can put even the best marriage at risk. An Italian study found that the odds that a marriage will last increase with every hundred yards that couples put between themselves and their in-laws. Italian courts found this evidence so compelling that they have ruled that a wife has a right to a legal separation if her husband is not effective in preventing his mother from "invading" their home, says Cambridge University psychologist Terri Apter, who embarked on the study of in-law relationships because of her own relationship with her mother-in-law. [28]

I'm lucky to have a mother-in-law who has four sons and is a sweet, loving, and easygoing person. From the very beginning when we were married, she told me, "I don't want to mind any of your business." All she wants is to spend some good family time together whenever we are able to. All her daughters-in-law appreciate her and love her dearly.

~ RESET PERSPECTIVE ~

Our Korean family culture is too tightly interwoven to be healthy or sustainable. Let's take a look at how Western families deal with this highly complex and emotional mother/daughter-in-law relationship and discover some of the things we can do to ease the tension and live a little bit more independently.

Give your child unconditional love with no attachment. You love your child and raise him to be the best person he can be, but once he finishes college, you have to let him go. Give him your blessing to go wherever he chooses. Let him spread his wings and find his new nest and new adventure in life. As hard as it may be, know that you will still be part of his life, and he will fly back and see you whenever he can, not because it's an obligation but because he wants to.

It's time for you to live your life! Parents, you have sacrificed so much for your children. You have done enough. It's time for you to detach your emotions as much as you can from your child and live your own life. This doesn't mean you will love your son any less, but because you love your son, this is necessary. Your grownup son is not yours anymore to guide or take care of, especially after he is married. Once your child finishes school, your obligation to support him has been met. It's quite common for Korean parents to buy a home for their marrying children. Unless you have more than enough money for a comfortable retirement, don't stretch yourself too thin financially.

Almost half of Korea's elderly live in poverty, a fact I was shocked to learn. Korea has the worst senior poverty rate among developed nations. The elderly end up poor for several reasons, but one of them is that most of their life earnings go into their children's education. There is no guarantee your children will be able to take care of you. There's a strong possibility that they may struggle to make a living and have difficulty caring for their own spouses and children. Once your children are not dependent anymore, it's time to think about your own well-being and the security of your retirement. Indeed, the sooner you prepare for this, the better. No more endless giving to your children if you are that kind of parent. And don't give anything that you don't consider a gift—that you think of as something they will "owe" you for, now or in the future.

Much family disharmony is caused by the giving and taking of expensive gifts. Once you give something large, it's natural to expect reciprocation in some way. The daughters-in-law can complain about their mothers-in-law but may feel obligated to listen and follow the mother-in-law's wishes since she has spent so much money. So unless you are planning to be an ungrateful daughter-in-law, don't expect or accept more than small tokens of affection. In the West, they say, "There is no free lunch."

DEAR MOTHERS-IN-LAW:
Thank you for your sacrifice and devotion in raising your son(s). I hope they brought much happiness and joy while you were raising them. I hope you have a peaceful and respectful relationship with your daughter-in-law. But if you are one of the mothers-in-law who is suffering and living with a disappointing daughter-in-law, maybe you could try to look at things a little differently so you can manage the relationship better and be more at peace with your own life.

The mother-in-law/daughter-in-law relationship generally starts with anxiety on both sides. You have had experience with it (most likely), and she has heard stories. Except in those rare cases where there is a natural and happy affinity between two women, there's an adjustment to be made. Your family is not what it used to be, and it will never again be like it was.

You may feel that your life's work is slipping away. You may feel betrayed when your son takes his wife's side or doesn't support you on your issues. It's only too easy to think that she is influencing him, changing him, but it's more likely that she is just making you aware of how he has already changed. If it's a good marriage—and that's what you want for him—she now knows him better than you do. You know the little boy and the adolescent, but she knows the man he is now and the man he hopes to be. If you want to know your son as an adult, get to know your daughter-in-law. Perhaps you remember how cautiously you navigated your own husband's family when you were a young bride. You may not think she's being as cautious—and maybe she isn't. Times have changed. But it's also possible you don't "read" her expressions and comments correctly. Most newly married women want to get along with their husbands' families. And most people are also good at hiding their fears. She's not the same as you—of course not. She's still a young woman feeling her way through life, hoping to be happy.

If you do choose to argue, please be aware that you are hurting your son and his marriage by putting him in the middle. Your son's wife needs to be respected and come first in his life, even before you if that choice has to be made. I know that you may be taken aback or shocked at hearing this. This may be an area where culture has moved on, and you wish it hadn't. But in fact, it's always been true that a marriage is strong only if both people are getting what they need. You wish your daughter-in-law to make your son happy and healthy, to take as good care of him as you do your husband. You want her to be a good mother if they have children. Please try to remember that to do these things, your daughter-in-law needs to be taken care of by her husband. It should be a mutually respectful and equal relationship. Do you feel that your marriage is not—or was not—equal? When I look at the marriages of some older people in my family, I would say that the wife did not have enough input and did not get the respect she deserved, especially in her youth. But we can't change the past, only the present.

In the present, you may want your sons and daughters-in-law to visit you more often and take care of you. Probably they are trying, but they are dealing with many challenges, desires, and responsibilities of their own. They are also setting up their own house and merging two different individual minds and ways to create one family. There's tension in that, but also joy. Do you remember what it felt like?

Your daughter-in-law was raised in a different household, with different rules and expectations. It's that difference that can lead to anxiety and a feeling that something is lost—but it can just as easily be seen as something gained. Maybe you're a better cook than she is, or maybe you just have your ways, and she has hers. She may have learned slightly different recipes or preparations of traditional dishes, or wants to try her hand at something she heard about. Mothers-in-law often feel like this is disrespectful to them. A mother-in-law may feel competitive with her daughter-in-law's mother or anxious about any influences that come from outside. Try to see it as your family getting bigger: something you are still a part of.

Undeniably, we are seeing some traditions and societal views evolving. The world is changing; women have new roles to play, and that affects marriages and families. This doesn't mean your sons and daughters respect you less or love you less. It's just that the nature of our duties and obligations are in flux. People always strive to live more harmoniously, with less friction, and that is what your children and their spouses are doing. You may not agree with them about everything. You may think things were handled better in the past. But they are adults now. If you want to have a good, loving relationship with them, listen to them and respect their thinking. Probably you won't agree with every idea they have. That's normal. But show them the courtesy of keeping it to yourself if you think they are wrong. They will love you for it and be grateful for your open-mindedness and understanding.

After your children finish school, it's a whole new stage of life. It's always sad when they leave—of course, you miss them—but it can also be an opportunity to make new friends, reconnect with old friends, start a new hobby, travel, or learn things that you were always interested in but never had time for. It is never too late to start living for yourself. Don't feel that you are being selfish! An active mind and body will keep you healthy and happy. Don't clutter your thoughts with resentment, anger, or disappointment about what your daughters-in-law are doing or not doing. Live your life and let them live theirs.

With much love,
A Daughter-in-Law

DEBT OR NO DEBT?

Amy Chua, the Chinese American John M. Duff Professor of Law at Yale Law, is the author of a controversial book *Battle Hymns of the Tiger Mother* (2011). She received death threats and was criticized heavily after *The Wall Street Journal*, an international daily newspaper based in New York City, published an article about her book titled, "Why Chinese Mothers are Superior."[29] In the article, she said something I found very interesting.

"Chinese parents believe that their kids owe them everything. The reason for this is a little unclear, but it's probably a combination of Confucian filial piety and the fact that the parents have sacrificed and done so much for their children. Anyway, the understanding is that Chinese children must spend their lives repaying their parents by obeying them and making them proud. By contrast, I don't think most Westerners have the same view of children being permanently indebted to their parents. My husband, Jed, actually has the opposite view." (Jed is an American, also a professor of law at Yale.)

'Children don't choose their parents,' he once said to me. 'They don't even choose to be born. It's parents who foist life on their kids, so it's the parents' responsibility to provide for them. Kids don't owe their parents anything. Their duty will be to their own kids.' This strikes me as a terrible deal for the Western parent. "

Our Korean parents think the same way as the Chinese parents do since Korean society's moral and social rules are also based on Confucianism. So which side is right? Do we have to spend our entire lives paying back our parents or do we owe nothing to our parents?

I'm in the middle. I don't think parents should be keeping score and asking their children to pay back for raising them. Nor should children demand help once they are grown. Neither parents nor adult children should insist on specific amounts of time or gifts/money from the other or play one spouse against another. I don't think I would want to go to a family gathering if I was treated as a second-class citizen and just stuck in the kitchen cooking and cleaning the whole time. Let the men do the dishes! Family gatherings should be a time of remembering, laughing, and celebrating, spending time together with those you love. That's so much more important than anything else. Of course, that's not always possible—conflicts between people are inevitable, and sometimes problems or illnesses can make even loving families feel more stressed around each other. The aim in being together should not be obligation, or keeping score, but enjoyment.

A MOTHER'S SPEECH

Angelina Jolie, actress, filmmaker and humanitarian, received the Jean Hersholt Humanitarian Award at the 2013 Governors Awards. I was quite moved listening to her acceptance speech and I want to share it with the mothers who want their children to know they have the potential to reach beyond themselves, to have empathy for others, to be leaders. She began by speaking to her adopted son, Maddox, from Cambodia, who was present.

"I'm not going to cry. I promise. I won't embarrass you. You and your brothers and sisters are my happiness. There is no greater honor in this world than being your mom...." Then Jolie talked about her own mother.

"My mother loved art. She loved film. She supported any crazy thing I did, but whenever it had meaning, she made a point of telling me that is what film is for. She never had a career as an artist. She never had the opportunity to express herself beyond her theater class, but she wanted more for us than she had had. She wanted Jamie [her brother] and I to know what it is to have a life as an artist, and she gave us that chance. She drove me to every audition, and she would wait in the car for hours and always make me feel really good all the times I didn't get the job. When I did, we would jump up and down and scream and yell like little girls. She wasn't the best critic since she never had anything unkind to say, but she did give me love and confidence, and above all, she was very clear that nothing would mean anything if I didn't live a life of use to others. I didn't know what that meant for a long time.

"I came into this business young and worried about my own experiences, my own pain. It was only when I began to travel and look and live beyond my home that I understood my responsibility to others. When I met survivors of war and famine, of rape, I learned what life is like for most people in this world and how fortunate I was to have food to eat, a roof over my head, a safe place to live and the joy of having my family safe and healthy. I realized how sheltered I have been, and I was determined never to be that way again.

"We are home. Everyone in this room is so fortunate. I have never understood why some people are lucky enough to be born with the chance that I had to have this path in life and why across the world is a woman just like me, with the same abilities and the same desires, same work ethic and love for her family, who would most likely make better films and better speeches, only she sits in a refugee camp and she has no voice. She worries about what her children will eat and how to keep them safe and if they will ever be allowed to return home. I don't know why this is my life, and that's hers. I don't understand that, but I will do as my mother asked. I will do the best I can with this life to be of use. To stand here today means that today I did what she asked, and if she were alive, she'd be very proud."

4

Fathers

He was there when I didn't understand, he was there when I was wrong, he was there when I cried, he was there when I lied. For some reason my dad was always there, when I needed him the most. His love was never ending. And now that he's gone, there is an emptiness in my world but not in my heart.

—MICHAEL JORDAN

I DON'T KNOW MY DAD

My half brother Jon has four children, three boys and one girl. Their names are Randy, Bill, Julie, and Jim. We have never lived in the same city, so I didn't really get a chance to know them. They were living in Wisconsin when I came to Chicago in 1980. Jon was running a martial arts studio on the second floor and a restaurant below the studio. Even though we were brother and sister, there was such an age gap between us that we never knew what to say to each other. He went to Germany when he was in his early twenties and came to the U.S. in 1967.

Despite the many decades he has lived in Germany and America, he still is a very traditional Korean man. He was never really Americanized.

This is the case for the many first-generation Koreans who come to the U.S. as adults. He is a quiet and hardworking person who started several businesses over the years and lost them all. Unfortunately, hard work alone is rarely enough to succeed in a competitive landscape.

Some years ago, I went to Seattle for a conference at Microsoft. I spent a weekend at Julie's house and got a chance to see everyone for a short time. I remember a conversation between my brother, Jon, and his son Bill, who was working in lead development and software architecture at the Nordstrom headquarters in Seattle.

We were in the car driving somewhere, and Jon was telling Bill what an idiot he was for not taking a job at Microsoft when he had the chance. Jon continued, "You graduated at the top of your class from one of the best business schools in the country, and you're working at a department store!" To Jon, Microsoft was the best company to work for in the U.S., the equivalent to Samsung in Korea. Working for a big corporation meant having financial security. A few minutes into this conversation, I couldn't stay quiet, and so I said, with some anger in my voice, "*Oppa* (brother), Microsoft is not the only place Billy can work. Nordstrom is probably the best company in its category in the retail industry. Maybe Bill doesn't want to work for Microsoft!"

While this conversation was going on between Jon and me, Bill didn't say a word. He was calm and pretty much brushed it off as if we were talking about someone else. I was the one who got all worked up in Bill's defense. I couldn't stand the insult to Bill, regardless of the fact that Jon was his father. Looking back, I think I was probably mad at all Korean fathers and mothers who talk to their sons and daughters this way.

Bill has been a co-founder of a mobile software company for the last seven years.

I have always been impressed with my nephews and niece. I wonder how they grew up to be so well-balanced and intelligent when they were raised in such a militaristic and oppressive way. If I were one of them, I would be full of anger and resentment toward my parents.

Recently, I interviewed Bill for this book. "Many Korean parents tend to be very oppressive," he said. "They are not very affectionate. A lot of parents are not compassionate with their kids. Obviously, not all of them, but it seemed to be common among Korean families. The majority of Korean families don't talk among themselves about who they are as people. I can honestly tell you that I know I'm not the only one who grew up as a stranger to my Korean family. In this culture, you don't really know your parents; they don't want to talk about themselves or tell you anything until they're really old and get nostalgic. Then they want to reminisce, and they need someone to talk to. It's the same thing with most of my Korean American friends. Their fathers never told them anything; basically, they don't know them as people. They don't know how they grew up. They don't know what challenges they faced. Meanwhile, the kids feel like their parents don't know anything about them either. You grow up as strangers. It's really sad. I don't think we are the only culture like this, but we are definitely worse at 'family togetherness' than Western culture."

A recent study in *The Hankyoreh* found that South Korean children spend an average of six minutes a day with their father. By contrast, Australian fathers spend seventy-two minutes, U.S. fathers seventy-six minutes, and Japanese fathers nineteen minutes.[30] There is no way this does not have a very negative effect on Korean children.

Recently, in the U.S. media, there has been a lot of talk about how millennials (the generation born between 1980 and 1998) don't know how to deal with ordinary human conflict because they've been so coddled.

There should be a balance as in anything in life. You have to guide your children. They need to be directed, and they need discipline; they need to be aware of the needs of others (including parents). But they also are vulnerable and learning about the world, and deserve compassion and respect for their newly forming selves. Even those who want to make conscious choices about parenthood have trouble sifting through the ideas, advice and parenting styles—while also attending to the rest of their lives. You want to prepare your children for the challenges of life, to make them strong and resilient, but you don't want to stunt them emotionally or turn them into enemies.

My nephew said, "Korean parents tend to just dictate something for you to do. They don't explain or convince you why you should do this thing. They just say: do it. Then you kind of feel like a slave. I don't know what it is. I think there is a communication problem. They just don't talk to each other. Fathers, mothers and the kids: none of them do."

Bill added, "They are ashamed. It happened to my brothers. Any time kids lose their way, the parents basically crucify them. They don't support you. The saddest part about that is that what if your kid was struggling with something that they could overcome? What if they were poised for greatness, but they just lost their way for a little while… which happens all the time. Look at all the successful people who lost their way at one point, like President Obama, who rebelled a little as a teenager, smoked pot and so on. They went into the wilderness before they became successful. What's typical in the Asian story is that when kids lose their way and stumble, the parents basically just get rid of them. They just disown them. Then what happens is that when that kid arrives into success, the parents cannot rejoice in it because the whole time they were beating the kid down, telling him that he was a loser and a failure.

"I don't know why Asian parents do that. I don't know where that comes from. They don't have any patience for their kids. They have to know that their kids are going to struggle at some point; that's when you need to support them. So when they do succeed you can rejoice in their success. The Asian concept of shame is kind of weird. It is bad. I don't know why Korean parents are so quick to condemn their kids…."

Our Korean parents belittle their children in front of their friends or other people without thinking there's anything wrong with it. Julie used to teach Korean middle school girls. She says, "They have the worst self-image issues. I remember I had an overweight friend at the Korean church I went to. Her grandmother would come up to me all the time and say, 'You are so thin and pretty, but our baby is so ugly!' That's so typical of Koreans."

I'm sure many of us heard this from our parents. "Why can't you be more like her, why aren't you this or that?" When you grow up think-ing you are always inferior to someone, it's impossible to feel good about yourself or have the self-confidence to live your life fully. Our parents need to realize this kind of talk is demeaning and destructive to children's self-esteem. Everyone is special in his or her own way. We don't have to be alike and look alike. Let's face it—conformity is kind of boring.

Children are very sensitive and responsive to situations around them. If you have an aggressive and demanding parental style without giving your children reasons for what you do, they will rebel and resent you. Human beings, regardless of their age, want respect. So when you belittle or treat them like they are idiots, of course they will rebel—sometimes vocally, sometimes silently—or suffer as what little self-esteem they have gets destroyed. They will keep a distance from you, and once that distance has been created, it will be hard to close. Nobody wants to be talked down to no matter how young she is.

Children may or may not want to do something if you explain the reason for it, but you will at least have a chance to persuade them and win their cooperation rather than have them obey out of fear. And even if you do have to put your foot down about something, they will remember later that you took the time to explain, and they will remember your explanations. Years later, you may hear your child say, "You know what? You were right. I'm glad you made me do that." But you will never hear that if you don't make the effort to let them know that overruling them was done for specific reasons: safety, their future well-being, others' needs, whatever it may have been.

Your home should be not just a place to eat, rest, and sleep, but a place where you can share your frustrations, disappointments, and happiness with your family. For the children, it should be a place to be encouraged and supported as much as possible, not criticized and shamed if they happen to fail. They need that support to get up, gather the emotional strength, and do better next time.

Many fathers don't realize what an enormous impact they have on their children's lives, even if they know how important their own father was. A funny thing happens: if their fathers made them feel small, they still feel small when they become parents. They think their greatest contribution is to bring home money. Many studies show that when fathers are involved in childcare, kids become more confident, concentrate better, are less aggressive and suffer less from anxiety and depression. [31]

"Mothers and fathers give different stimuli to their children. While mothers tend to use more emotional words and play emotional and linguistic games with their children, fathers tend to use logical words and play more physical, active games with their children," said Lee Young-hwan, a professor of childhood education at Chonbuk National University. "Children who are influenced by both, therefore, tend to develop in a balanced way." [32]

FATHER SCHOOL

I don't want to give the impression that the absence of fathers in children's lives has not been the subject of serious concern and attempts to change. There have been a number of specific interventions aimed at making Korean fathers more responsive. One is the very popular TV show *Superman is Back,*[33] which is initiating an improvement in the relationships between fathers and children by turning it into a challenge: can these celebrity dads look after their kids without the mother's help for forty-eight hours? This show is a lot of fun and a great help. But, dear fathers, you don't have to wait for a TV show to teach you how to be a good dad. You don't wait for other role models to do things. You want to be a role model for your children now. Don't waste any more time!

Another, older initiative, Father School, began in 1995 at the Duranno Bible College in Seoul. The mission was to end what the

Father School guidebook calls "the growing national epidemic of abusive, ineffective and absentee fathers."

"Traditionally, in the Korean family, the father is very authoritarian," Joon Cho, a volunteer for the Korean Dads 12-step program, said in an interview with the *New York Times*.[34] "They're not emotionally linked with their children or their wives. They're either workaholics, or they're busy enjoying their hobbies or social activities. Family always comes last."

Father School now operates in the United States as well, designed to help Korean immigrant fathers whose Americanized kids wonder why their fathers aren't more like those they see on TV or at friends' houses. Now there is a Father School in fifty-seven American cities. The school is a four-day immersive experience that introduces concepts of openness and vulnerability, where the men talk about their relationships with their own fathers and with their children, practice hugging, and write loving letters to their families. One of the ways it works is by having previous graduates mentor current students. Often the wife is the person who demands her husband attend, but it is the bond between the men, newly aware that their feelings of distance and loneliness are very common among their peers, that makes the difference.

I wonder if my father would have benefitted from a program like this. He wasn't oppressive. He was a gentle and kind man. I know he tried to be a good father to me, but I can't say we had a close relationship. The only time I remember any meaningful conversation with him was when I talked to him a couple of days after my parents had a fight. I was about twelve years old. My mom was accusing him of things, and my dad wasn't very responsive. I don't remember the nature of the fight, but I must have been on my dad's side. I asked him, "Dad, how come you don't say much when Mom accuses you of things? You should fight back!" He answered me in a quiet and logical manner as if I were his equal or his friend. "You know what happens when two stones clash with each other? It makes a fire. I don't want to make it worse by attacking her back." I wish we had had more conversations like that.

Many Korean fathers know that their children need them and want to do a better job. "According to a survey by the JoongAng Ilbo, which targeted 500 working fathers with children younger than twelve years old, 98.4 percent answered that fathers should put more time into childcare. Additionally, more than half, 58.9 percent, also said fathers could have a positive influence on their children.... Yet nearly half of respondents, or forty-eight percent, answered that their wives take on all the childcare responsibilities.... Notably, eight-six percent of the 500 respondents attributed long working hours as the primary reason for their lack of participation in child-rearing."[35]

It doesn't take a lot. Even a few extra minutes reading to your child, telling her you love her, driving her to school or just asking about her day can make a difference. And the rewards for the father are as great as they are for the child. We make so many sacrifices for our children; why shouldn't we also enjoy the pleasure of their company, their trust and affection, the kind of solid relationship that makes life meaningful?

Most of Carlos' and my close friends are younger than we are. Many of them have children aged from two to 10 years old. So we get to observe and participate in their family activities. One of the things I see that's very different than Korean families is how much the fathers are involved in raising their children. How much love and affection they show them. My friend Anja's husband, Roland, is a good role model. Anja and Roland have two beautiful daughters: Lina, my goddaughter, who is four years old, the funniest little person I know, and Julie, the singer, five years old. They live in Switzerland, so we only get to see them about once a year, but we talk on Skype regularly. Every time we get together, Roland amazes me with how patient, fun, and loving a father he is to his daughters. He is their best friend, and the girls love him dearly.

Enric is the father of Lucas, who is three years old. He loves cars and gives generous big hugs to family and friends. We were at Lucas' birthday party recently. Enric told me with a big smile, "He has my heart." Last summer in Barcelona, Quim showed me a list he made of all the unique words that Martina, his sweet and shy four-year-old daughter, says. The words were not English or Spanish, but they sounded very interesting, and they each had their own special meanings. Unless you spend quality time with your children, you won't notice the imaginative and cute habits they develop while they are growing up. I remember asking Per, my Danish friend who has two children (Erik, nine years old, a Lego king and puzzle genius, and Freddie, creative, seven years old), "How do you feel being a dad?" He said, "It's surprising how much I love them. I had no idea."

In most societies, mothers and children have much closer relationships than fathers and children. This is changing in America and Europe, but there is still a long way to go, and Koreans have even farther to go. Certainly, there is a special bond with the person who carried you in her body and was around a lot more in your infancy. But children need more than one person can give, and in particular, they need fathers. Many Korean dads think their role is to support the mother and to support the family financially. But even if a family follows the traditional path, and the mother stays home tending to the children, the father is part of the family's emotional life. He can't be in the home and not be important to his kids.

To a child, a distant father is a rejecting father—even if the man believes he is deeply devoted to his family. That perceived coldness can be as damaging as actual abuse, particularly since few people recognize the harm being done. [36] Children crave attention, and they will often choose negative attention over no attention at all. This is one reason children get in trouble at school, commit petty crimes or take drugs. Dr. Ronald Rohner, Professor Emeritus at the University of Connecticut, and Director, Center for the Study of Interpersonal Acceptance and Rejection, stated that perceived rejection by a parent in childhood has a strong and consistent effect on personality and development. Children and adults everywhere—regardless of race, culture, and gender—tend to respond in the same way—with anger, hostility, numbing and mental health issues of various kinds."[37] An involved father makes a difference in his children's life in every area—academic, career, relationship, health and happiness.

"Emerging evidence from the past decade of research in psychology and neuroscience is revealing that the same parts of the brain are activated when people feel rejected as are activated when they experience physical pain. Unlike physical pain, however, people can psychologically re-live the emotional pain of rejection over and over for years," Rohner said.

DRINKING FATHERS

While I'm surrounded by warm and loving fathers of my generation and younger here in the U.S. and Europe, I read articles about the after-work drinking culture in Korea and how it's encouraged by superiors and co-workers. According to the *Daily Mail*, "South Koreans drink more alcohol than Brits, Russians and Americans put together, a new report has revealed."[38] I don't know the reasons why Koreans drink so much, but one generally accepted one is that after-work drinking is a way for members of a culture who are raised not to talk about themselves, raised to be "strangers" even at home, to break down emotional inhibitions and forge the kind of friendships and camaraderie that make it easier to work together. "I didn't like it in the beginning," said Charles Lee, a Korean-Canadian who came to Seoul to work for a South Korean company. "I was like, 'Why are you making me drink something when I don't want to?' But once I understood the meaning behind it, I appreciated it more. There are just some things you can't say at work or talk about over lunch—people who talk about work at lunch are losers. But when someone offers you a glass of soju, it's an invitation that means that they want to listen to you."[39]

The problem is that alcohol-soaked conversations, no matter how personal, are not nearly as effective in creating bonds as sober ones. For one thing, you don't remember everything, or you remember it patchily. And for another, your brain is not really taking in the experience. It feels good, but the sense of accomplishment that you get—the "click" of learning something when you face the fear of intimacy, take a chance and connect with someone—doesn't happen in a drunken conversation. You have the memory of closeness, but you haven't actually learned how to do it, so you are no better at communicating with the people who matter the most: your family. At best, alcoholic conversations remind you that you're human and that connection is possible—but that is a very weak substitute for real relationships.

The first thing that came to my mind when I read about the Korean drinking culture was, "What about the family? Don't they want to go home and spend time with their families?" Maybe they do, maybe they don't. Every family, every marriage, has its own problems. For sure, there are some men who avoid their wives because of conflicts. The whole question of marital communication is huge. But whatever the problems in the marriage, the influence of culture is very strong. The surprising thing I hear is that some wives even encourage their husbands to go drinking for political reasons. Wives want to ensure that their husbands don't miss out on any opportunities to impress their bosses or his team members, which could be directly related to securing the next promotion. They ask, "Who went drinking? Who did you go drink with? Why don't you go drink with that person? It's so and so's birthday. I'm going to get a present. You give him the present, and if he is drinking, make sure you go with." They are determined that their husbands do whatever it takes to secure the next promotion, no matter what effect this has on home life. Thomas Kim, who travels to Korea regularly, thinks that there is a lack of family values in Korea. "If they don't have a vision for something for their family, they don't go home. I think the value is not instilled that spending time with family is a good thing."

Peter Kim, who worked in Korea for several years, said, "There is a lot of peer pressure to drink and drink a lot. A lot of Koreans are trained that way. That happens in America too. In college, they have frat and kick parties, but culturally, Westerners say it's okay not to drink. In the workplace, we cannot make anybody drink. In most of the corporations in America, you don't drink that much with coworkers."

And what about health? Alcohol is one of the leading causes of chronic liver disease in Korea and can lead to heart attacks, strokes and other medical problems. But even on a daily basis, drinking imposes a huge burden. Drinking once in awhile is fun, but every night? Waking up early after a night of drinking sounds kind of like hell to me. Don't we need to return home to relax and recharge so we can start fresh with renewed energy the next day?

Many Korean men accept frequent hangovers and liver disease in order to have an illusion of friendship and bonding with co-workers without ever learning how to be loving husbands and fathers. Most of them grew up with fathers whose responsibility started and ended with making money for the family. The rest was the mother's work, including raising the children.

As with any relationship, if you don't spend enough time together, one to one, you won't get to know one another. You won't have intimacy. It becomes a kind of robotic relationship. I'm not talking about just being in the same room and everybody watching TV together. That's not connecting; that's coexisting. I'm talking about engaging in activities together and having daily conversations. It may take a few drinks to get your co-workers to open up to you, but children are born ready to love and trust their parents. All you have to do is spend time with them as they grow, listen when they talk, pay attention to their problems and their moments of joy. Find out who your children are. See how you can help them. Be supportive and encouraging. Be present in their lives.

If you have never done it, and your children aren't toddlers anymore, it may be awkward in the beginning. They may already feel self-conscious around you as you do around them. They may respond to your first attempts dismissively. This is because they don't yet trust your desire to better the relationship or simply weren't expecting your behavior to change. They are used to you as you have been, and they may not even know what a good father-child relationship is like. The important thing is making an effort slowly and consistently. As always when you start something new, take a small step each time and keep doing it until you feel comfortable and it becomes second nature.

I believe that what we become depends on what our fathers teach us at odd moments, when they aren't trying to teach us. We are formed by little scraps of wisdom.

—Umberto Eco

IT GOES BOTH WAYS

Children need to think of their fathers differently, too. When my father went bankrupt, I remember thinking badly of him, blaming him for the breakup of our family. He didn't fulfill his responsibility as a father, so I thought of him as less of a person. There wasn't any empathy at all, only one hundred percent blaming. Since young teenagers rebel against their parents even without any significant family issues, it was easy for me to blame my father and be angry, considering the circumstances. Now I look back and wish I had let him know that no matter what happened, I still loved him.

We lived separately after the bankruptcy. He lived alone near the city of Incheon and passed away without his wife or daughter near him. My mom left for Chicago, and I was living at my uncle's house in Seoul. My heart aches every time I think about how I didn't get a chance to tell him that I loved him.

We had a Korean intern many years ago. Yoon Kim was a senior student from the School of the Art Institute of Chicago. One day we were talking, and I was curious how much she had to pay for her tuition since she was a student from abroad. She told me the cost was over one hundred thousand dollars per year, including living expenses. I was shocked. Knowing how many Korean students were in the U.S., I couldn't imagine the burden on the families. But the thing that surprised me was how Yoon Kim responded when I said, "Wow, your dad must work very hard to pay for your college!"

She replied, "Of course, he has to work hard. That's what dads are supposed to do." She expressed no gratitude or real appreciation for how fortunate she was to be studying in Chicago. I have no doubt that she feels that she is entitled to receive everything she has. It's not just

Yoon Kim. Many young people feel the same way. I was one of them. Growing up as an only child in the house, I was a little spoiled. I just assumed that my parents should give me everything I needed. I didn't consider how hard parents work to provide for a family. Typically, we say that you don't appreciate your parents until you have your own children. But I believe we should teach our children regularly to practice gratitude for the things they have and have empathy for other children and people who have less. I believe that, with help, they can develop a personality that's more balanced and learn to connect with others in more mature ways. I wish I had had someone to teach me about gratitude when I was young.

GOOSE FATHERS

Yoon Kim was a college student. But many Korean and other Asian children leave their families, or at least their fathers, much earlier. Goose fathers—"gireogi appa" in Korean—is the term used for fathers who work in their home country while their wives and children live abroad so the children can learn English and avoid the harshness of the Korean school system. Like a wild goose, the father flies in to visit once a year. (A wealthier man, who can visit more often, is referred to as an "eagle father." A man too poor to visit at all is called a "penguin father.")

There are hundreds of thousands of families living this way. China, India, and Korea send the largest number of international students to the U.S., but Korea stands out, because so many of the children are elementary, middle, and high school age.[40] The mothers generally accompany the children while fathers stay behind to work and support the family financially, although occasionally the child goes alone. "The unnatural phenomenon of wild geese daddies is a clear sign of something wrong in our society," said Kim Seong-kon, a professor of English at Seoul National University and President of the American Studies Association of Korea, quoted in an article in *The Korea Times*. [41]

Between 2004-2011, an average of 20,000 families per year left Korea to live in the U.S., Canada, the U.K., New Zealand, or Australia for education. One online survey in 2015 showed over seventy percent of these fathers were suffering from depression, alcohol problems and inadequate nutrition.[42] They endure this because they believe they are doing the best thing for their children. But are they?

Probably some families and individual children are better equipped to handle this type of living arrangement than others. People are different in their mental, emotional and physical abilities. But even those who get through it well lose something irretrievable—childhood with their fathers, fatherhood with their children, marriage with their husbands. I believe children's education is important; I know it's hard to make a good living today, and I understand the fears parents have about increasing competition. I'm not sure, however, that these families are aware of what they are sacrificing, or the effects that sacrifice will have in the years to come.

CHINESE FATHER AND SON

One day I was putting on makeup in the bathroom when I heard a story on the radio that I remember to this day. It was about a Chinese father and his son, Larry, who were living in the U.S. The father owned a Chinese takeout place and worked fifteen hours a day.

The parents never tried to teach Chinese to their son, and the father didn't speak English. The parents thought: we're living in America so why bother teaching him Chinese? The mother spoke English, but the father didn't. So father and son couldn't communicate. They never had a single conversation. Larry couldn't even keep eye contact with his dad because it was just too awkward. They'd glance at each other and look away quickly.

His dad worked so late that Larry would go days without seeing him. When they did have some time together, it wasn't quality time. It was the opposite. When they were eating dinner together, and the mother was not home, they would just be picking up the food and not saying a word the entire time. The dad only asked two questions of his son: Did you eat? Are you healthy?

His dad became like a wall to Larry. He felt his dad didn't love him, and that made him angry. Larry started to feel nothing for him. He thought, "If he doesn't care for me why should I care for him?" Then his dad had to move back to China because the construction business he owned there started making more money than the restaurant in the U.S. Larry was fourteen years old.

The father left a goodbye letter for Larry. The letter explained how he struggled tremendously to just write the words on paper; however, he felt that it was a father's duty to mentor his son. He went on to say how he was so happy when Larry was born, and that his arrival gave him a brilliant outlook on life. He wanted Larry to not pressure himself too much in school.

"As long as you are unafraid of working hard, there will be a path for you. I cannot speak English, and I've been able to support my family all these years, so relax and do your best. Thank God for giving me the courage to write this letter to my oldest son. I believe deeply that to gain anything, you must surrender something; conversely, anything that is surrendered will give you something back. Pardon me for sharing."

Pa."

Towards the end of the letter, Larry was crying. He felt so guilty for all the ill feelings he had had towards his dad for all those years and for not understanding him. His father had been with him and worrying about him. He envisioned his dad standing by the hot oil, cooking year round to make sure they had a place to live and food to eat.

The letter totally changed how Larry saw his father. But he didn't respond to the letter. Larry wasn't mature enough to know how to respond. Instead, he decided to study Chinese.

Six years later, his Chinese still wasn't fluent, but the producer of the story hired a translator and coached Larry in how to read the letter he wrote to his dad. They recorded his reading it so it would sound perfect. They called his dad in China and played the recording for him in the language that he and his son now both understand. Here is part of the letter:

"Dear Pa,

I have read your letter countless times since high school. I treasure it and read it sometimes when I feel down about myself. It makes me feel better about myself, about family. But the most important thing about the letter was that for the first time I felt like you were speaking directly to me and I was so surprised by how emotional you were. When I read that letter I thought here is someone I care about and appreciate and I want to get to know better.

I had so many questions for you at first. What was your childhood like? What did you do for fun? Who were your friends? Did you know you were going to be working in the Chinese takeout restaurant for two decades? Did you enjoy it? Did it mean anything to you? Then I realized that everything I thought about you my whole life was completely wrong and I felt guilty that I never tried to get to know you. I'm so sorry but it's not too late. Now I know a little bit about who you are, I want you to know who I am. Where I live, where I like to go to, who my friends are, what I like to do, what instruments I play. I'm learning Chinese now in school so hopefully one day we can actually talk about all these things for real, face to face. Until then I'm happy to simply know how much we care about each other. I love you, Pa."

After a few silent moments, Larry's dad answered, "Well, I'm quite touched. I haven't quite caught up to my emotions at this moment. While I was listening to your letter, I felt a sense of contentment. You are not a boy anymore. I'm very relieved that you can express these things with me through the letter."

Then Larry asked, "When did you feel that you couldn't communicate with me anymore?"

His dad answered, "If you were hungry, I'd give you food, but anything beyond that was impossible. Those were painful moments. I hope that you don't have to make choices like this between your family and your work. I hope you have a happy family and I hope you have a different family than I did. Thank you, my little boy, for saying this." The dad continued, "I do feel regretful and guilty as a father and husband that I wasn't able to take care of the family."

Larry replied, "It's okay now. I love you. It's been a really long time that I waited to say this."

His dad replied, "You are like me. I'm not very good at expressing. I like to hold my feelings and my thoughts to myself. Maybe we can both work on that together. I am thousands of miles away from my son, but I feel like I'm sitting next to you for the first time."

Larry and his dad text regularly now. The producer says she read the texts, and they aren't deep. It's just normal communication. Before this, Larry thought he would feel closer to his dad if they talked about who his dad's friends were when he was young, what his dreams were. But their texts are just the small things you text with anyone you love. His dad reminds him to buy his mom a present for Mother's Day and complains that his little brother is ignoring his texts. He tells Larry to be careful walking home late at night. Larry texts, "School is good. The weather is starting to cool down." His dad asks him how his new job is and tells him to make sure to take care of himself and eat more food. Larry sends him a thumbs-up emoji.[43]

This story really warmed my heart. How they misunderstood each other for so many years! If it weren't for the letter, they might have stayed strangers. What a tragedy that would have been. Language was the main obstacle in Larry and his dad's relationship, but Larry would have learned Chinese if his dad had talked to him more when he was little. Most children who grow up in dual-language families learn two languages easily. But the dad didn't want to speak Chinese to him.

You see this in many immigrant families. The children will naturally speak what the mother does, or what the parents speak together, but that won't happen if one language is not heard regularly, if there aren't regular father-child, mother-child or family conversations. Parents will avoid speaking their native language around the children for several reasons. The desire to fit in can be overpowering. They also believe that the more the children speak English, the stronger their English language skills will be. My nephews and niece weren't encouraged to speak Korean at home while growing up, even though their parents spoke Korean to each other. Today, my niece has children and would like them to know Korean, but since she doesn't speak it herself, it is more difficult.

Once people have lived in a new country for a while—how long depends on the individual or family—attitudes often change. Parents realize that young children can easily learn to speak two languages because their brains are like sponges—and that this will be a great advantage to them, not only in talking to family but throughout their lives. Often they will make a great effort to ensure the children don't learn only English. All of our European friends speak their native languages at home with their children while the children speak English in school. It takes a conscious effort for them not to stray from their routine of speaking the native language at home. Often the child will resist in the beginning, but the benefit is worth the pain. Being bilingual opens doors to a variety of business and cultural opportunities. It is a good investment in your child's future.

Larry's father didn't realize that knowing Chinese would have been a benefit for his son. He also didn't realize that even if his son's only use of the language was to speak to him, that in itself would have been worth it. Like so many Asian fathers, he didn't know that he mattered as a person, as an emotional presence, to his child.

Don't let what happened to Larry and his father happen to you. Stop waiting around for a big moment to say, "I love you" to your children. Affection and love from parents are what makes for a happy childhood. There is nothing better you can give to your children than letting them know how much you love them, letting them know who you are, and finding out who they are—as unique, fascinating people. Nobody can predict the future, whether your or anyone's children will be happy, successful adults or not—but we can make choices in the present. As well as guiding and supporting our kids, we can enjoy them.

Life is about little things, sharing and talking about little things. That's how we connect. If a father is not around to get to know his children, both the father and children will feel the pain or become numb to each other's emotions. Bridging the gap can easily develop into a lifetime challenge. In the same way, a lively, loving relationship when your children are small will resonate through their lives and your own.

5

Black & White

Run if you see a black person when it's dark!

When I first arrived in Chicago in 1980, my mom, who came to this Midwestern city four years earlier, told me: If you see a black person when it's dark, you should run.

I've never forgotten that. All I knew about white and black people was what I had learned from the movies—there were very few foreigners on the streets of Seoul in my childhood. And in the movies then, the white people were rich, good looking, successful, while the black people were mostly servants or criminals. I learned about America, Europe and Africa in school, but again, what I learned about Africa—the frequent famines and the primitive living conditions—was not as appealing as what I learned about the West. Everything that excited me—new technology, music, movies, fashion—came from the West. Therefore, before I had any experiences of my own, I had prejudice. I came to the U.S. just as racist as my mom.

WHERE IS THE EMPATHY?

I was eating dinner at my mom's house one evening a few years ago. The Korean channel was on TV. While I was eating, I barely paid attention.

Then all of sudden I found myself crouched in front of the TV, listening to the story with ears wide open.

It was a story about a Korean woman married to a Pakistani man. The people in the neighborhood were gossiping, pointing fingers at her, and openly making disrespectful comments to her just because she was married to a Pakistani. The whole time she was talking, tears were rolling down her cheeks. By the end, she was sobbing, and her pain slammed into my heart.

In 1990, I visited Seoul for the first time since I had left ten years earlier. I traveled with my husband. We were walking around Insadong Street, where many antique stores are located. Back then the street was far quieter than it is now. We stopped in front of a cart where a middle-aged man was selling antique-looking bowls and vases. I saw something I liked and asked, "How much is this vase?" He looked me up and down and said, in a scornful tone, "What are you doing going around with such a man?"

I was speechless for a second, then became really embarrassed and angry and walked away from the cart. My husband asked me, "What did he say?" I don't remember exactly how I replied, but I definitely didn't tell him what the man had said. I couldn't believe how he blurted out his judgmental opinion toward a potential customer in such a rude, ignorant, and presumptuous manner. He did it because I was a Korean woman with a foreigner.

Unfortunately, the only thing I remember from that trip twenty-six years ago is that incident, which left a bitter taste in my mouth. I didn't go back to Seoul for nearly fifteen years. Would I have gone back sooner if it weren't for that man? I don't know. I was buried in my work during those years, but maybe a happier experience would have enticed me to visit.

South Korea is a homogeneous country. Until recently, there were very few foreign inhabitants. Most Koreans consider this normal and probably would say that it's a good thing, making it easier for everyone to get along. Since I hadn't lived in Korea for so long, I didn't know if or how Koreans' treatment of foreigners had changed. After seeing this story of the woman married to a Pakistani on TV and remembering my own experience, I started to read articles about the attitudes toward and treatment of foreigners in Korea. I was very sad to discover that even though there are more foreigners living in Korea that has not yet led to more understanding. Racism is still open and blunt.

In July 2009, a drunken thirty-one-year-old man named Park was riding a bus, sitting behind two people. One was twenty-eight-year-old Bonojit Hussein, from India, a research professor at a Korean University, and the other was his Korean female friend, Jisun Han. Park started hurling insults at Hussein and his friend. "What a disgusting odor! You're dirty." More insults followed. Park called Hussein "Arab" and "smelly." He also asked Han, "Are you Korean? How do you feel dating a black bastard?" He continued with sexual and racist insults until Hussein and Han thought enough was enough. They decided to report the case at a nearby police station. To add insult to injury, when Hussein and Han attempted to file charges against Park, the police questioned the immigration status of Hussein, using "banmal" (a low form of Korean, similar to what one uses speaking to a child) and openly doubted that he was a university professor. Then the police treated Han with contempt for being with Hussein. On the other hand, Park was treated with respect even given his unspeakable, ignorant, and unruly behavior!

Hussein took further action and filed the first racial discrimination case in Korean history. The case was heard at the Incheon District Court, where Park was fined a thousand dollars. In the meantime, the case went to the National Human Rights Commission. In an article in the *New York Times* about this case, Han was quoted as saying, "Even a friend of mine confided to me that when he sees a Korean woman walking with a foreign man, he feels as if his own mother betrayed him."[44]

~ RESET PERSPECTIVE ~

We are all the same, we have same mind, emotion. Power and financial wealth create arrogance and delusion.

–THE 14TH DALAI LAMA

Each one of us, when we interact with foreigners, is an ambassador representing our nation. Park thought that his prejudice towards certain people justified his ignorant behavior, even though the other person did nothing to provoke him. Somehow he felt superior to Houssein, just based on his skin color. Park made the most common mistake Koreans make when they see a person of another race. They think that the other person is somehow different from them. They are a different kind of human. Of course, they come from a different culture, but that's the only difference between Koreans and any other race or ethnicity. Let's try to remember that.

They are exactly the same as us. We are obligated to treat each one of them with respect using the good Korean manners we would use with another Korean person. That's a basic requirement of being a good Korean/world citizen. Accordingly, conduct such as Park's shouldn't be acceptable in our society anymore.

What can we do, as individuals, to prevent this kind of ugliness from occurring again? When we witness this type of ignorant behavior, instead of being a bystander, should we speak up? It takes guts to stand up to a bully. Remember, though, Park was just drunk and not threatening violence. Nobody was in danger of being physically hurt in the encounter. I know it's easier said than done, but I believe many of us have the courage to speak up, to call out the instigator. This is the right thing to do.

I thought about what I would do if I had been sitting on that bus. I would have said, "Ajusee (Mr.), what you just said is offensive and rude! Leave them alone. It's not your business!" I'd say this in the nicest possible way. If he spoke insultingly to me and continued his hostility, I'd ask the bus driver to get the drunken person off the bus at the next stop. A person who bullies other passengers should not be allowed to ride. At this point, I would be hoping that some other passengers would follow my lead and make the same request of the bus driver.

ANYTHING BUT KOREAN!

My three nephews and niece were born in the U.S. and live in Seattle now. When I first came to Chicago, they were living in Janesville, Wisconsin. My brother Jon was working for GM (General Motors) and also owned a martial arts studio and a restaurant. I saw my nephews and niece a few times in their childhoods; they all seemed like normal, happy children. I never suspected what they went through growing up in two small cities in America.

"I was constantly bullied, but also they were afraid of us because they knew that we were a martial arts family." My niece, Julie said, "We just had to learn to accept it. We were constantly teased and made fun of. You just get thick skin. They called me 'slanted eyes,

Chinese, Japanese, you know you're not from here!' As I got older, it got worse. 'Oh, I heard your kind is cheaper! (as a prostitute).' They were real insulting on the bus.' Wisconsin is a very white state, demographically. When we moved to Indiana, there were more black people in our neighborhood. For about a year, there was a lot more mean and physical stuff, like shoving you on the bus. If you were in the seat they wanted, they would just shove you out of the seat. Things like that. When I was in sixth grade, we moved to the other side of the town—a white, wealthier part of town. It was better there, a different demographic. Then we moved to Seattle, and we had culture shock because there were so many Asians. And then racism pretty much disappeared.

"I was very angry at those people who bullied me. I think everyone has a different coping mechanism. I just ignored it. Of course, I got angry, especially in that black neighborhood. I had so much anger inside of me, but when I got older going to church helped me a lot. You know, just the healing—just letting things go. That's what happens when you become an adult. You either hold on to things, or you let them go. I thought when I was a little girl I would never get married because I've been bullied for being Asian. Nobody even knew what a Korean was. That's what I got a lot. 'What are you? Are you Chinese or Japanese?' 'I'm a Korean.' 'There's no such thing. What is that?' It's just ignorance.

"Oh, then they said, 'You're ugly.' As a girl, I knew I was ugly. In eighth grade, we had a sleepover and a boy—I still remember this—I don't know why they invited a boy. He was like 'I'll kiss everyone but Julie.' Looking back, it didn't even affect me. Because I had accepted the fact [that I was ugly], that didn't bother me. But then it was very interesting when I got older, and guys started asking me out. I was so shocked, I didn't know what to do.

"I was told 'ugly' and I was told 'pretty' so I don't put too much weight on those words. They're just superficial. I'm still the same person, and I'm glad I'm that way; it's not like I'm obsessed."

"So how do you feel about Korea now?" I asked Julie.

"You still feel the connection because you're Korean. At the same time, when I heard about the big ferry accident in 2014 [in Korea], it was so sad because people are so obsessed with money, they break the regulations. I was glad that my kids live here, not there. But I always tell Haley, my nine-year-old daughter, that I want her to have a lot of pride at the end. When I was a kid, I hated being a Korean. There is nothing I hated more. If I had one wish, it was not to be Korean because that was what all the bullying stemmed from. Having parents who look different and all of that. I don't want that for my kids. I want them to have a lot of pride in being Korean. At the same time, I don't want them to live in Korea. There's a high school program, and I want her to learn the language, but the plastic surgery and the culture and all that—. I don't want her to experience that. So I haven't decided."

I've wondered whether I was the target of racism living in America, but after listening to Julie, I realize how fortunate I was to live in a big city and to have moved here at the age of eighteen. I have hardly ever experienced any bad treatment for being Asian. I would never have imagined my nephews and niece going through so much pain in childhood. They don't even speak Korean. They are a hundred percent American inside. Despite that, they had to endure so much psychological torment and abuse at their most vulnerable ages. After hearing Julie's childhood story, I heard from several more second-generation Korean Americans about similar or worse experiences growing up in America.

Kwon Yul, the 2006 winner of *Survival,* the reality TV show, shared his longtime secret with his audience on the Korean program *15 minutes to Change the World.*[45] He struggled with psychological disorders for many years as a result of being bullied when he was in elementary school.

"The bigger kids would pick on me and some of my friends. What they would do is hide in the bathroom, and when we came in, they would beat us and then they would try to urinate on us. Even when these attacks stopped, I found myself so scared that I couldn't go to the bathroom in school or anywhere with other people around." His depression got so severe that he even started to think about ending his life until a tragedy happened to his brother's best friend who had moved to another state. This boy had a hard time making friends at his new school. He committed suicide. Kwon Yul decided to change himself by deciding what kind of person he wanted to be. He made a list of long-term goals, then broke them into smaller, short-term goals that he could work on every day. Looking at his fancy resume or seeing him on the show, you would never think that he had gone through such a period of despair.

Another Korean American reality TV show star, James Sun, who was on Donald Trump's *Apprentice,* also went through a hard period while growing up in a rural area near Houston in the early to mid-eighties. He remembers coming home and seeing his family's car tires slashed, with these words painted on the car: *Go back to your country*! He remembers walking to school with his mother because she wanted to protect him from other kids throwing rocks.

James is the CEO of a mobile technology company, but he also has become a passionate promoter of diversity and globalization. He speaks on these subjects regularly.[46]

Mia Park is a yoga instructor, actor, and drummer, a Renaissance woman. "I have so many stories very similar to your niece's. When I was growing up, I was so embarrassed being Korean. At least if I were

Chinese or Japanese, people would know who I was. I hated being Asian, and I hated to be Korean if I had to be an Asian. Then somewhere in my early twenties, I turned around 180 degrees, and I thought I really want to get involved in the Korean community."

I asked, "What was the turning point?"

Mia answered, "I think it was just being on my own, moving permanently away from my family. I went to learn Korean in Korea for thirteen months. I went to a very, very small liberal college in the U.S. There I took pride in being Korean. It was kind of cool. I was the only Korean person in this entire college, so I thought, 'Oh, I'm cool.' Something about that empowered me. Being on my own and realizing that it's okay that I'm Korean. Having my own identity."

I was curious what Julie would tell young people about why we shouldn't discriminate against people who look different. "I think it's just the lack of respect for other people's backgrounds and culture. It's completely wrong. I think there are some hardships that are good for you. They make you learn and get stronger. Any discrimination—I don't think any good comes out of it except to learn firsthand how wrong it is. I think it affects someone's identity, their confidence and future success even. When it's been going on for years, your self-esteem is low. It totally affects the long term. Especially when it happens consistently for years when you are little.

"We have a Girl Scout Troop. It is so different now. Haley's in third grade. Her school is very diverse. They promote it. There are a lot of cultural affairs and a lot of discussions about diversity. I think some normal questions are fine. She knows kids who say 'You look Chinese' or 'Why don't you speak Korean? Does that mean you are Chinese?' For the kids, I think those are fair questions. They're not doing it to be mean. They are kind of curious. She gets a little bit of flack about North Korea. Boys say, 'Oh, you are a North Korean.' Anytime it goes into the category of taunting instead of curiosity, I think it's completely unacceptable. I put it on the same level as bullying. Absolutely zero tolerance for bullying. I think we were bullied our entire childhood."

~ RESET PERSPECTIVE ~

It was hard to hear that these young Korean Americans received harsh emotional and physical wounds in their youth. Thankfully, they have come out of it and have become normal, happy, and successful individuals even though they may carry deep emotional scars for the rest of their lives. At least that's what happened to the people mentioned here. But I have no doubt that it was different for some other young Korean Americans who went through similar experiences.

I expect that hearing these stories about Korean children being bullied is as upsetting for you as it was for me. The lesson here is that everyone who is discriminated against, taunted, bullied, or insulted is hurt by it, sometimes very deeply. Dave Hazzan and other white and non-white foreigners living in Korea feel the same way, although adults are not as vulnerable as children. "It's upsetting when a white foreigner sees another non-white foreigner being a target of racism. It's a human issue. The key feature of being a developed country is that you accept foreigners."

A friend in Seoul asked me, "Isn't there racism in the U.S., too?" Yes, of course there is. There are discussions about race and racism every day in the U.S. on TV, radio, and on the Internet. There are all kinds of people in America. Good, bad, extreme, ignorant, any kind you can think of. There are pockets of people who believe things I find appalling. A majority of the educated people I have met on the coasts and in the big cities, however, promote and practice openness, tolerance, kindness, and acceptance. Otherwise, America wouldn't be a country of immigrants.

Donald Trump, the new president elect, worries a lot of people. He won the election by the antiquated electoral college voting system in America even though the democratic opponent, Hillary Clinton, won the popular vote by over 2.9 million votes. Trump gives a voice to hatred, fear, and disinformation in people. More racist incidents have been surfacing after Trump won the presidency. His winning was truly shocking and puzzling for many Americans and people around the world. Despite this surprising turn in U.S. politics in 2016, the West, in general, is way ahead of the rest of the world in its recognition of basic human rights—even if those rights are sometimes threatened or if some groups face discrimination. The West's equal treatment for all is a work in progress, but it's a work that most Americans and Europeans are committed to. Of course, people will have various opinions on what needs to be done and how it should be done. Yes, there are countries that are much worse than Korea in the area of human rights, but that's no excuse. Koreans are a proud people, eager to be part of the modern world even as we respect tradition. We should seek to be modern not only in our lifestyles but our thinking and behavior. Racism has no place in the kind of society we want. I don't believe most of my country's people, if they really thought about it and understood the consequences, would want to belong to a country considered deficient in human rights.

"What do you think Koreans can do to be less racist?" I asked Melissa Kim. "This needs better education and direction from the government. Again, lack of global thinking and perspective may be a reason. Many Koreans don't realize that Koreans are discriminated against when they go abroad. Once you have been in that position, then you wouldn't treat others that way."

ARE THE 'RIGHT' FOREIGNERS BETTER THAN US?

In general, Koreans classify foreigners as white and non-white. Many have an inferiority complex towards white people because of the dominance of Western influence in Korea. We treat white people with respect because the perception is that they are better looking and richer than we are. But we treat non-white people with less respect because somehow we assume that they are of a lower class—either in Korea or their home country—and we tend to look down on people who are less privileged. Older Koreans don't think of it as "racism," something negative to be overcome, but just common sense. Koreans haven't been forced to face the racial issue, in the way Americans and Europeans have.

One of our past interns, Ohyun, has been working and teaching in Seoul for a few years now as a graphic designer. His parents are Korean, but he was born and raised in Germany. We got reconnected via Facebook, and I wanted to know how he likes living in Seoul. He shared this experience with me.

He was to meet his colleague at a printing company. He was at a station but wasn't sure which exit to take and tried calling his colleague, but his phone was dead. He tried to borrow a phone from a stranger but wasn't successful. So, he was just standing there, smoking, thinking about what to do. Then he threw his cigarette butt on the ground. All of a sudden, a man came out of the station office and approached him, yelling at Ohyun using banmal (an informal way of speaking, considered rude when used with a stranger), asking him, "How old are you? What's your identification number?" (Koreans typically ask, "How old are you?" when they disapprove of your behavior in some way. It means that you should know better for your age.)

Ohyun realized what he did was wrong, but he still wanted to know exactly what was being said, so he replied in his bad Korean, "What did you say? Are you giving me a ticket?"

The man heard his bad Korean and asked, "What's wrong with you? Where are you from?"

"I'm from Germany." The minute the man heard that Ohyun was from Germany, his attitude changed 180 degrees. He said in a super-friendly way, "Oh, you shouldn't be throwing the cigarette on the ground. Is there anything I can do for you?"

Ohyun said, "Yes, actually I need to call my friend, but my phone went out."

The man said, "Oh, you can use mine!" Ohyun made a call and confirmed the exit. He thanked the man and started walking away. Then the man said, "You didn't tell your friend which station or where you are."

"It's okay, I already know where I'm going. I just had to confirm the exit number," Ohyun replied. The man wished Ohyn the best, and they parted. When he met with his colleague, the colleague told Ohyun, "I got this text message from someone saying where you were." Even when Ohyun told the man not to call his colleague, he went ahead and sent a text message making sure Ohyun found his way.

Ohyun couldn't believe the man's 180-degree change when he heard that he was from Germany.

But it's not as simple as white foreigner (or Western foreign country) good; dark-skinned foreigner/black, bad. Foreigners, in general, can run into trouble. Ryan, who is Canadian and Caucasian, came to Seoul to see the 2002 World Cup. He liked the city and decided to stay for a year.

Ten years later, still living in Seoul, now married to a Korean woman and with two beautiful babies, he shared some of his stories. "I love certain aspects of Korea. I love the food. I love the efficiency of how everything works. I love teaching and experiencing a new culture. But I hate raising a family here. Often I take my older son to a park and other children don't want to play with him because he looks different. It broke his heart when he saw this the first time.

"I came to Seoul and decided to stay of my own free will, but I won't let my children be ostracized by others because they don't look 100 percent Korean. My children will have a lot of difficulties growing up in Korea, and I won't let that happen." He said he was looking into moving back to Canada as soon as possible.

He also shared one incident that had happened to him a couple of months before. He was waiting for his wife outside of the convenience store one evening, and a drunk approached him and gave him a sucker punch to the face! Can you just imagine being on the receiving end of this sudden, unexpected attack by a stranger? You could easily say, "Oh, he was drunk," but this wasn't a drunken brawl of the sort that happens in most big cities; this was a man hitting another person, who had not bothered him or said anything to him, for no reason other than that he was a foreigner.

I was very sad to hear that Ryan's love for Korea was turning into bitter resentment and anger towards Koreans' hostile behavior toward other races. Ryan also commented that Koreans are one of the most educated people in the world since almost ninety percent of the people go to University, but "So many Koreans act so ignorant." That made me wince.

~ RESET PERSPECTIVE ~

XENOPHOBIA AND GLOBALISM DON'T MIX!

What would you say if your Korean child was in school with a foreign or different-race child? Would you encourage your child to be friendly—or would you get angry or afraid if he or she wanted to play with that child? If your answer is the latter, think about it. Think about what it means to teach children to scorn other children. The world is getting smaller, and your Korean child may well be working with foreigners or living in another country someday. How suited for that reality will he or she be? In America, a lot has changed in the last thirty years. Many more school children and university students study with Koreans, Chinese, Russians, Africans, Indians and Europeans, as well as the different races and national backgrounds that make up America.

As a result, recent college graduates are much more comfortable in global business roles than their parents would have been. Often, they have friends throughout the world, as I do. This offers a person much more opportunity, not just in business but also in life. The more you know, the more aware you are of different ways of doing things, different customs and different belief systems, the more creative and confident you will be. Encourage your child to play with other children who look different if they have an opportunity. They may be hesitant or shy, but your child can have his first global experience simply by reaching out to another child who looks very different from him or her.

On the other hand, when you are disrespected as a human being, the insult can cut very deep. For some people—the young, the fragile, those to whom this has happened many times before—it can be extremely difficult to recover from. Even one experience can be traumatizing. Human beings have a natural wariness toward strangers or those who look or act differently, which can develop, with cultural encouragement, into immense cruelty. It's time that we realize real humanity lies under the skin.

We need to stop judging people by their appearance and making accusations when we know nothing about the person—as the antique vendor judged me. When you judge people, it shows what kind of person you are. It shows your ignorance or worldliness, your good-heartedness or the opposite. You may say, "Oh, he is an ignorant old man. Just forget about him." But it's not that easy to forget. Let's not blurt out to a stranger what we think of him or her. Let's not insult strangers as if we know them. Let's stop being a frog in the pond. Let's be kind and have empathy, not just for our friends and family but for strangers and all human beings. Be on the right side, the human side.

IT'S A PRACTICE

When I first moved to Chicago, I wasn't necessarily a friendly person. I was serious and cautious. I wasn't too crazy about small talk at parties. I thought people talked way too much when they had nothing important to say. It probably didn't help that I didn't know the language well, or any American etiquette. I felt self-conscious about making mistakes that resulted from my lack of understanding of the culture.

My first invitation to an American family event came from my mom's landlord. His name was George. When he came to collect rent from Mom, I told him in my poor English, "I just came from Korea." He said, "Wow. Welcome to America!" He stayed for a cup of coffee and answered many questions I had. Before he left the house, he said, "You should come to my family's dinner next Sunday!" Then there I was, having my first American family dinner with a group of ten or more white people sitting around me. Everybody was very nice and pleasant. Nobody asked, "Who is that Asian girl? " or "Who invited her?"

Literally, I was just off the boat, but they made me feel like I'd been to their house several times before. I felt awkward because I wasn't familiar with American table manners and I didn't want to draw attention to myself while we were eating. George invited me to some other gatherings after that, but I declined. I liked him, but I didn't want him to think I was interested in him as anything other than a friend.

In those early years, I came across several people who made an impression on me. I didn't necessarily know them in person or even well. Some were just acquaintances, and others TV talk-show guests, but they seemed genuinely kind. I admired how they talked and treated people with consideration, no matter their status. I decided I wanted to be like them—a kind, friendly person, a good human being. Gradually, and consciously, I made an effort to overcome my discomfort with new people and be genuine and kind. Well, as they say in the U.S., "fake it until you make it." You have to start somewhere and kindness translates very well across cultures. More so than politeness, which has different rules in every society, true kindness is universally appreciated.

Being kind to everyone, regardless of who they are, is now one of my core values. Whether it's a cleaning lady or a CEO, a garbage collector, a shopkeeper, a stranger who looks funny—it doesn't matter. Black or white or Asian. I'm nice to everyone unless they give me a reason not to be. The thing is, energy is contagious. When we encounter a person who is kind to us and respects us as a person, we automatically want to be nice to the next person we run into, even though it might be someone we meet for a couple of minutes on the street.

When I asked my Danish friend, Per, what he thinks of judgmental people, he answered, "You have to judge others in order to navigate your life." I agree. We judge others. It's part of survival. That's what we do, but the question is how and when? Do we judge others instantly, too fast, without knowing who the person really is? Do we have a habit of judging others constantly? If the answer is 'Yes' to one or both questions, we need to practice something else and it's important. When you meet a new person, try seeing that person as a person first. You may ask about work or education—that's just what people do in certain settings—but don't use that information to decide how you are going to treat the person. Try seeing the person's spirit. Is the person someone you can have a meaningful conversation with? Is the person warm, kind, trustworthy?

Per is correct in the sense that we have to be careful who we become good friends with, who we date or marry and who we hire to work in our company. Most of us need to network and are naturally curious about what people do. I'm not saying you should pretend it doesn't matter to you. But if we can start from a place of openness, remembering that each person is a human being first, we may be surprised at how we can connect with people of all kinds, even those with whom we think we have little in common.

I'm not sure exactly how long I was trying to become this new person, this "American," but before I realized it, I felt comfortable talking with strangers and didn't mind the small talk. I actually appreciated the small talk! That's how people connect—through exchanges of simple, everyday subjects: traffic, weather, TV shows, complimenting someone's hairstyle or sweater, remarking on the obvious to let each other know we are in this together. Eventually, it came naturally to me to talk with people without judging them by race, gender, or other physical characteristics, just as one human being to another. When I realized that this is how I interact with people, I felt like I had grown as a person.

Treating all people equally instead of based on cultural preoccupations is a learned behavior. It takes effort in the beginning and may feel phony or uncomfortable, but you will find it gets easier, more natural and more rewarding. I asked Jisook Hong who has been traveling the world extensively, "What kind of new Korean image should we be projecting to the world?"

She responded, "Actually I'm not interested in something *as a Korean*. I'm more interested in things as a global citizen. Whether somebody is Korean or not doesn't matter to me. I hope Korean people will have more global perspectives and think as citizens of the world. Not discriminate against other people, not be too proud of being Korean but be more humane and have more humane views on everyone, regardless of who they are. Contributing to the world, not just Korea. We should definitely change. We should be more global as a people."

ONE BAD APPLE RUINS THE WHOLE BARREL?

Another aspect of prejudice is the kind that develops when one jumps to conclusions based on a very tiny sample. When an English teacher in Korea, Christopher Paul Neil, was arrested in 2007 in Thailand for child molesting, Korean people started looking at all English teachers in Korea with suspicion. Based on this one case, we started to think most of the people who come to Korea to teach English are losers in their own countries— that they came to Korea because they had nothing better to do. Of course, the English teachers felt that they were not being treated fairly or respected. They were offended by the entire country's reaction to this one criminal's behavior.

To those English teacher candidates, the teaching job in Korea is just another employment opportunity. They are not losers. These people are probably more open-minded and adventurous than other young adults in their countries. Wanting to travel to a country where the culture is completely unfamiliar and foreign is challenging and exciting, as you can imagine. It's a life-changing experience. They don't come to stay forever. Some do, of course, stay longer than they expect—or forever—because of circumstances: meeting someone they want to marry or being offered a better job. But the reason they travel is to earn money in a place where everything is new— the food, the scenery, the people—where they can learn about other ways of living and looking at the world. It's very disappointing when what they learn is the pervasiveness of the human fear of those who are different.

I want to be clear that this trait is human, not confined to East or West: if one person in a group (generally, a minority group) behaves badly, then the entire group gets blamed for it. This happens frequently throughout the world, in many different situations. It happens because it's easy to jump to this kind of conclusion. Suspicion of the stranger is hardwired into our brains. Current scientific thinking is that this is the case because it's quicker to jump to conclusions than to carefully analyze a situation, and at one time this speed was essential to survival. There have been a number of books written about this lately. (One of the best is David Kahneman's *Thinking: Fast and Slow.*) It's useful to understand where these impulses come from, but that doesn't mean we have to give into them. The human tendency to constantly categorize what we see is part of our great success as well as being the cause of many social problems.

I have mentioned Elif Shafak before. Here is another quote from her TED talk.[47]

My mother became a diplomat. So from this small, superstitious, middle-class neighborhood of my grandmother, I was zoomed into this posh, international school [in Madrid], where I was the only Turk. It was here that I had my first encounter with what I call the "representative foreigner." In our classroom, there were children from all nationalities, yet this diversity did not necessarily lead to a cosmopolitan, egalitarian classroom democracy. Instead, it generated an atmosphere in which each child was seen—not as an individual on his own, but as the representative of something larger. We were like a miniature United Nations, which was fun, except whenever something negative, with regards to a nation or a religion, took place. The child who represented it was mocked, ridiculed and bullied endlessly. And I should know because during the time I attended that school, a military takeover happened in my country, a gunman of my nationality nearly killed the Pope, and Turkey got zero points in [the] Eurovision Song Contest.

Has this ever happened to you? Have you felt responsible for what someone of your race, nationality, gender or political party did or said? I'd be surprised if you said no. Most of us identify with one group or another (usually many groups) and feel personally involved when someone in that group does something wrong.

I was watching the news one day, and a Korean person was arrested for drug-related charges. They showed his mug shot. Instantly, I felt ashamed and wished he weren't Korean. When the Korean teenage student Seung-Hui Cho killed thirty-two people and wounded seventeen others in April 2007 at Virginia Polytechnic Institute and State University, I felt horrible for the victims, but I was even more horrified that the shooter was Korean.

In September 2014, Philip Cho, a twenty-eight-year-old living in Chicago, lost control of his white BMW and crashed. He fled the scene, leaving his four Caucasian passengers—his friends—in the crumpled car. Before he left, his friends asked him to call 911, but instead, he hailed a cab and abandoned them. The accident left Kelsey Ibach paralyzed from the waist down. The worst part of this accident was that, before taking off, Phillip Cho asked his injured friends to cover for him—asked them to pretend the accident was a hijacking. I was utterly speechless with dismay. His friends told the truth, and now he is known as a "big coward" in the news and social media.

The 2014 ferry accident near Seoul where almost 300 people died is seared into the memory of every Korean person. It was sickening hearing about the captain being among the first to escape the sinking boat, along with crew members, when hundreds of passengers depended on them—on their specialized knowledge and experience—for their lives. It was also, of course, part of their employment responsibilities to care for passengers.

Any American hearing these news reports might come to the conclusion that there are many cowards and criminals among Koreans. Imagine if all Americans started to form bad opinions of me and looked at me with scrutinizing and cautious eyes because another Korean person committed a horrendous crime. I was a little bit afraid to go out right after hearing the Virginia Tech massacre news, because I'm Korean, like Seung-Hui Cho.

The *New York Times* printed a long article on May 7, 2015,[48] about nail salon owners exploiting their employees. Most of the owners are Korean and Chinese. Koreans own seventy to eighty percent of the 2000-plus nail salons in New York. The main point of the story was about how little money these manicurists were being paid, and how unfairly Koreans treat Chinese and Hispanic employees. Sadly, Chinese owners treat even Chinese employees poorly.

In the interviews, many of the Korean owners said things like "Spanish employees are not as smart as Koreans, or as sanitary." "They don't want to learn more." They make these types of remark without realizing how this makes them look! They look ignorant and arrogant, which is a really bad combination. How others view them is something that is very important to Koreans, but often we don't have the self-awareness to realize that what we are saying makes us look uneducated and unkind.

Imagine that American people reading this article are discovering just how racist and cruel Koreans can be. We are exposed! One salon owner made the Hispanic workers sit in silence while the Korean manicurists were free to chat. One manicurist from Tibet recalled a former job at a Brooklyn salon where she had to eat her lunch standing up while Korean employees were eating lunch seated at their desks.

These nail salon owners abuse their employees by not paying their wages and making them work twenty-four/seven. This type of labor abuse exists in many Third World countries. Many business owners who immigrate bring inhumane business practices to the U.S. or other countries. Most of the Korean immigrants and their children work and study hard to build their lives and make a name for themselves in their fields. Some Korean immigrants bring down the Korean image—what we try so hard to build up—without realizing how wrong their practices are.

Even though millions of Koreans live in America, the language barriers and the demands of making a living mean that most of them don't watch or listen to the daily news or pay attention to the important current issues. They don't learn about the values and the social atmosphere of their new country. My mom came to the U.S. at the age of fifty-five. By the time I arrived in 1980, she had been living in the U.S. for four years. She didn't speak any English, and she only socialized with her Korean friends. She worked for Korean businesses where she didn't need to speak English. Even though she has lived in the U.S. for many years now, she hasn't truly gotten to know the people or the culture of the country she calls home. When we don't have the opportunity to interact with people who are very different from ourselves, our understanding of the world stagnates.

When you come to the U.S. as an immigrant, I believe it's important to make an effort to learn about the culture. It may take a long time, but it's better to do it little by little than be completely in the dark. Immigrants come to the U.S. mostly to better themselves economically, but it is very important to respect and learn about the social values of your new country. (The same is true of the foreigners who decide to live in Korea.) We will always be Koreans in our hearts, but it is also necessary that we try our best to be aware of and understand the customs, culture, etiquette and current events of the city and country we now call home. Immigrants have a social responsibility as residents and citizens of the new country. The Internet is an endless resource. There are many Korean organizations in the big U.S. cities and some in smaller cities and towns as well to serve the Korean communities.

A few days before leaving Seoul for Chicago in 1980, I had to take a mandatory one-hour class in Seoul offering basic information on living in America. A person came into the room and explained about how to find an apartment and how car manufacturers engineer cars to break down after three to five years and a few other pieces of information that weren't really helpful. You can find out this sort of thing when you arrive, and it will be more likely to be tailored to the specific rental market where you will be living, for example.

This class would be a good opportunity to educate new immigrants coming to the U.S. about basic labor laws and important social issues in America. If someone is hired to give a talk to Koreans who are leaving Korea, he should speak about current and relevant issues. Providing information about how to look for an apartment and how to buy a car is important, but it's more important to help new immigrants understand that they are going to a very different culture. To understand what they need to know to adjust well will require sustained work. It would be very helpful and useful to give them an overall picture of what social issues, customs and etiquette they will have to learn if they want to fit into their new American communities. A couple of examples are saying "Sorry" when you bump into someone by accident while walking or in a store. Personal space is very important for Westerners. Also, saying, "Excuse me" when you have to pass someone in a narrow grocery aisle or any small space is a must. Holding the door for someone who is behind you—coming in or going out—is considered basic manners. If you ignore these customs, people will think badly of you and might even say so.

The salon owners making racist comments had no idea that one of the worst things that can be said about a person in the U.S. nowadays is, "You are a racist." (Of course, they should also not be racist, but often the first step in overcoming one's racism is learning that other people find it unacceptable.) Reversing bad images created by a few Koreans can take many years.

~ RESET PERSPECTIVE ~
Every race, country, even every family, has good and bad people, smart and stupid, beautiful and not so beautiful, rich and poor, generous and stingy. You can see how silly it is to judge a whole race or group of

people when you hear of a criminal act perpetrated by one person from any nation or race.

In regard to the Canadian teacher: when any business hires an employee, the applicant has to go through an interview and screening process. This often involves background checks. Even if this is done thoroughly, following the correct procedures, some employees will still turn out to be not qualified for the job or not meet expectations. Having a few unqualified or bad teachers in a school is quite normal. Having a serious offender on your payroll, criminal or otherwise, is less common, but still happens. People with these tendencies are secretive and can fly under the radar for a while.

Carlos thinks there is another way we can look at this judgmental habit of ours. People use one individual's bad behavior as an excuse to expand on an already existing bias towards that group. One individual's act is used as an excuse to justify hatred, fear or discrimination. Regarding the English teacher, it's not the case that yesterday we liked all English teachers and only after hearing about the incident of Christopher Neil, Koreans started to dislike or think negatively about English teachers. It built over time, primarily on the traditional Korean distrust of foreigners (particularly those who are not from a wealthy country) and on a lack of understanding about the reasons propelling young Westerners to places like Korea. This adventurous spirit, where unusual experiences are more than, or just as, important as building a successful career is not yet part of Korean culture. Since, for a Westerner, teaching in Korea (or Japan or China or Peru) isn't part of a clearly defined career trajectory, it was too easy for Koreans to accept that such teachers are either "losers" or have immoral motives.

FAVORITISM
Favoritism is another side of prejudice, as we saw in the anecdote about Ohyun. Favoritism is prevalent and a daily occurrence. One thing that

always shocks non-Koreans is the way that Koreans give compliments or show prejudice openly, shamelessly, without any consideration for bystanders. While an individual is receiving a compliment or treated with prejudice, people nearby watch it without reacting. This happens so often in the classrooms or at work, it seems natural. You don't think there is anything wrong with it.

When I was in junior high, the teacher sat the students who paid their tuition early near the fireplace during the winter. People who paid late sat away from the fireplace. When I was in senior high school—a different teacher, a different school—the same thing happened. The students who paid early sat closer to the front and ones who paid late sat in the back of the classroom. While I sat near the fireplace and in front of the classroom, on the receiving end of the favoritism, I remember feeling something was not quite right about the arrangement. Looking back, I'm wondering about the long-term psychological effects on the students who had to sit in the back or away from the heater.

In many of the classes in Korea, it was clear to everyone who the teacher's favorites were. Sometimes the favoritism was because of looks. Other times, it was paid for. Giving presents/money to teachers was pretty normal when I was growing up. It was thought of as showing appreciation to the teacher as well as saying, "Please take good care of my daughter, please pay extra attention to her." I know my mom did it a few times. Whenever she gave something to the teacher, I remember being given some kind of a compliment in front of the whole classroom. It always made me feel awkward.

When I was in my second year in high school, my mom came to visit me from Chicago. This was the period where I was waiting for the paperwork to be processed to go to America. So, my mom was living in Chicago, and I was living in Seoul. Mom invited my teacher to have lunch with us, and she brought a small gift for him, a kind of fancy cigarette lighter. When the teacher and I went back to the classroom, it was very clear that the teacher wasn't very happy that what he received was not money.

~ RESET PERSPECTIVE ~

When we judge, we form an opinion based on our own knowledge and experience, which can be very limited. We are drawn to sensational stories and transfer the emotions we feel about them—disgust at a child molester, for example—to a larger group of people. There is something satisfying about this emotionally unless you happen to be a part of that larger group. Then it feels terrible and frightening and deeply unfair. It takes work to consciously remember that.

Every time I talk with someone about my Korean experiences—the ones I've written about above—they all have similar stories. If you live in Korea, these things are quite normal, but for people coming from outside, especially from the West, these experiences are shocking. These incidents make Koreans look like such prejudiced people, even when things turn out favorably for the Western foreigners. They realize that Koreans don't treat their own people as nicely as they do white Westerners, to whom they show overwhelming kindness and respect. To grow as a society, we need to break the cycle of prejudice. Let's be nice and respectful to everyone.

SUMMING UP

After I read a part of my first draft of this chapter to my husband, Carlos, he answered eloquently: "All humans are racists. Acknowledging that is part of the truth. The fact that it is wrong doesn't eliminate the fact that it is within us. It's the same as the fact that we war against each other. We kill, we are greedy; we cheat; we are racists. We do all these things because they are within us."

I asked him, "How do we get over being racists then?"

"It's not about not being a racist, but about becoming more tolerant. Tolerance is what enhances peace and love, what improves the human condition. But the racism within us has to be overcome by tolerance. The racism as a gene, as a behavior, it is not going to go away. You have to train yourself to subdue it."

What he said made sense to me and put this complex race issue in perspective. Just as we try not to cheat, steal, lie—whatever we shouldn't be doing—we should try not to be a racist. There's no point in being ashamed of our natural human impulse to categorize. I'm thinking of how so many people are criticized today for being "politically incorrect" about race—or gender or sexual orientation—when often they didn't intend any malice and maybe didn't even understand why someone was offended. And, let's face it, anyone can make a gaffe. The point is, having feelings about race that aren't 100 percent perfect is not a sign of a degenerate character or a cold heart. It's the human condition—sometimes a human failing. We can change our minds. We can learn tolerance and learn to look beyond the skin, beyond what we were taught.

I don't imagine we can scrub racism from the planet, from Korea, or even from our hearts. Humans are stubborn that way. But let me tell you from experience—there is a wonderful pleasure in finding out that you can make a connection with someone from a very different background, someone you once looked down on or up at, were scared of or just didn't understand. There's really nothing to compare it to. The biggest beneficiary of this change will be you.

6

Nature or Nurture?

Biology is the least of what makes someone a mother.

— OPRAH WINFREY

THANKS FOR SENDING ME TO NORWAY!

One of the things I like the most about Western living is that most people don't judge you based on your education or family background. Where you come from doesn't matter. Who you are now and where you are going is more important. Now, some Americans would argue with me about this. If you have a degree from Harvard, you will be looked at differently from the person with a degree from a mid-ranked state university, or the person who grew up in a trailer park and didn't finish high school. But compared to what I experienced growing up in Korea, and what I've seen in Korea on my visits back and in conversations with people living there now, the scale of that judgment is very different.

This applies to any form of early misfortune, including being adopted. In fact, children adopted as infants in the U.S. are not thought to have suffered any misfortune, and it is even considered socially incorrect to assume that parents who adopt because they are unable to

128

have biological children are at all unlucky. This is one of those areas in American life where one truth—that it is painful and disappointing to learn you are infertile—is put aside for the sake of a more acceptable truth—that the vast majority of Western parents who adopt fall madly in love with their children and feel blessed to have them.

Over the years, I have met Korean adoptees from Sweden, Norway, and several in the U.S. Every single one of them seems happy and is doing well in life. Until I met a Korean adoptee in Stockholm, Sweden, seventeen years ago, I didn't realize so many Korean orphans were sent to Scandinavian countries. Since Koreans have deep prejudice towards orphans, the general population doesn't have much knowledge about the orphans in their own country. It was said that at one point, South Korea's biggest export was babies. South Korea was a pioneer in international adoptions starting from the end of the Korean War in 1953. There was a sizable humanitarian effort to rescue war orphans and Amerasian babies. More than 200,000 orphans were sent to the U.S., Canada, Australia, Switzerland, Sweden, Norway, Denmark, France, Germany, and Luxembourg. Here are a few of their stories.

Siri Willich was an orphan who was adopted into a loving Norwegian family in 1973, when she was one year old. I became friends with her in Miami. She is a jewelry designer and a fashion designer who is busy being a wife and mother and traveling between her Miami home, New York for work, and Norway to visit her family.

I asked her about how often she thought about her birth mother. She said, "It's something I always thought about, but very early on it was explained to me that I was abandoned on the street. So I can never find out. I kind of settled for that. It was never anything like some other adoptees say, 'It's like a piece of my heart is missing...' I was curious but I truly love my parents, and I think of them as my real parents.

"I knew I was adopted as soon as I was able to look in the mirror. But my dad, a child psychologist, and my mom always talked openly about the fact that I'm from Korea. They used to take me to the Korea Association when I was three and four years old for parties and gatherings for the Korean children who were adopted during the 70s. It was just part of life and has never been an issue.

"I did talk with my dad when I was younger about going to visit my birth country. He told me that he would take me to Korea if I wanted to go. I didn't really want to. I'm not sure exactly why— if it was out of fear of hurting my parents or not… but I didn't want to go for some reason.

"I was twenty-eight, and it was Christmas Day. I was flying out of Bangkok. I was on my around-the-world trip. I was talking to a man on a plane, who turned out to be a Korean. Coincidently, he used to work with Holt International Adoption Agency in Korea during the seventies as an escort, bringing the orphan babies to their new homes in the Western countries." This man might have been the very one who brought Siri to her new home in Norway. Siri kept in touch with the man. He is the reason that she decided to go to Seoul for the first time.

The irony is that while she is a hundred percent pure Korean physically, she was a hundred percent Caucasian inside—more accurately, a hundred percent Norwegian. She felt very strange when people were talking to her in Korean. I asked her, "Do you have anything to say to Korean people?" She said, laughing, "Well… Thanks for sending me to Norway! You can always question how much is nature and how much is nurture. Definitely, I would have been a different person growing up in Korea." Siri is proof that it doesn't matter where you come from. You become how you are raised. She is truly happy to be Norwegian, and she doesn't see herself as anything other than Norwegian.

She added, "If you grew up in a family where you always felt like an outsider then you might feel the need to find your roots. I never felt there was a void inside that needed to be filled."

Hilde Reljin, film director and founder of Uncontaminated Olso Art Fashion Festival, is another adoptee who grew up in Norway with a wonderful family who loved her and her brother, also adopted from Korea. When we first started our conversation in March 2015, she talked about the similarity between women in Norway and Korea. "Norway is very far away from Korea, yet the culture is quite similar in a way. We both have a kind of honest and rough mentality. There is a saying that Korean women are very strong. Norwegian women are also very strong but more liberated in better ways than Koreans. We [Norwegians] don't have to disguise it, in a way. "

Hilde's parents put a fund aside for her to go to Korea when she turned eighteen, but instead she used the money to move to LA. "I wanted to go to school and for my education; LA sounded much more fun. I went to study special effects makeup. The school was right in the middle of Koreatown. For me, it was a huge shock to see the Korean people and the culture so close up from having seen none. I remember I didn't necessarily like it so much because there was a lot of prejudice. I was very bold. I'd walk out on the street with my strange makeup on. I was never shy. I had incidents where Korean men who were fifty or sixty years old would come up to me on the street and tell me I was the shame of their culture. I remember thinking, *What culture do you think I'm part of? Definitely not yours.* So that was my first meeting with Korean culture. It was a negative experience, but it was still kind of interesting."

"Did you make any Korean friends in LA?" I asked.

"No, I was too involved with school."

Hilde worked as a makeup artist for many years in the fashion industry and still has an agency in New York. She now directs film with her ex-husband, who is Norwegian. She works with many Korean and Japanese clients, but she still hasn't been to Korea. She went to Shanghai and Hong Kong with her Korean client/friend in November 2014. Everybody was asking her where she was from. She said, "I'm from Norway." They asked again, "No, no, where were you born?" Hilde answered, "I was born in Korea." Then they said approvingly, "Oh, yes!" To the Chinese people, the fact she grew up in Norway was of no interest, but being born in Korea made her a hot chick. Then Hilde realized how much influence on China Korea has nowadays. (As any Seoul resident knows, Korea has become a favorite tourist destination for the Chinese.)

I asked Hilde if she feels like she is a white person with blue eyes and blond hair as Siri does. She said, "I used to think that but after living in New York for eighteen years, living in the capital of cultures, you don't really think you are anything anymore. I feel like I have no country anymore. I feel I'm very international."

She adds, "Korea is a very Westernized country but the culture is so set back and old. Korea is the only developed country where they still send the orphan babies to other countries because they themselves don't want to adopt them."

Marissa Webb is another Korean adoptee in U.S. She was the global creative director of Banana Republic, a major clothing retailer in the

U.S. and now has her own clothing label. She and her three biological siblings were adopted when she was about four years old. She has no birth certificate; therefore, she does not know her exact age. Her adopted parents didn't have extra money, so she worked at a grocery store in middle school and put herself through college. She started her career designing jeans at Ralph Lauren.

Kristen Kish is a crowned winner of Top Chef, a popular and very respected cooking competition reality show in the U.S. She became the second female winner in the history of Top Chef. Kristen was adopted when she was four months old by an upper-middle-class family in Michigan. She worked as a model in high school. Even with supportive and loving parents, she struggled to find her identity and went through a period of soul-searching before she seriously started her career as a chef. She gets emotional when she talks about her birthplace and very much looks forward to connecting with her roots.

She has a sweet and vibrant personality. She has many fans. I am one of them, not because she is another Korean, but because she seems well-rounded, witty, and has a good attitude about things. She is much younger than me, but one can always learn something from anyone, regardless of how young or old the person may be. My attitude is opposite to the Korean way of thinking, which is that the young can learn from their elders, but learning never goes in the other direction. I haven't met Kristen personally, but I'm looking forward to dining at her restaurant someday.

Paull Shin became the first Korean-born state senator in the U.S. (Washington State). He was born in 1935 in Korea and orphaned at four years old. He lived on the street until he became a houseboy to a group of U.S. Army officers during the Korean War. When the war ended, he was nineteen. One of the officers adopted him and took him to America. He had never been to school and knew little English, but he was able to complete a GED in eighteen months, eventually earning a master's degree and Ph.D. from the University of Washington.

Sadly, not all adoptees have happy stories. Susanne Brink, adopted into a Swedish family, suffered abuse and racism in her adoptive home and country. The story even became a 1991 movie titled *Susanne Brink's Arirang*.

~ RESET PERSPECTIVE ~

Judging a person does not define who they are. It defines who you are.

The interesting thing is Norway was a homogeneous country until not too long ago, and yet Siri and Hilde grew up with no negative experiences as a result of being the only non-white people in their communities. They experienced almost zero racism, to the point that they thought of themselves as white even though they knew they were different. But their "difference" was something they saw in the mirror or heard from their parents when they asked about their origins—it didn't come from other Norwegians, as either open or subtle discrimination. Of course, their schoolmates could see that they were of Asian heritage, and probably many of the kids were curious and asked questions—but nobody thought the girls weren't Norwegian.

Korea is a homogeneous country, too, but our treatment of people who look different is very different from that of Norwegians. How ironic and blessed for Siri and Hilde that they ended up going to a country where the values are rooted in egalitarianism and equality after being rejected by a country that couldn't offer them any of those values.

In the West, every time you meet someone who was adopted and you start to talk about family things, he or she will say, "I was adopted!" There is absolutely no shame, not even a hint of desire to hide the fact. It's very natural to tell new acquaintances that you were adopted, and people respond non-judgmentally, showing no prejudice. If someone does respond with any kind of prejudice to a person after finding out he or she was an orphan, that person will be considered to as having a character flaw.

Lisa Oh* is an international creative talent recruiter whom I met through working on a project for a Korean company and who has become a close friend. I'm so glad that she and her husband in Seoul adopted their baby Jiwon. They love the new baby like their own. I hear the same thing from all the parents and adoptees I have spoken with and know of; the parents and the children become your own. Also, it seems like having an open conversation with the child/children about the adoption early on is more natural and healthy for all relationships than trying to keep it secret. I can only imagine that, when things are hidden, and the children get older and are surprised by their true identities, it can create confusion and resentment.

I have no doubt that there are some unhappy adoptees whose family circumstances led them to feel blame and anger towards the adoption system, and others with legitimate complaints about the circumstances and documentation surrounding their adoption. But based on every adoptee case I have seen—and my own life experience as a Korean and an American—I think how lucky and fortunate they are to have a chance at a normal life instead of being left at an orphanage in Korea. Even after orphans become adults, Korean society treats them with prejudice and shuts doors on them. Both orphans and adopted people in Korea face extreme prejudice—which just doesn't happen in the U.S. and Europe. It's a non-issue.

Biracial Korean people are also the target of discrimination. In an *LA Times* article, Janet Mintzer, president of Pearl S. Buck International, said, "My impression is that there is more discrimination against Amerasians in South Korea than anywhere else in Asia and that it has not improved significantly. "

Yujin Lee, an actress and model, hid the fact that her father was an American G.I. until 2003. Lee grew up in Seoul. She was a good student and a beautiful child. Yet everybody pitied her. "They said I would come to a bad end, maybe end up in a brothel, because I was of mixed blood," Lee said. "Even my mother felt sorry for me. She still does. Even if I became president, she would feel sorry for me. That's Korea."[49]

TO HELP OR NOT TO HELP

I was very surprised to hear about the Special Adoption Law that was passed in 2012 in Korea. The law, initiated by some grown adoptees, requires unwed birth mothers to register their babies in their family registry. The intention was to help returning adoptees locate their birth parents more easily. In some (rare) cases, Korean children who were found on the streets because their families had fallen into poverty and disarray, or were given to orphanages by fathers who didn't consult the mothers, ended up in the U.S. or Europe while still having family in Korea who wanted them. This sort of thing happened during the dark years after the war and into the 80s; it is impossible to guess how often it happened, but all indications are it was infrequent. In any case, in a much richer Korea, it is far less likely to happen. Today ninety percent of abandoned babies are born to single mothers who don't want anyone to know about their pregnancies. The shame of unwed motherhood, if it became public knowledge, would have a serious negative impact on their ability to marry or get a good job. So this law, which forces young mothers to register the child in their family registry for the baby to be adopted, results in the mothers choosing secret abandonment like the baby box or leaving the infants on the side of the road. [50]

Some of the adoptees also wanted to prevent foreign adoptions. These have been restricted for a number of years since the 1988 Summer Olympics in Seoul spotlighted Korea and what the government considered a national embarrassment—how many children were adopted out of the country. Today, there is a larger number of grown orphans. As of 2015, there were approximately 17,000 children (birth to nineteen) living in government facilities.

The Special Adoption Law was passed before social attitudes caught up to those of Western countries. As we know, changing the ingrained mindset of thousands of years doesn't happen overnight. If you prevent overseas adoptions, and Koreans don't want to adopt these babies, where will they go? Why would you prevent these babies from the possibility of a bright future unless you can offer them one yourself? More Koreans should adopt as Lisa Oh and her husband did. But we Koreans don't want to adopt. The attitude is, "Why do we want to raise somebody else's baby?" The importance of bloodlines is deeply rooted. Even though some parents do adopt, many hide it from their families and the adopted child, shielding them from the prejudice against orphans in Korea.

Ph.D. student Hollee McGinnis, has studied orphaned Korean children and founded Also-Known-As, a nonprofit organization for adult intercountry adoptees in New York City. She says that many Korean families today start out with the intention of being open about their adoptions, but because of the social difficulties the children will face—bullying, ostracism—eventually change their minds. (This is especially true if they have the opportunity to move to a new town.)

The choice these parents make is understandable, but what this means is that people aren't nudged to change. People don't know that the child their child plays with is adopted. They don't get a chance to witness the family love that is apparent in Western adoptive families. There's no social pressure for those who might be inclined to bully or ostracize to take a hard look at their—or their children's—behavior.

Yet more than two hundred thousand families on the other side of the world opened up their hearts, wanting to take care of these babies and raise them as their own. The vast majority of those children would be loved, well cared for, educated—and would grow into global citizens whose Korean heritage would only enhance their understanding and opportunities. The fact is that while there are people who suffer because they grow up away from their birth families and culture, there are just as many, if not more, who benefit from being adopted. We all process the idea of 'identity' a little differently. There are some unhappy adoptees, and everyone's story is unique. But unhappiness and feeling like you just don't fit in also happen in biological families. I'm not downplaying the pain or struggle some of these adoptees went through. Nor is it anything to be proud of, sending so many Korean babies overseas. But I believe that until the Korean people have a change of heart, so that most orphans end up in loving homes and are welcomed into society and treated fairly, as any Korean wants to be treated, preventing foreign adoption is saving face at the expense of children's rights to a life of love and opportunity.

By 2026, one fifth of Koreans will be more than sixty-five. This is a dramatic change that will put greater burdens on our society—and especially on our young people. Considering how much we need them, not only to care for the elderly but to carry on the culture and accomplishments of the Korean people, let's consider cherishing all who are born here, in whatever circumstances. Let's extend compassion toward those who grow up as orphans and learn to see all families, biological or otherwise, as worthy of our respect and support.

7

Women

If the hen cries, the house is ruined.
If a woman is educated, she is not going to listen to her husband.
If a woman is smart, she will have a hard life.
(Korean proverbs)

There is a sentence in Korean that starts "You as a woman, what do you know." (*Yujaga morel andago.*) As you can imagine, these words give me a chill. They sound painfully belittling, disrespectful and saddening to women.

Yes, we women have come a long way, and I'm so thankful that I wasn't born in my mother's or my grandmother's generation. There were times in Korea where wife beating was acceptable. Basic education was denied. A woman's best achievement was producing sons for her husband's family. If she failed to produce sons, the rest of her life was marked as a disgrace; she even had to look the other way if her husband took a mistress to have a male heir. She was supposed to accept it—as her fault or her fate—if he divorced her.

We women have come far, but it seems that we Korean women still have a long way to go. *The Economist* reports that South Korea has the strongest glass ceiling of all the OECD nations.[51] Only about ten percent of all managerial positions are held by women, and the gender pay gap is thirty-nine percent, making it the highest in the OECD.[52]

I know what this means for women who are working hard to get ahead, and it makes me sad. Moreover, I'm questioning why this is the case. What are the stumbling blocks for Korean women to move ahead?

My friend Jane, who lives in Seoul, told me in one of our Skype calls: "*Unni* (older sister), I'm being discriminated against by my housekeeper!" Jane is now in the middle of getting her second masters degree in design education and raising her adorable baby girl, Lina.

I asked her, "What do you mean?"

She said, "She serves the best part of the fish or meat to my husband and only gives me the scraps."

I burst out laughing at her complaint. I said, "Why don't you tell her then?"

Jane said, "She takes care of Lina so well. I don't want to lose her." Jane is afraid that if she confronts her housekeeper about how she is being treated, the housekeeper might quit, and Jane doesn't want that to happen. So she eats whatever she is given and accepts the situation with a sense of helplessness. The truth is, Jane understands deep down that her housekeeper is of an older generation and doesn't have much education. There is no reason to bring up the issue or argue with her when she knows that she won't be able to change the housekeeper's lifelong belief that women should be nice, submissive and take care of their husbands as if they are the kings of the house.

OUR MOTHERS AND GRANDMOTHERS

To the younger generation, it may sound like ancient times, but we still live with or remember the women for whom this was a typical situation: The husband would get the best of everything, then the older brother, younger brother, then finally the sisters. The mothers got whatever was left.

My mother was born in 1921. I came as a surprise toward the end of her childbearing years. She never received much education, like most women of her generation, while her two brothers were sent to school and given opportunities to make their own lives. She was never even given a proper name because she was a girl. My grandparents named her "Kannan," which originated from "Kan Nan Yi," meaning "just-born baby." So it's not even a name, just a reference to an apparently less-than-special event and a huge disappointment to the parents. My mother always hated her meaningless name and gave herself a new one as soon as she was able.

Though she was resentful of these particular things—her name and lack of education—she accepted her fate of being born in a time when that was common for Korean girls. I have no doubt that if my mom had received a proper education, she would have been far more successful than her two brothers. There are strong women everywhere, and my mom is one of them. Until she became elderly, she was the hardest working person I know; she has tremendous integrity and discipline. She got things done, whatever it took.

I'm ecstatic to hear that the number of Korean families wanting only a baby boy, or a baby boy first, has declined significantly and is becoming almost a non-issue. In fewer families is the birth of a little girl a disappointment, or at best a less exciting event.

A few years ago, I had lunch with my mother and a Korean girl-friend at a restaurant. (My mom is hardly the most extreme Korean parent; I'm using her as an example because she is the one I know best, and because her mindset represents the majority of Korean women of her generation.)

My mom brought up the subject. "Why don't you have a baby?"—even though I was beyond childbearing age. She went on to say, "A woman with no children is not functioning as a woman." I was shocked to hear my mom's statement about her own gender. I've spent my life studying, working and learning about the world, 'functioning' at a high level in many ways. Then I felt bad for my girlfriend, who was older than me and had been single for a long time. I just couldn't believe my mom said we women were only good for having babies. Did she think my whole life has been useless?!

I had been taking care of my elderly mom for many years. Shopping for groceries, taking her to doctors' offices, visiting her three or four times a week—doing whatever she needed and wanted done. My half brother, Jon, who lives in Seattle, wasn't able to do much due to distance. A few years ago, the management office of the senior citizen building where my mom was living asked her for the name of an emergency contact. My mom was about to give my name; then her Korean neighbor told her that she should put my brother's name because it should be a son's name on the record. My mom listened to her and gave the name and number of my brother, who is thousands of miles away—2,043 miles to be exact—and whom she hardly ever sees! I was speechless when she told me this. The old mindset overrides the most basic logic or common sense.

HOW MUCH HAS CHANGED?

I got to watch a Korean TV show while visiting my mom one day last spring. It was called *Achim Madang*, the KBS morning talk show. I'm going to attempt to tell you the story here since it's been a while and I don't remember the exact words but the core of the story remains clearly in my head. The guests were two families with young teenage daughters talking about everyday family matters and relationships with each other. Surprisingly, this one show addressed several of the topics I'm covering in this book.

The teenager in one family talked about wanting to be a chef. The family also talked about how the father scolded the daughter for coming home with an injury from falling off of her new bicycle. The father threatened her, saying, "You won't have a bicycle anymore if you fall one more time!" He explained his state of mind when he said this. He was upset that his daughter hurt herself. And he thought, "Oh well, she is just a girl; she doesn't need to know how to ride a bicycle." His daughter didn't say much about that incident, but you could easily sense her resentment towards her father. It appeared there was no regular communication between the father and the daughter except through the mother. She talked to him on behalf of the daughter. The father and daughter were living in two separate worlds, and the mother was the bridge. The mother said, "He always says no, so she doesn't open up to her father anymore."

The other family's daughter was asked, "What do you want to be when you grow up?"

She answered, "I want to become a senator because when I see politicians on TV, I don't like how they conduct themselves, and I think I could be a better politician than them."

I was elated watching these two girls with such bold and can-do attitudes at such young ages. I was sad that there are still many fathers who box their daughters into rigid roles, thinking they should play and stay safe and be domestic because girls are fragile, helpless and can't do many things. The daughters' desires and dreams were being rejected in their very own homes when these girls needed encouragement and cheering on from their fathers: "Yes, you can!" The past, present and future were living in parallel under one roof, the daughters' present frustrations and future hopes clashing with the father's mindset of caring for his daughters. He doesn't understand them or the world they are growing into.

PLAY SOCCER!

I spent one afternoon with Dr. Gye Young Park, Director of the Pulmonary and Diagnostic Laboratory at Illinois Hospital, and Dr. Lucy Park, pediatric allergist, immunologist, and pulmonologist there. Dr. Lucy Park is also Executive Director at The Sejong Cultural Society in Chicago. The organization is very active in promoting Korean culture in the United States. They reach out to the younger American generation through contemporary creative and fine arts. We went to listen to a talk by Chang-Rae Lee, Korean American novelist, author of *Native Speaker* and professor of creative writing at Stanford University, and chatted over a sushi lunch.

Dr. G.Y. Park has a daughter and a son. He told me that the subject of gender equality has been on his mind for some time. "I realized and learned a lot from watching my daughter growing up with a mindset that's completely different from my own. I grew up a certain way, but my daughter thinks differently. We had many conflicts, but over the years my thoughts started to change. I tried really hard to decide what is right and what is wrong.

"My daughter was five years old when she came to the U.S. Back then, I probably thought maybe she could be a teacher or have a job that's safe and respectable. But now she can be anything she wants to be. The worst part about women in Korea is that they don't realize they are being discriminated against. They are limited to the role of what women should be and nothing else. So even when they grow up and start working at a company and they get discriminated against, they just accept it, rather than thinking that it's wrong.

"When I was growing up, I wasn't allowed in the kitchen, but my wife raises our children, a boy and a girl, equally. My daughter and I sometimes have confrontations. My daughter will ask me, 'Dad, why do you do that?'

"I grew up in very traditional ways. So things I do or I say consciously or subconsciously are very traditional Korean ways. My daughter and I went to Korea. My daughter saw many things she didn't understand. She would say, "Why is he just sitting down? Why isn't he helping his wife?

"The mindset starts early on. They have to be raised with the mindset of equality as my children were. My daughter played soccer in America. When she went to Korea to learn Korean one summer, she saw boys were playing soccer at lunchtime while the girls were playing with jumping ropes. She went and joined the boys and played soccer, making four goals. Everybody was shocked. The last day, when she was leaving the class to return to America, everyone wrote on the farewell card. Most of them, including the boys, wrote how much they were impressed by how good of a soccer player she was.

"The gender equality mindset needs to start at an early age as possible for both boys and girls. So they grow up thinking men and women are equal. Women can play soccer if they want to and be good at it.

"Of course, there is a gender gap here too in America, but in Korea, there are many things that are just out of the question. For example, there is a big hospital in Korea called Asan Medical Center. These days there are a lot of women medical students in Korea, but in Asan Hospital, there was only one female doctor in a division I was meeting with. So I asked her, 'How come there are almost no female doctors here?' She answered, 'Oh I wasn't aware of that.' So women themselves don't realize they are being discriminated against. Women are the ones who need to make the changes, but they don't realize the problems. They are just used to the way things are done and accept the sameness."

"When I was going to medical school in Korea," Dr. G.Y. Park said, "There were many things said about women among professors: 'You don't work with women, women are to play with.'"

Dr. Lucy asked Dr. G.Y. Park, "Which year did you graduate?" He responded, "I graduated in 1990."

Dr. Lucy Park said, "I graduated in 1975. Which means there hasn't been much progress. After three years of medical school, we do a one-year residency training. The professors used to call the male students *Park Seonsaeng* (teacher), but they would call female students Miss Park. Some professors would say openly 'Hey, why don't you just go home and take care of children? What are you doing here?' When I graduated university, I went to my pediatric professor and told him I would like to be a pediatrician. He told me, 'We don't pick women.' Even after hearing that, I could've pushed through and gone ahead using my high scores, but after hearing that answer, I was angry. I decided to go to America."

"That's why we have to make women soccer teams!" Dr. G.Y. Park said, laughing.

Not all intelligent, capable women can leave Korea because their work culture doesn't accept them or mocks them. Those male professors who made sexist, offensive comments to Dr. Lucy Park—and the ones making such remarks now, though I hope no one does—need to realize that these attitudes are no longer acceptable or tolerated.

"When I was in high school," Dr. Lucy Park said, "My mom told me to go to medical school. So I went to talk with my teacher for consultation. I told him, 'I don't want to go to medical school, but my mom wants me to go to Seoul University (the best university in Korea). I was expecting him to say, 'No, you can't go' or 'You are not qualified.' But he told me, 'Oh that's a great idea!' So I was surprised. Even my friends told me, 'That's out of the question!' I later found out all the friends who could have gone to Seoul University with me, instead ended up going to Ewha Womans University Medical School. Automatically, they assumed they weren't good enough to go to the best university."

In 2013, a CNBC *Financial Times* article reported, "Many foreign executives say that Korean women seem to be smarter than men with higher communication and adaptation skills," says Kim In-hye, head of the Seoul office of Russell Reynolds, an executive recruitment group. "However, many women here still work in the back office rather than the business front lines as they prefer stability to risk-taking."[53]

There is constant talk about how much things have changed,[54] but the data still reflect that many still carry the same mindset and resist a different view of women in Korea. I have no doubt things will continue to get better, but let's not wait around for someone else to make things happen. Let each one of us participate in the change whenever we see an opportunity. Korea and the world need all of the talents of both men and women. But the first beneficiary will be you. There is an incredible amount of joy and satisfaction in discovering and accomplishing things that you didn't realize you were capable of. So please don't give up before even starting!

HOW OLD IS TOO OLD?

My friend Jane (the one with the old-fashioned housekeeper) was, in her late thirties, working for an IT company in Seoul. Some people at the company said to her, "We need to send you for Goryeojang." What is Goryeojang? It's a folk legend, apparently of Chinese origin, and considered now to be fictional. As the story goes, in the Goryeo Dynasty (918–1392), people would take parents over seventy up the mountainside to die. This tradition was called Goryeojang. A 1963 Korean movie of the same name, produced and directed by Kim Ki-young, has kept the story current in people's minds.

This is pretty shocking even as a legend, considering how highly regarded elders are in Korean culture. Goryojang, if it was ever practiced, happened under extreme poverty and food scarcity to save food for young people. In Jane's story, the men at her work were saying that in their opinion, she was of an age to retire even though they acknowledged Jane as a highly valued employee in the company. They were implying that they wanted to work with young and pretty women—so it was time for Jane to retire.

Around that time, Jane's company was hiring a PR person. Jane knew an excellent candidate whom she recommended to the company, but this woman didn't get hired even though she was very talented and highly qualified. The reason was that she was too old. She was forty-one years old! The fellow decisionmaker told Jane, "Even you are a Goryeojang—and she is older than you? There will be no more discussion about this candidate." A second later he asked, "Is she pretty?" Then he said, "No, that doesn't matter. We don't want to work with a woman who is older than us. It's out of the question."

All these comments were said in a joking manner, but the content of the conversation and the employee selection process was very real and clearly shows the company's culture of severe age discrimination.

Jane added that another reason for not hiring older people is the Korean tradition of respect for elders. People assume that when they hire someone older than them, they will have more difficulty managing them.

Isn't it sad that women learn and master skills, and their experience is treated with such contempt? (Of course, this happens to men, too.) Why does a company—or a country—think that human capital is of no value just because the person is older? The insecurities of the young are not a good basis for running an enterprise that should care more about merit and performance. Women's insecurities and fears give legitimacy to the way men behave—so the practice is rarely questioned, at least openly. But when you look at it rationally, what you see is employees putting feelings that have nothing to do with the job ahead of the needs of the business. I understand that most men grow up with this culture and don't take time to think about it, but they should. We all should.

Another story from Jane's company: they were in the process of hiring an interior design firm to remodel the entire space. One of the firms under consideration was acknowledged by all to be the best, but in the end, they decided to go with another company. Why? The owner of the design company was over fifty, and they gave the job to someone younger, saying that they didn't want to work with a grandma. There are age and gender discrimination in the West, too, of course, but in the West, attitudes are more fluid, and even fifty or sixty years ago, exceptions were made for talent and proven success.

~ RESET PERSPECTIVE ~

What should be obvious is that when people—men or women—reach the age of forty, they are just coming into their prime. That's when they start to perform at their highest capacity and contribute at a higher level. They are able to make decisions with confidence, based on substantial and varied knowledge. That's a huge asset to a company. You want to work with people who can bring the best results for the projects, regardless of their age. Young people bring new ideas and boldness. They are best able to see or intuit changes in the culture. Older people have perspective and the advantage of experience: what worked and what didn't, how the clients reacted last time, how the market behaved, what the dangers are. This is in addition to their technical know-how and well-honed skills. Companies—enterprises of all kinds—need both kinds of people. (I should add that age is not a hard and fast descriptor. There are so many young people who think and act like old people, and there are many old people who think and act young. It truly depends on the individual.)

The practice of dismissing someone with qualifications based on the assumption that "It will be difficult to work with an older person" is simply wrong. The employees in our design company joined when they were young. I have to tell you, some of them have been pretty difficult to work with. Chuck Rudnick is a Group Creative Director at Foote, Cone & Belding, an ad agency in Chicago. He is an old friend and creative partner of Carlos from back in the agency days. Chuck sums it up well by saying, "As a rule, people who are easy to manage are mature, respectful, and willing to admit they don't know everything – this is true regardless of age."

When I talk about age, in this context, I'm not even talking about a sixty- or seventy-year-old person, who may be slowing down (though

I know plenty who aren't). I'm talking about a forty-year-old person being considered "old" and not getting the opportunity, even though she was the best candidate for the job! In particular, I'm talking about a forty-year-old woman. In her book *Do Not Marry Before Age 30*, Joy Chen says, "You don't find successful head hunters who are early or mid-thirties. Most successful headhunters begin this part of their career in their forties or even sixties. It takes wisdom, maturity and judgment to guide a search toward a best outcome."

On Forbes' list: "The World's 100 Most Powerful Women in the World 2014," ninety-plus women were over forty. The majority were between fifty and sixty-eight. These were women like Angela Merkel, Hillary Clinton, Nancy Pelosi, Sheryl Sandburg, and Arianna Huffington. Just imagine if these women hadn't been given the chance to pursue their careers, dreams and passions. None of them would have achieved what they have achieved.[55]

WE ARE NOT WORTH IT
Do you know who our worst enemies are in the pursuit of our goals and our happiness? Ourselves. We Korean women are so accustomed to being treated as second-class citizens in our society. Imagine if anyone suggested, "You are not a second-class citizen. You are as valuable as a man. Your contribution to society is just as important as any man's. You have the courage, and you can do anything you want." Would we believe it? Unfortunately, it seems like we women often don't know or realize our value because our mothers and grandmothers and great-grandmothers thought the same way. We were brought up to not think much of ourselves, and we watched as our fathers and other men treated the most important people in our lives, our role models, as less than. At least that's how it used to be until not too long ago. My mom didn't have many expectations for me. She just wanted me to have a life that was

safe, steady and easy. She imagined a very limited and simple life for me. But I wanted to know, experience, and create life and things beyond my current existence in this world.

In our grandmother's generation, if women failed to deliver sons, they were treated like servants by their in-laws. They had let the family down and, therefore, the only respect they could have hoped for was denied. Living in an environment like this made women accept and believe that they were inferior to men. You can see this ingrained bias in the earlier examples. Jane is only served crumbs and scraps by her housekeeper in her own house because the housekeeper believes Jane's husband is much more important, just because he is a man. Jane, a woman like herself, does not deserve the best parts of the meal. Women have had less and are considered less.

WE ARE AT THE BOTTOM!
Korean girls and boys study equally hard and take the same vigorous academic path until they graduate university. Korean women receive more than fifty percent of bachelor's or master's degrees awarded by Korean universities. We're smart, we put in the time, and we should be proud of that. But then what happens? Women work for a few years until they get married. Most women don't worry too much about advancement. They assume that they will quit their jobs and become stay-at-home moms if their husbands make enough income. For many smart young women, to marry such a man is the goal. But why should you study so hard for so many years just to have a good university name on your resume and marry well? What is the point of all those years of hard work and accumulated knowledge? Just to pass the tests? Isn't that a waste of effort? I don't mean to devalue the importance of entrance exams but whatever is waiting at the end of all the tests, for women in South Korea, seems grim. Even though there are many brilliant and successful women in

South Korea, there are still fewer, many fewer than there should be from a global perspective.

Korea is ahead in one respect: it has strict laws promoting gender equality. Kinam Park, the executive director at The Korea Foundation for Women (KFW), told me that the laws are excellent—but they are neither followed nor enforced. Whenever there is a problem related to discrimination, whether it's sexual harassment or unfair practices regarding promotion or pay, people handle it as a personal issue. They suffer, quit their jobs or move to another location. The problems never make it into the public arena to be discussed. They don't become social issues. And to deal with any particular case legally is a huge and costly undertaking with the outcome uncertain. So what can women do to change things?

In the West, when a sexual harassment case is won, the company pays the victims. A well-publicized case involves 21st Century Fox, run by Rupert Murdoch. The company reached a twenty million dollars settlement with Gretchen Carlson, an anchorwoman who sued Roger Ailes, the powerful CEO and Chairman of Fox News. He has since stepped down. The best way to prevent sexual harassment is education. Companies are legally required to provide sexual harassment education for all their employees, and they face penalties if they do not and a subsequent sexual harassment suit is filed.[56] The suits function as warnings and to emphasize the consequences of bad behavior. If a company wants to create a healthy and productive working environment for all employees, sexual harassment education should be treated as very important business training.

Whatever they do must begin with an understanding of what the problem is, how it truly affects people, and how other societies have dealt with similar conditions. Let's start with the constitution, because it represents what many intelligent and important people have thought matters—on paper anyway. The 1948 Constitution of South Korea states:

"All citizens shall be assured of human dignity and worth and have the right to pursue happiness. It is the duty of the State to confirm and guarantee the fundamental and inviolable human rights of individuals." (Article 10)

"All citizens shall be equal before the law and there shall be no discrimination in political, economic, social, or cultural life on account of sex, religion or social status." (Article 11.) Wouldn't it be wonderful if this were true in our society? Why do you think these ideas are spelled out in our constitution if they are not something to strive for?

Globally, women now outnumber men in university graduation rates. The numbers are ninety-three men per 100 women. In the U.S., sixty percent of managerial positions are held by women.[57] Many scholars believe that women hold the key to lifting countries out of poverty: women's small businesses and crafts can make the difference between bare survival and a family thriving, with the children doing better than the parents. There are also horrible things happening to women around the world, from the 300 schoolgirls kidnapped by Boko Haram in Nigeria to the stoning of women for alleged sexual crimes in Pakistan. The leading cause of death for women fifteen to nineteen is complications related to childbirth. At the same time, in many places where girls and women were historically oppressed, there are signs of change. I'm thinking of India with its recent outcry against rape, and the Nobel Prize won by Malala Yousafzai for her advocacy of education for girls. Her activism provoked a man to shoot her.

None of these atrocities are taking place in Korea—nor am I suggesting that they will—but they are a reminder of where disrespect for women leads. They nudge us to be better and stronger, to make use of the opportunities we have, in education, social mobility and career, and not to be held back by fear of disapproval or failure.

Sometimes it can be easier to protest when things are unbearable. In Korea, our lives are pretty good, compared to much of the world. Yet our country, our society, has demonstrated in recent decades that change is not only possible but is something exciting and desirable. Of course, we want to do things our own, "Korean" way, but that doesn't have to mean the way we've always done things. Every dynamic society grows and evolves. History demonstrates that one thing humanity does spectacularly well is learn from other cultures.

MOTHERS AND CAREERS

I understand that not all women want both career and family. Some people are happier in the domestic environment because of their temperament and talents. Introverts—especially those with a great interest in early childhood development—might welcome a chance to avoid the public sphere and focus on their offspring. Some women use cooking, entertaining and homemaking as a way of being creative and building family and community. Everyone does it differently. If becoming a mom was your dream, and you are completely satisfied with your life as it is, that's fantastic. But if there is anything else you want to do in life, anything that makes you wistful, makes you long for the chance to try your hand and test your skills, you should go after it. It may not be easy. You may not succeed. But what if you do? What if that dream becomes reality?

I live in a big city in the U.S., surrounded by professional women. Carlos and I decided not to have children, but most of our close friends do. Inger is a group creative director who works for an ad agency in Chicago. Anja is a senior consultant at a marketing firm and a professor in Bern, Switzerland. Fiona is an artist in Barcelona, Spain. Elke is a designer in Austria. Raquel is a transplant surgeon in Chicago. Ann-Marie is a pediatrician in Miami, Florida. Jisook is an executive director at a wellness center in Seoul; Valeria is an architect in San Francisco. I could list many more friends and acquaintances in the U.S. who are moms and continuing with their careers.

They are incredibly dedicated mothers, still their jobs are a crucial part of their identities. I can't imagine their talents and knowledge not being utilized, and they can't imagine themselves not working while raising their children. Most of them work full time.

I want to be clear that I'm not putting down or disrespecting mothers whose decision is to be full-time moms. But I'm challenging those of us who assume automatically, without further consideration, "After I have a baby I'm going to stay home."

One of the few full-time moms whom I know is Sonia Angres, mother of two, who was a Director of Recruiting at Thoughtworks when she quit to be a stay-at-home mom. "I have a big regret about not working. I do. I feel like I'm smart, and I have a lot to offer, but I'm sitting here at home now. I'm not going to be able to show the world what I have to offer because I have been home for ten years. I'm scared that no one's going to hire me. If they do, I'll have to start all over, and that is a big fear for me. My kids benefited from me being at home. But I see other kids who went to daycare, and they are fine. I gave up my career for them. For my career trajectory, I always think what could I have been, what would I be now if I had stayed working…"

I wonder how many Korean women are living their lives to the fullest, utilizing their intelligence, education, and skills to achieve their dreams. I once saw a video by an English teacher in Seoul that resonated with me. She asked her young female students about their future career plans. She was surprised when some of her students answered with hopes for their future children's career plans, not their own. The implication was clear—they desired to live their dreams through their children, rather than pursuing their dreams themselves. Are they giving up before even trying? How many Korean mothers set aside their career ambitions and interests for their children? Your children learn from watching you live. Of course, you will do your best to raise your children, but don't forget to live your own life, as well. Your children will be proud to have a mom who pursues her interests through her career or, if not a traditional career, then through important volunteer work, arts work or other passions. There's no one right answer when it comes to parenting. Every child has different needs at various phases of childhood. Every mother has different maternal and career needs. The important thing is to be a woman who creates opportunities for herself to have a more fulfilling life.

MEN AND WOMEN IN BUSINESS

The reality is that women working in the corporate world—and other sectors as well—often face pay discrimination, sexual harassment, blatant and subtle sexism, and a thick glass ceiling. It seems there are many more challenges for working women in Korea than in Western countries. That's why Korea is ranked last for women's equality at work.

Japan is in pretty much the same position as Korea when it comes to the gender gap. Highly educated women settle down as housewives, relying on their salaryman husbands to support the family. Many prefer this system, and the reasons are understandable. The overworked and stressful salaryman's life is not something every person wants.[58]

Jeanna Haw, an American-born Korean who worked for the Clinton Foundation and at one of the major pharmaceutical companies in the U.S. as a global manager in strategic alliance, mostly dealt with corporations, government and universities, working with people at a high level. She consulted for the Korean government when they were setting up a centralized biotech system in Korea.

In 2005, she was in Japan to have a meeting to explore a possibility of working with Japanese companies for a multi-billion-dollar project. She was the team leader of the project and was with her team of ten men at the meeting. When she went into the meeting room, the Japanese men they were meeting with didn't even acknowledge Jeanna's presence. They were all senior managers, directors, VPs from an assortment of R&D/clinical development, commercial, and licensing departments. One of the men started talking to one of Jeanna's team members who was standing behind Jeanna. He completely ignored her. It was like she wasn't there. Jeanna's team told the Japanese men that they needed to speak with Jeanna, not them. Well, what made them behave so unprofessionally with Jeanna? Were they so unused to dealing with a young woman at such a high level that they just couldn't accept her? Maybe they were among those Japanese men who think they are superior to women and refuse to work with one— especially a young Korean American woman? Who knows? Jeanna didn't inquire. The whole experience was so distasteful and disrespectful that Jeanna decided that she wouldn't be working with them in the future.

Helen C.*, working as a consultant in Seoul, was at a meeting one day with many high-level executive officers. There was one female executive; the rest were males. As the meeting progressed, it was clear to

Helen that the woman was the most intelligent and capable among the people at the table. The amazing thing was that every time she spoke, she was challenged by the men. They did their best to discredit her opinions. At the end of the meeting, it appeared as if the main purpose of the meeting was to oppose her position in every way possible. Helen felt that the message these male executives sent to the woman was: "Let's see how far you can go.... You are a woman and how well are you going to do? We are not going to allow you to succeed."

After witnessing such one-sided, unfair, discriminatory situations, Helen couldn't help thinking that such men have no integrity. They show no respect to other human beings when they put down and attack someone simply to gain the upper hand—and do this because she is a woman. As a result, Helen saw these men as small and petty. She lost her respect for them. You can imagine how often this kind of situation occurs in Korean companies where women face glass ceilings.

Perhaps these men think that women will respect them anyway if they succeed, or that it doesn't matter what women think, but they are wrong. The days of respecting men no matter how they treat women are past or passing. Men are shooting themselves in the foot with this behavior and don't even know it.

Helen C., who worked with several major corporations in Seoul, told me, "Men have a hard time with a woman being promoted. Men help each other be promoted. That's one of the many reasons a lot more men are in high positions than are women." This is the old boys' network in Korea's corporate culture.

SHOOTING YOURSELF IN THE FOOT

The Harvard Business School newsletter had a long article on how Korean companies don't hire many women, no matter how qualified.

The multinational firms are more than happy to snatch up the best female candidates for their international branch offices. It's been a trend for many years. Foreign companies are taking advantage of Korea's labor market where women are not hired for managerial positions.

In the article, Harvard Business School professor Jordan Siegel discussed teaming up with Lynn Pyun of MIT and B.Y. Cheon of Hanshin University and the Korea Labor Institute to conduct a research study titled "Multinational Firms, Labor Market Discrimination, and the Capture of Competitive Advantage by Exploiting the Social Divide."[59]

The result was eye-opening. In the study, the researchers set out to prove the following hypothesis: "Firms, both foreign and domestic, that do more to hire and promote women to positions of managerial responsibility will see higher levels of profitability." After analyzing financial and employment data from hundreds of medium-sized and large companies, they proved their hypothesis. "The results are pretty strong that even when you control for anything that's fixed about a company, it appears that increasing your female managers leads to higher profitability over time," said Siegel.

The Western business guidebooks for strategic and practical information on doing business in Korea advise seeking top female candidates who are underutilized by their own country due to the rarity and infrequency of opportunities for professional advancement in many Korean companies.

Korea has a deep talent pool of highly educated, highly qualified women with advanced degrees in business, engineering, economics, and foreign languages—all useful in corporate management. But we are handing over the talented female leaders to foreign companies and helping their bottom lines. Do you see how the traditional way is working against us?

WOMEN'S ATTRIBUTES AND CONTRIBUTIONS IN THE WORKPLACE

It is time that Korean companies realize the value of women in the workplace. Not as worker bees with lower wages but as managers and leaders. Men and women are equal in intelligence and general ability but bring different strengths to the workplace. Some of the attributes of successful women: they have a heightened sense of justice; they have more empathy. An empathetic approach helps in building relationships, within the company and with clients, vendors and others. It has been proven that, in general, women are more resourceful and more intuitive than men, and better at multitasking. Men are more likely to be linear thinkers while women are multi-dimensional thinkers. Women get along better with others but are just as competitive and decisive when it matters. Most importantly, having all these attributes makes them good communicators. [60]

Journalist Hanna Rosin has given a TED talk about how we are now going through an amazing and unprecedented moment,[61] with the power dynamics between men and women shifting very rapidly. For every two men who get a college degree, three women will do the same. In 2010, women became the majority of the American workforce for the first time. They're starting to dominate lots of professions as doctors, lawyers, bankers, and accountants. In 1965, only seven percent of new medical school graduates were female. In 2014, it was 47.5 percent. Over fifty percent of managers are women these days.

The number of women CEOs is also rising. To name a few Fortune 500 corporations with women in charge: General Motors, Xerox, Oracle

Corp, DuPont, Yahoo, Campbell Soup, PepsiCo, Hewlett-Packard, IBM. The list goes on....

Connie Chung, writing of the undemocratic nature of the Korean family in *Korean Society and Women: Focusing on the Family*, said, "The bias is rooted in the belief that men and women are inherently different in character and ability, and that this difference favors the male; the female is the "weaker sex of the species." These perceptions delegate such qualities as wisdom, courage, leadership, tenacity, and cool-headed reason to men, while reserving prudence, sacrifice, selflessness, patience, and overabundance of sensibility to women."[62] This is not specific to Korea. All over the world, West and East, women have been seen this way, and the reasons why have a lot to do with the biology of childbearing, male aggression and territoriality, and other factors that still influence our lives, thoughts and desires, but do not set actual limits. The limits are the result of human choice.

Most jobs today do not require sex-specific skills. The ones that, arguably, do, like firefighting or military action (or wet-nursing), are not what I'm discussing here. Corporate jobs, professional jobs, jobs in the arts and media require analytic, organizational, creative and communication skills, which both men and women possess.

Of course, some men (and women) still believe that men are, overall, smarter than women. But research paints a different picture. The British researcher Adrian Furnham, a professor of psychology at University College London, did a meta-analysis of some thirty studies.[63] What he found was that men and women are fairly equal. "Men tend to score higher on certain specialized skills, such as spatial awareness." (Which is why they are often better at reading maps.) "Women score higher in terms of language development and emotional intelligence. Most experts agree that there is no major overall difference in regard to gender and intelligence."

But Furnham's most interesting finding is not the (old) news that the sexes are roughly equal. It's that, on average, women underestimate their IQ scores by about five points while men overstate it. This kind of explains the greater male ego! Men, no matter their intelligence, think they are smarter than they are. And women think their intelligence is lower than it really is. Why does this matter? Because thinking you are smart has everything to do with confidence. In particular, thinking you are smarter than the woman next to you allows you to justify your higher pay, more frequent promotions and the fact that you just appropriated her idea as your own.

It also gives you an understanding of why men can react so angrily to the idea of women's equality. Finding out you're smarter than you thought you were is a pleasant surprise—finding out the opposite (or fearing that you will find it out) is quite a different thing.

YOU HAVE TO TAKE IT

Let's think about how women's status has changed in Europe and the U.S. over the years, how it's changing now and will change in the future. In England and the U.S., women were not allowed equal inheritance until 1922. In the U.S., women didn't have the right to have bank accounts without their husband's permission until the 1960s.[64] German women won the right to vote in 1918, American women in 1920. French women didn't have this right until 1946. In Korea, the year was 1948. Of course, voting is only part of the picture. It wasn't until the second half of the twentieth century that employment rights and "personal" rights (sex, childbearing) were widely discussed. The United States took the lead, probably because the Civil Rights Movement sparked a lot of thinking about equality and because, as a nation of immigrants, tradition is less powerful.

But if you look at the history, what you see is that nobody came to women and said, *Guess what, we were wrong to see you as less than. You're just as smart and capable as we are.* The men asking for women's help in the Civil Rights Movement and the fight against poverty didn't say that, nor did they say that in nineteenth and twentieth century England when people were protesting the class system. What happened was that women—who were very involved in all this activity—said: Wait a minute. Why am I fighting for the rights of others and not for my own rights? What about me? Why do I work and help and sacrifice and still get treated as inferior? There's a famous quote from Black leader Malcolm X. "Nobody can give you freedom. Nobody can give you equality or justice or anything." The rest of his statement is often quoted as, "You have to take it." But what he actually said was, "If you're a man, you take it."

Kind of ironic, isn't it? I would like to say, "If you're a woman, you take it," though *how* the women in a particular society take power is perhaps very different than what Malcolm X had in mind. In America in the 70s and 80s (and continuing), the women's movement used marches, protests, legal battles, and a lot of private activity: consciousness-raising groups and conversations with spouses, peers, and family members. Books and articles were written and the (scientific, philosophical, religious, political) discussion about what gender differences exist was contentious and lasted for decades. It wasn't easy for those forward-thinking women, and it was especially difficult for women who weren't really interested in protest, who took no pleasure in conflict—who just wanted to live their lives, using their talents, making their own choices.

Gloria Steinem, the most famous feminist in America, was promoting her book *My Life on the Road* on a TV show called *Chicago Tonight*. She was asked what advice she would give to young women today. She said, "Don't listen to me. Listen to yourself!"

In Korea today, we have the advantage of being able to look at this history and read these books, and most importantly see what the outcome was: many more women in positions of responsibility and power, more women working, and more women fulfilled and happy as a result of working. It's not that I think Korean should be just like the U.S. or Western Europe. We will do things our own way. But will it be a Korean woman's way—or a Korean man's way? Can't it be both? Recent history indicates that when women are given a choice, a larger percentage of them want to work and use their unique gifts than has been the case in our traditional society. Korean women are half the country. What they want matters.

~ RESET PERSPECTIVE ~

But before we can change anything about women's situation in Korea, we women have to realize something. The forces that hold you back are not only external—though that's where they originate—but internal. Only you can dismantle the internal barriers.

Don't allow yourself to be convinced that you can't succeed. Once you decide you can't do something, it is very hard to get out of that mindset. Removing that "I can't do it" voice is the first step. It can help to talk to other women, both those who have fought successfully to become who they want to be and those who are still struggling. If you can, reach out to the women who have achieved something similar to your goal in life. Don't be afraid to approach these women. Yes, some will be too busy to speak to you; some may even be dismissive. What's important is not so much concrete help—though that's great—but the validation and encouragement you get as a woman who believes in herself. I also suggest finding like-minded women and starting a networking group. It's so easy to do these days with the Internet, creating connections through Meet Up groups or Facebook. This is especially helpful if you are young or just starting your career. Then you as a group can reach out to the women who have achieved something. Perhaps they will come and give a talk—or you could host a luncheon or seminar for them.

Balancing work and family is not easy. It's always a struggle, and it's a very personal one, touching on your most intimate feelings and your most private doubts. But it's not only personal—the ease or difficulty of this balancing act depends on public policy. Denmark is one of the most progressive countries in the world for gender equality within the work place. Danish family policy explicitly champions the "dual-earner family"—with extended maternal and paternal leaves, during which the employee is paid and guaranteed a job upon return. Cash benefits are also paid to parents for each child.[65]

Can you imagine if Korean mothers had the same help from society? If Korean fathers felt they could take the parental leave that their companies offer to care for infants and toddlers without repercussions? The Danish system is in place because the Danish people wanted it. Korea—or the U.S.—could do the same thing.

Korean mothers may feel guilty and worry that family members, colleagues or neighbors think they are bad mothers for leaving their children with someone else. Research has shown though, that children of working mothers do just fine. The *New York Times* recently reported on a study, which involved 50,000 women in twenty-five countries, showing that daughters of women who worked were more educated, earned more, and were more likely to be in supervisory positions.[66] Mother-love is the same, wherever you live, whatever you do for a living. Of course, parental time with children is important and precious, but so is time at work, and time with other adults—for both parents and children.

An important part of true equality for women is respecting what women already do with such passion and commitment—childcare. It's one thing to say that children are so important that they need their mothers' constant attention and another to really believe that children matter and make it possible for them to thrive, whether they are at home, in school or in care. No one woman can provide everything that a child needs in terms of stimulus, activity and perspective. A mother's love may be unique but her daily teaching, communication and inter-personal skills are not. Children benefit from learning about the wider world and having relationships—just as adults do. Throughout history, children have been involved in the workplace, been cared for by many adults including older siblings. The society we have today doesn't allow for many of those experiences. Instead we have—or could have—day-care centers with smart, licensed teachers; outdoor play; arts activities; and socialization. While parents are earning a living and contributing to the greater good, children are having varied experiences and making new friends.

Of course, there can be problems. Parents have to be careful in choosing where to leave their children. But they need to have those choices. Companies and government should work together to provide accessible daycare, held to high standards, for working women. Men and women should both be involved in setting those standards—just as they are in setting educational standards. Daycare is an opportunity for Korean parents to think about what it is they want their chil-dren to learn, other than academic subjects. Cooperation? Kindness? Creativity? Goal-setting? Tolerance? Self-reliance? These qualities can be fostered by good daycare, as well as—and in some cases better than—family life.

Sheryl Sandberg, Chief Operating Officer of Facebook wrote a book you may have heard of: *Lean In* (2013). [67] She is one of the most successful woman CEOs in the U.S. corporate world. She urged female graduates to embrace leadership and change the world they've inherited. Sandberg's advice to young women is to be more ambitious if you want to stay in the workforce. She frames her thoughts in encouraging terms— "What would you do if you weren't afraid?" This gets at a major reason for women's success lagging men's. Self-doubt. Social forces, parental example, direct experience—so much conspires to make women uncertain of their abilities. Even women who've done very well in school and at whatever jobs they've had often think they're missing some invisible ingredient that makes leaders, innovators, or even solid, well-respected professionals. It's just not true. You have doubts—so do men. You aren't perfect—no one is. You have a lot to learn: brava for knowing that!

In 2015, Sandburg's beloved and supportive husband, Dave Goldberg, died at the age of forty-seven. This tragic event illustrates another good reason for women to work—you never know what will happen. You may be called upon to take care of yourself and your children. Self-reliance is always a good idea. Even if you choose to stay home, having a skill you can fall back on bolsters self-confidence, sets an example for your children, and provides another layer of security for the family.[68]

WHAT IF THERE WERE NO BABIES?
There is another aspect to this story that is equally important. Many young Korean women either can't afford children or decide there is too much stress involved in being a parent and a career woman. Instead of trying to find a good childcare solution, they decide not to have babies

at all. They are reacting to a twofold social condemnation: if you have children and work, you are a bad mother; and if you have children and work, you are a bad employee. Many Korean mothers, like Korean fathers, are afraid to take parental leave even though granting such leave is the company policy. The boss will be unhappy if they do, and will argue and resist; co-workers will also be unhappy because the mother's workload gets shifted to them on top of their already heavy workloads. A comment on an article about this subject said it very well:

> The difficulty of juggling work and family life makes some people quit work and become full-time housewives. After all, women are the butt of criticism: When they stay single, they are under pressure for marriage; When they get married but have yet to have a baby, everyone tells them to get pregnant; When they have babies, everyone says that women put a burden on the shoulders of their husband to bring home money; When they get back to work after giving birth, they face a hell where husbands don't lift a finger in doing housework and women are the ones who have to take off work whenever their child gets sick; If something bad happens to the children, people scold the woman, saying, "Does your career matter more than your child?" What a pitiful life for women.[69]

"WITH NO CHILDREN, IT'S GAME OVER – FOREVER."[70]

These are the words of Joel Kotkin, a journalist who covers demographic, social and economic trends around the world. He's talking about companies that either don't offer maternity or parental leaves, or offer them but make sure that very few people take them. This is hard on parents—and children—but if it goes on too much longer, it will be hard on everyone. It's not simply a matter of an individual or a company's short-term economic interest. What he's talking about is what happens when social forces conspire to make childrearing/childcaring too difficult and expensive for the average person, and people respond rationally—by not having any children.

Korea's population is aging. Soon (by 2026) nearly twenty-five percent of the population will be sixty-five or over.[71] There will not be enough young people to support the elders and carry on the economy. Domestic markets will shrink, labor shortages will be widespread, and this will trigger social and economic problems of all kinds. This has already become a reality in Japan. Japan's many decades of growth has stopped as its workforce begins to shrink. A 2012 report by the Japanese National Institute of Population and Social Security Research (PSSR) predicts a forty percent decline in Japan's population, assuming medium fertility projections, by 2060.[72] The same thing could happen to us.

As a business owner who knows what it's like when key employees are absent for periods of time, I completely understand companies' position on this issue. However, we need to step back and look at the bigger picture. Yes, it's a short-term additional expense and inconvenience for a company to have to hire temporary help, but creating a discouraging work environment for mothers and fathers taking parental leave will do only harm in the long run for the society and country.

It takes a village to raise a child. – African Proverb popularized by former First Lady, Senator, Secretary of State and presidential candidate Hillary Clinton.

Be a boss who is supportive to moms who are afraid and worried about their job security. Be a boss who is happy to hire the extra help, so the co-workers don't get resentful of the person who is absent. Let moms work at home if necessary. In this Internet age, there are alternative ways to get work done. Many jobs don't require a person to be at work all day long. The companies should make it easier for parents to have children because there are so many who won't. These children are our future.

When I think of Sonia Angres, I'm reminded that society and corporations need to create paths for women to reenter the workforce after raising children or after a divorce. Yes, they may be five or ten years behind, but those were not wasted years. One learns a lot raising children—patience, conflict resolution, efficiency, and simple maturity. And at forty or forty-five, a woman has a lot of healthy years left to contribute.

Fathers also need to participate in domestic work. For a working mother to go home after working and then do the domestic work and take care of children is unfair, to say the least. I hear and see so many fathers watching TV while the mother is working around the clock at home. In our house, I cook, and my husband does the dishes. Seeing a man in the kitchen doing dishes is not a pleasant sight for my mom. Nothing I can say will change her opinion. The young and old generations will have to agree to disagree on this subject. Our parents' generation don't want to acknowledge that things are changing, that gender roles are not set in stone—and that we are not going back to how things were.

AZUMMA SPIRIT

Yet I also believe we have a lot to learn from the previous generation. We make fun of Korean Azummas for their look and their behavior, but they are the same as us—just older. Azumma literally means a married or middle age woman, but it also carries a lot of derogatory connotaions. A stereotypical Azumma is a short woman with a short permed hairstyle who will shove you out of the way to get a seat on the bus! This Azumma stereotype is evolving as a new generation of women are becoming Azummas themselves. The fact is, Azummas were us when we were less educated and less affluent. They were just fighting for survival. They lived their lives like bulldozers, pushing through until they got what they wanted. They did whatever it took, without fear or shame. Modern Korean women have the same strength and determination; they just have to dig a little deeper to find it. I suggest we grab hold of that Azumma spirit and that Azumma resilience to move forward. We aren't pushing for survival as the Azummas were, but pushing to share the fruits of the Korean miracle, to claim our part of the modern, technological world and the fast-paced, dynamic careers our mothers' sacrifices helped create. It is often true that a woman becomes more daring with age, having finally shut off the voices that tried to muffle her spirit. Look at me; I'm writing this book![73]

OTHER WOMEN AROUND THE WORLD

Let me tell you about a few of the inspiring women I discovered in just one week in 2015.

In 2005, Dame Elle MacArthur, a British sailor, sailed solo around the world non-stop, breaking the world record. As you can imagine, she had to sail through horrendous conditions. She described one of the worst moments: "We are forging ahead of a huge storm. Within it, there was eight knots of wind, which was far too much wind for the boat and I to cope with. The waves were already forty to fifty feet high, and the spray from the breaking crests was blown horizontally like snow in a blizzard. If we didn't sail fast enough, we'd be engulfed by that storm, and either capsized or smashed to pieces. We were quite literally hanging on for our lives and doing so on a knife edge."

In some parts of the world, half of the women lack basic reading and writing skills. The reasons vary, but in many cases, literacy isn't valued by fathers, husbands, or even mothers. Laura Boushnak, an Arab photographer and educator, traveled to countries including Yemen, Egypt and Tunisia to highlight brave women—schoolgirls, political activists and others. One of the activists she interviewed in Tunisia said, "Question your convictions. Be who you want to be, not who they want you to be. Don't accept their enslavement, for your mother birthed you free."

These countries may be way behind us economically but the women's struggle for a better place strikes a chord in me, and I hope in you. We all have the same hopes and dreams: security for ourselves and our families, freedom to choose our path in life, meaningful work, respect, and happiness.

I see so many brave and fearless women everywhere. I have been learning Spanish for the last nine years. To learn and retain a language, you have to speak it regularly, or you forget it. Since I don't have much opportunity to speak it, I try to watch Spanish TV for thirty minutes at least four-five times a week. Last week, I was watching a Spanish news magazine program called *Al Punto.* The host, Jorge Ramos, was interviewing Gloria Alvarez, who is a young Guatemalan political scientist and radio broadcaster. Alvarez made a speech at the Youth Parliament in Zaragoza, Spain, opposing the corrupt Latin American governments and championing populism. Populism is a political philosophy that focuses on standing up for the rights and interests of the common people. She was brilliant and inspiring with her don't-mess-with-me attitude. [74]

This week, I watched Maria Corina Machado in Venezuela, a leader of the opposition to dictator Nicholas Maduro, demanding that Maduro step down—even though speaking out like this may put her life in danger.

In Jerusalem in January 2015, twenty-nine-year-old Knesset member Stave Shaffir, Israel's youngest lawmaker, made a speech against corruption and for budgetary transparency that made headlines in the

Israeli press. Her fearless and commanding speech was cheered and watched by liberal Israelis countless times. [75]

According to the Federal Aviation Administration, there are 8,175 women commercial airline pilots in the U.S. There are so many professions that for a long time were considered automatically as "men's jobs." But if you have curiosity, passion, and the willingness to go for it, you have more possibilities than what's in front of your eyes. So dream big!

Of course, there are many women around the world who have accomplished amazing things. I could list them, but the point is that within one week's time, I learned about so many admirable women. Several of them are standing up on behalf of their people. One of my heroes has been Aung San Suu Kyi, a Burmese opposition politician who was detained under house arrest for almost fifteen years. (While imprisoned, she won the 1991 Nobel Peace Prize.) The first time I saw her being interviewed on *60 Minutes*, a popular TV news magazine show in the U.S., her bravery and intelligence resonated with me. I have followed her career ever since. It is inspiring and moving that there are so many women of courage and intelligence in our world! When they decide to lead based on their convictions, there is no stopping them.

The fact is, the world is changing, and changing fast. In Pakistan, a schoolgirl wins a Nobel Prize for insisting on the right to education for girls. That wouldn't have happened in the last century. In Scandinavia, the future is already here. Denmark takes female leadership so seriously that every sizable company in the country must have concrete goals for how much it intends to increase the share of women in management. Companies have to describe what they will do to achieve this goal. The government expects companies to have plans and to implement those plans.

Japan, which is very much like Korea in its attitude towards working women, has recently made a big change. The authorities have stated that the country's business climate is being undermined by the lack of women in leadership roles. Innovation is being stifled and talent lost. They are frank in saying that Japan cannot afford any longer to ignore women's brains and ability.

I have no doubt that Korea will come to the same realization and women will advance in the workplace and society. But the question is: how long will it take? How long will we be at the bottom in charts of the global gender gap? I don't know about you, but I'd prefer Korea lead. I'd prefer the young women of today and the girls in school have a chance at career success—using their minds to their fullest ability—rather than putting it off for another generation.

LOOKING AHEAD

I asked Gul Hwang, who is a well-respected industrial designer and a professor at Hongik University in Korea, "When do you think Korea can take a leadership role in the design world instead of being a follower?" He responded without any hesitation, "When girls take over. That will be the turning point. If you go to top schools in Korea, there are many more girls than boys. In the past, they used to control the ratio. They wanted half boys and half girls. That's gone away. Girls are much smarter nowadays. They are much more independent; they are more aware of the reality. Boys are still like the big babies. They grew up in a way that they can't stand criticism. I think the most noticeable turning point will be when the females take over the management or manager roles. This is going to happen sooner than later mainly because we have such a low birth rate. One way to resolve that is actually bringing more opportunities for the girls to get into industries. If you look at anything, girls are more competitive."

I have a suspicion that many men recognize the capability of women but want neither to acknowledge it officially nor cheer the empowerment of women because they feel threatened. As we see the rising number and range of women's roles in all sectors around the world, there is no need to prove to men that women are smart enough, decisive enough, courageous enough.

Men who think otherwise need to change their attitudes and start supporting, encouraging, and partnering with the women around them instead of getting in the way. Because when women get ahead, we all benefit.

One of the dinner table conversations I often have with friends focuses on how, if we had more women leaders in the world, there would be a lot less conflict, fewer wars.

Joseph Nye, a former U.S. assistant secretary of defense, Harvard professor and author of *The Future of Power,* wrote: "Former U.S. President George W. Bush once described his role as 'the decider,' but there is much more to modern leadership than that. Modern leaders must be able to use networks, to collaborate, and to encourage participation. Women's non-hierarchical style and relational skills fit a leadership need in the new world of knowledge-based organizations and groups that men, on average, are less well prepared to meet."[76] Obviously, this doesn't mean that any women leader is better than any male leader. And just because we have a woman president or a black president doesn't mean women or blacks as a group will advance. It simply means that we are wisely extending the pool of candidates to more than gender or race specific. Talent and bold leadership have no gender. We will need all the peacemakers we can find!

I truly believe the society can grow and be happier when more women get involved in all professions. Korean women are more than capable and have the power to do it. If she has the desire, let her!

8

Man's Best Friend

KINO

Kino follows my husband around like a shadow. He might not be sitting right next to him, but he has to be sitting somewhere in the same room. They look like they are connected by an invisible thread. Kino gets very jealous of anybody who hugs my husband, including me. Whenever he sees us hugging or making an attempt to hug, he instantly launches himself between us, separating us with his wriggling twenty-two-pound body, which cracks us up every time. Kino is also very curious about things we do. Whenever we have contractors come to the house to repair something, he always stands in the middle of the work area, or glues himself right next to the contractor staring at and examining the problem. He watches every move the repairman makes with such intensity; it's as if he is learning how to do it himself. Of course, we have to move him out of the way, but it's hilarious how he loves to observe and wants to get involved in human activities.

Every morning, Kino waits patiently for Carlos to wake up. The second Carlos opens his eyes, Kino jumps on the bed and buries his head in Carlos' chest with a happy yip and a wagging tail. Then he twists and turns his body, waiting for Carlos' big morning hugs. Carlos says to Kino, "Good morning, baby! Did you have a good dream?"

When we leave the house, Kino stays on the top of the stairs with stretched neck and sad eyes. His expression is so desperate that it makes our hearts ache. And when we get back—every time—he is so full of relief that he starts to run around the house with a ball in his mouth, celebrating our return. Do your children do that?

This six-year-old, long-haired, white Havanese terrier that we adopted from the animal rescuer in 2011 has captured our hearts and become an integral part of our family. We love his joy in living and his "Don't mess with me" attitude. He makes us laugh out loud with his quirky habits. Often I'm amazed at how incredible this little animal is and how much we love him. We almost can't imagine our lives without Kino.

YUKI

We had another dog before Kino. Yuki passed away in December 2007. She was a sixty-five-pound yellow Labrador, a sweet and loving creature. Unlike Kino, Yuki was very obedient and wanted to please us. We thought she was irreplaceable—the best dog ever. Then, four years later, Kino came along with a completely different personality. He is even funnier than Yuki.

When Carlos said he wanted a dog, I thought he had lost his mind. We were in the middle of a big move, transitioning from a rented office to our own small, three-story bank building near downtown Chicago. We had boxes everywhere, and I mean everywhere, and weeks and months of organizing and settling down ahead of us. People say moving is one of the most stressful things in life, and I can assure you, I was very stressed. But Carlos wouldn't back down about getting a dog, though I did my best to talk him out of it. When we need more hands, the last thing we should be doing is creating more work and spreading ourselves even thinner, I argued.

I want a dog, he said.

I want a dog, he said. Eventually, I gave in, with certain conditions. 1. I'm not taking the dog out for pee and poos. 2. I'm not walking the dog. 3. I'm not cleaning up after the dog.

Basically, Carlos had to do everything to take care of the dog. With these agreements in place, we started puppy shopping, using the newspaper. There was no Internet to search in 1996. We found a puppy store that had two 3-month-old Labradors. We didn't know back then where to get a puppy other than a puppy store, but now we know it's not a good place to get one. There are so many dogs at local animal shelters that need to be rescued.

After seeing the advertisement, we drove to the store immediately and spent three hours playing with two puppies, one male and one female. The male one had the cuter face, but he had major hiccups. The female was very playful, running around with toys in her mouth, knocking down the water bowl, making trouble. Clearly, she had more energy and seemed to have more personality. I also liked the idea of a female, and so we decided on her. I still remember how happy Carlos was in the car on the way home. I felt like we had just adopted a baby.

So, we started life with the new puppy. Carlos named her Yuki, which means 'snow' in Japanese. It was a name of a character in a book my sister-in-law was reading. Carlos liked the sound of it. The first three nights, Yuki cried. It wasn't barking, more like whimpering. We placed her cage in our bedroom on the floor, away from the bed. The owner of the puppy store recommended we use the cage for the first few weeks, until she was housebroken.

I couldn't sleep, which was very upsetting. I need my eight hours to function. I had to go to another room. Then, the fourth night, all of a sudden the crying stopped. Carlos had moved the cage onto the top of the bench at the end of our bed so that Yuki could see us. Being in the same room wasn't enough. She felt insecure not having us in her field of vision. That was my first ' wow' moment concerning how badly this four-legged creature wanted to connect with us, how much she depended on us for her emotional and physical security and survival.

Puppy-training is hard work. Realizing that Yuki felt security and comfort being near us, Carlos slept with his head at the foot of the bed, closing the distance between his head and Yuki's. We didn't lock the cage door so when Yuki wanted to go to pee in the middle of the night, she could hit the door with her paw. The door would hit Carlos' head, waking him up to take her outside. But the first few days, Yuki pooed and peed in the cage sometimes, and that smelled not just awful but awful to the point that I couldn't even breathe! By nine o'clock in the morning, Carlos had done two loads of laundry and had taken Yuki out at least twice. Carlos really held up his end of the bargain and took care of Yuki like the best dad in the world.

We were worried in the beginning that Yuki was going to chew our furniture or other things around the house, but the only thing she ever destroyed was a pair of Carlos' favorite summer sandals. We came home one day and saw those sandals all chewed up on the floor. Carlos was very upset. We sat her down in front of the chewed-up shoes and scolded her, saying how bad a dog she was, repeating and pointing at the shoes, "Bad dog, bad dog!!!"

Oh boy, you should have seen her little face. She felt so bad, afraid, and guilty. She sat like a statue. She didn't even seem to breathe. That was the first and last thing that she ever destroyed in her twelve years.

Months passed. Yuki and Carlos became best buddies. Carlos took ten pictures of Yuki for every one of me. I have to admit I was a little jealous of the dog, but I couldn't stay jealous for too long. Yuki was so beautiful, smart and funny that she just melted my heart with her sweetness. They say dogs only have one master. Yuki and Kino both picked Carlos as the master right away. I'm assuming that's because he took care of them and spent more time with them. It didn't matter. I started to love Yuki almost instantly, seeing how innocent, playful, fun and loving she was. Not to mention how adorable she looked. She pretty much had all the qualities we love about human babies.

Yuki used to work as a messenger in the studio. (One of the good things about having your own business is you can bring your dog to work if you want to. We even allowed another designer to bring his dog to the office so they could keep each other company.) I'd page Yuki on the phone from my office on the third floor. She'd come, and I would place a letter or document in her mouth and say, "Take it to David!" (Or John, or Sandra.) She immediately would take the letter and go down to the first floor where that person was. In an office of ten people, it's not an easy task for a dog to remember everybody's name and face on different floors, but Yuki had no problem with it. It brought a lightness and warmth to the office to see the dog trotting back and forth, pulling her weight and so proud of it.

When Yuki had arthritis towards the end of her life, she couldn't walk up the stairs to the second-floor bedroom anymore. One night, we found her standing in the middle of the stairs, unable to move. She had attempted climbing the stairs, but the severe pain in her legs made her stop. Carlos picked her up and carried her to our room and put her bed next to ours. I remember her big sigh of relief—how happy she was to be near us. For Carlos, who has a back condition, carrying a sixty-five-pound dog up and down the stairs every day was not an easy task. After all these years, I still tear up when I think about the day we had to put her to sleep.

"YOU GUYS EAT DOGS!"

A few times in the past at parties or in classrooms where I used to take Spanish or Japanese, some people I've just met will ask, "Where are you from originally?" When I say Korea, the next question is: North or South? Believe it or not, most Americans don't even realize that North Koreans can't travel outside of North Korea. Then they say, "Oh, you guys eat dogs!" Most of the time, they say this jokingly or with a little bit of a laugh since it's obviously an accusation. I immediately start defending Koreans. "Only very few people eat dogs. I don't know anyone personally who eats dogs in Korea. Chinese and Vietnamese eat them too....." I want to lessen the shame by pointing a finger at other countries where they eat dogs as well, but no matter what I say, it is a truth, and I can't help wishing it wasn't.

When I was growing up in Seoul, we had dogs, but I never bonded with them or loved them like I did Yuki and Kino. The last dog we had in Seoul was named Brownie. In 1975, my father went bankrupt. We had to move to my uncle's house. My mom sold Brownie to a person who bought and sold dogs. I still remember how she made him promise not to sell Brownie to a dog restaurant. She wanted to make sure he went to a loving home.

Then twenty-one years passed, and I had my own dog. This time I fell in love completely. Once this happens, your feelings toward dogs, cats and other animals change dramatically.

Yuki and Kino made me realize how intelligent and emotional dogs are. I was surprised at how much they add to our lives. Many of our friends have babies, so I have spent a lot of time with little humans. I think of dogs as being like two- or two-and-a-half-year-old children in regard to their intelligence and behavior. All they want is to be fed, to play, and to be close to the owner who loves them. Kino follows my husband to every room he goes into, including the bathroom. If Carlos closes the door behind him, Kino will sit outside of the room and wait anxiously until he comes out. Yuki did the same thing. These simple, innocent qualities of dogs make animal lovers want to protect them as fiercely as we want to protect our children.

Forty percent of U.S. households own at least one dog, and most of the dogs are treated as family members. The press writes stories when the president's family gets a dog. Bo, a Portuguese water spaniel belonging to President Obama, is referred to as the "First Dog." Quite often, when Carlos and I are walking Kino, we run into other people walking their dogs, and we fall into conversation with them, talking about our dogs as if they are our children. It becomes obvious right away that we share the same love and passion for our pets. My experiences started me wondering why the bond between dogs and humans is so much stronger in the West than in Asian countries. In the West, dogs are almost always inside with their owners, because the owners know that the dogs want to be near them. Many people even let their dogs sleep with them in bed. Dogs are taken for walks every day, interacted with, and played with in the park. The owners will spend half an hour or more throwing balls for the dogs to fetch. At any American beach, especially in the morning and evening, you will see dogs running happily, chasing the waves and rolling in the sand. Dogs love to run and play, and most owners go out of their way to provide this for their animals. If they have to work long hours, they often put the dogs in doggie daycare especially in the big cities. I know many people who spend nearly as much on this daycare as a parent of a toddler might.

In Korea and other Asian countries, it used to be very different. Many dogs were confined to doghouses and some still are. It just breaks my heart to see them tied to a short leash all day, for years, for their entire lives. Now I know how much they love to run, play, be touched and loved, and just be near humans. Until recently, Koreans mostly kept dogs to guard the house from thieves. People didn't get to experience the very human qualities of dogs—especially their incredible affection and gift for happiness—because the animals didn't interact with people at the level they do in the West. I know that the Western way of being with dogs wouldn't work everywhere. I understand limited living spaces often don't allow room for dogs. And yet I think people are missing the best part of dog ownership by keeping their dogs at a distance. I'm glad things are changing. High-rise living is quite common in Korea nowadays. I'm happy to hear that many pets are indoors with their owners. There are even several dog cafes in Seoul where people can go have a drink and hang out with dogs.

When you develop a relationship with dogs as people do in the West, letting them live off the leash, allowing them to love you and be playful, you gain a whole different appreciation for them. You learn their personalities—and they do each have a unique personality, less complex than a human one but just as individual. The dog becomes your friend, your family, a creature that you want to take care of because he or she gives you so much love, loyalty, devotion, laughter, joy, relaxation…

Recently, I have run into several people who have pets as emotional therapy, prescribed by doctors. The basic gift of companionship and unconditional affection can be just the right therapy for a condition like debilitating depression. Numerous studies have shown that owning a dog extends your life.[77] Dog-owners have lower blood pressure, less heart disease and longer life spans.

I'm the receiver of this gift every day. I get stressed out easily, but every time I look at Kino, I smile because he is just so damn cute and does so many funny things. Just a couple of minutes of playing with him and hugging him makes me much more relaxed and at ease. If you don't have a pet, you can look at some of the millions of dog/cat videos on youtube.com. Pet owners capture the funny and adorable things their pets do, many of them so hilarious that for days after I laugh out loud by myself just thinking about them.

Dogs are not our whole life, but they make our lives whole.

—ROGER CARAS (AMERICAN
WILDLIFE PHOTOGRAPHER AND WRITER)

CULTURE OR CRUELTY?

While I was doing interviews for this book in Seoul in 2012, I learned that many Koreans don't want to hear Westerners criticizing the Korean culture of eating dogs. Of course, nobody wants to be criticized, and we have to be mindful of that. Getting people angry isn't very effective, not to mention that as soon as you criticize someone, you have to realize that they will be criticizing you right back. But I want to say something about the idea of "culture" as something special that needs to be set apart. Certainly, terrible things have been done because other peoples' cultures weren't recognized or valued. But the other side of that is that just because something is a tradition, a part of culture, does not mean it is beyond criticism.

There are many hideous crimes committed around the world in the name of "culture." Female Genital Mutilation (FGM) is practiced in Africa and in some parts of Asia and the Middle East. When a girl is still a child, her clitoris and labia are cut out, often using a stone or other primitive implement, with a lot of blood, pain and terror, and often a lifetime of complications, including difficult childbirth, incontinence and constant or recurring pain, not to mention the loss of sexual pleasure. Another hideous cultural practice against women is bride-burning (dowry death). In Bangladesh, India and Pakistan, young women are murdered by their husbands or their husbands' families because of their families' refusal to pay additional dowry. Even though this is illegal, it still happens often, especially in India.

I strongly believe that "this is our culture, how we've always done things" is not an acceptable defense for violence against human life. Nor is it an acceptable defense in the case of cruelty to animals.

My husband suggested that maybe I shouldn't write about this issue of Koreans eating dogs. It's that controversial. But If I evaded this subject, I'd regret it. I'd stay angry and sad for not having done anything to change this not-so-proud part of our culture.

Many Koreans say, "We eat only *nureongi* (the dog breed raised to be eaten), so it's okay." But we have seen all breeds of dogs sitting in the cages in front of dog restaurants. In 2012, CARE, an animal protection organization in Seoul, did extensive research on Korean beliefs on this subject. They interviewed 1,000 regular people and people in the dog industry at pet farms, pet auction houses and dog farms. The conclusion was "there is no difference" between pet dogs and dogs raised for their meat. The report shows that this idea was fabricated by the industry itself to make people feel better and less conflicted about the consumption of dogs and to maintain harmony between its dog meat customers and pet owners.

Also, as people in the West would say, dogs are dogs regardless of breed. Others argue that we eat cows, chickens, pigs, and other animals, so why not dogs? But no other animals are as close to humans as dogs are. The dog is called "Man's best friend" in the West. Humans domesticated dogs tens of thousands of years ago. We trained them over hundreds of generations to work for us, to love and obey us, to trust us. We also domesticated cattle, pigs, sheep, goats and chickens, but we chose dogs (and cats) to be our companions. As well as guarding sheep, catching rats, flushing birds and other "jobs" dogs have held, they have been our friends, slept at our hearths and guarded us, often at the expense of their own lives. In many times and places, people have left babies and small children to be watched over by dogs. No cow or chicken would be very good at that.

Some of the Koreans who eat dog meat believe it has medicinal benefits. There is no scientific evidence for this. It's the same with the shark fin eating in Hong Kong and China that is still popular — there is no evidence to support that shark fin soup does anything, and yet every year, millions of sharks, 100 million a year, are caught, only to have their fins cut off. The rest of the shark is dumped back into the ocean to die a slow death.[78] There are specific dates every summer to eat dog soup in Korea to beat the heat. Interestingly, the Chinese do the same thing, but they eat it during the winter because they believe dog meat stimulates internal heat, making it a food to stave off winter's cold. It's all myth and superstition.

HOW IT LOOKS

Another thing to think about is how the Western condemnation of dog-eating cultures affects the world image of Koreans. Even though only a small percentage of Koreans eat dogs, the idea that it is okay to eat dogs in Korea places us in a very negative light. Because Westerners raise their pets like their children and we Koreans eat them, we are automatically perceived as barbaric and/or primitive. Do we really need this reputation? I know that we very much care about our image in the world. Our dog-eating tradition doesn't help us.

The main question is do we really have to eat dogs now? Don't we have enough meat to eat? We were hungry a hundred years ago and hungry during the war. In desperate times, we had to eat whatever we could find. But in the twenty-first century, there are endless options for what to eat! This is a tradition that we Koreans can live without. Most importantly, we can't afford to be perceived as backward, barbaric, cruel, and heartless by Westerners when we want them to learn about our culture and people, when we want them to visit our beautiful country.

My American and European friends know that I'm writing on this subject so they send me magazines and links to articles and photos relating to the cruel treatment of dogs, mostly from China and Korea. Some of the articles I've received are about how the Humane Society International is offering Korean dog meat farmers an opportunity to get out of the business by helping them switch from raising dogs for meat to raising crops.[79] One big story that was covered in U.S. media last year was on the annual Yulin Dog Meat Festival in Yulin Guangxi, China, where people consume 10,000 to 15,000 dogs during the 10-day festival. TV cameras showed dogs in the cages that looked terrified and filthy. These are dogs that are often starved and abused and have no social interaction with people or other dogs.

I received a Facebook link one day showing a photo of several hundred dogs packed in tiny cages being shipped to dog restaurants around China. This photo generated so many hateful comments toward the Chinese. I'm only going to list a few of the Facebook comments. Some of them were too hateful and scary to repeat. Also remember that people use strong words when they feel anger or extreme emotion. Unfortunately, this photo generated such emotions.

Sickening!!!!!!!
Cruel and inhumane!!!
This is something so unbearable, I'm still shaking!!!
The Chinese are so barbaric!! How can they be so heartless!!!
God bless these animals. Appalling!!!
The only way you can live with doing this is if you're dead inside. I can't believe they eat dogs and all this time I thought it was a myth.
Ahhh, I always knew it was true! I hate Chinese food and the times I have eaten it. It makes me sick. Poor animals....
They steal house pets and they abuse them. It's disgusting. Chinese and Koreans must stop this horrific treatment of animals!!!

Ryan Allin, who lived in Seoul for over ten years and who did research on this subject, told me that in the countryside, the dogs are beaten to death before being cooked. People believe that the meat is tastier due to the adrenaline the dog's system pumps out before they die. The industry's other methods of death include electrocution and draining the animal's blood from its body while the dog is still alive.

WHAT CAN WE DO?

I understand that opinions are split among Koreans, and this is a very controversial topic. I'm relieved there are several organizations dedicated to ending the dog-eating practice in Korea. Most of these organizations are based in the West. Dogs saved from being butchered are shipped all the way to America to find new homes. It makes me wonder: how come dog owners in Korea don't do more? If you have a dog you love, how can you bear it? When I look at my funny, sweet, bright-eyed Kino and think of dogs being beaten to death…well, that's why I'm writing this. I can't bear the thought.

I remember seeing a dog soup restaurant near the market in our neighborhood when I was a young teenager. I passed by it a thousand times without thinking anything of it. I didn't know too much about dogs then. There are many animal lovers in Korea raising dogs with love and care. I'm thinking those dog lovers also must not be thinking much about it.

Soyoun Park, the founder and president of CARE[80] (Coexistence of Animal Rights on Earth) in Seoul, said, "There are several reasons for eating dog meat, even for people who don't normally eat them. You go out to dinner after work with your boss and colleagues. Your boss says 'Let's eat dog soup' and you can't say, 'No, I don't want to eat it.' Some young women eat dog meat thinking it's cool. 'I can drink. I can eat dog meat. I can do all the things that guys do.' Some people say, 'As long as I don't eat my dog, it's okay.'"

I hope we start to pay more attention to this issue. We urgently need a bigger movement to ban this practice. We are turning off the majority of people in the West with this one tradition. It is a practice that interferes with and contradicts everything we want to say and share about our wonderful traditions and culture. This practice makes Korea look like it is still in the Third World. Soyoun Park added, "I think most Korean people don't realize how much our culture of eating dog hurts the image of Korea internationally." The report shows less than three percent of people are aware of how this tradition damages Korea's national image.

According to the CARE's report, about four percent eat dog meat regularly and about thirty-five percent have tried it at least once in their lifetime. Even the relatively small number of Koreans who still eat dogs is too many. Western civilization has shared with us and the rest of the world so much: automobiles, planes, modern fashion, literature, films, music, modern medicine, kitchen appliances, electricity, cell phones, TV, etc.... oh boy, that's almost everything that we enjoy and can't live without even for one day!

Let's give back one small thing. Let's not eat dogs. And let's say, ' No more dog meat!' to anyone who eats, serves, or sells it. I'm certain that millions of Westerners would open up their hearts and minds to Korea if this happened. I can't wait for the day that I hear there are no more dog soup restaurants in Korea. Then I will be able to die with a smile on my face.

9

Happiness

In my early twenties, I was focused on going to college, building a career, buying a house, and settling down. Those things went well for me, but at a certain point in life, I started wondering: Is this what life is all about? Am I happy enough? Where did half of my life go? I couldn't get rid of the feeling of emptiness.

I wasn't dissatisfied with my job or my husband. On the contrary, I was quite happy with both. There wasn't some specific painful thing from the past I had to work out (though of course there are always things to work out). What I was facing was something very common: the realization that happiness is not the same as success, that happiness is elusive and hard to define, and that society and our families don't always give us useful advice about this.

I'm not a religious person, even though I used to go to church when I was a teenager in Korea. The truth is, I only went so I could sing in the church choir. I decided to go to church again, as an adult, to see if I could find some answers and explore my spiritual side. I talked my friend Shirley into going with me. The church was in Lincoln Park, Chicago. We went every Sunday for one year. After the year was up, I still felt the same emptiness and got zero answers to my questions. I stopped going to church.

THREE-EYE CULTURE

While I was questioning my own life's meaning and happiness, I couldn't help thinking about the psychological well-being of Koreans in general. I saw an article describing how Korea is at the top of the list of suicide rates among the developed countries, right below North Korea.[81] We can all understand why there are so many suicides in North Korea. North Koreans are blinded and handcuffed by a dictator, living their lives in a bubble, not knowing what's outside of their world. Those who do know what's out there can't escape without risking torture and death. But South Korea? We have so much! Our economic growth has been miraculous, and there is a great deal of individual freedom. We have culture that is becoming well-known and exciting cities, yet we are scarcely better than North Korea when it comes to achieving happiness. So many people on both sides of the peninsula, whatever their objective circumstances, have lost their willingness to go on.

In 2012, when I was visiting Seoul, I was crossing the street via an underground tunnel near Jonglo Station. As I was walking, I noticed a middle-aged couple sitting on the ground against the wall. They weren't beggars. They didn't have any container in front of them for people to put money in. They were just sitting like they had no place to go. The woman had her head buried inside her folded arms. The man was staring into the distance. Their faces were dirty, and their clothes were shabby. I don't think I have ever seen people with such a defeated look, other than in the movies. They made a huge impression on me. I wonder to this day what happened to them. What's their story? How many other people are in a similar situation?

Andrew Bae, who owns a gallery in Chicago's River North arts district, travels to Korea often. He represents a very few selected Korean artists and a couple of Japanese artists. I was at his gallery one day, and we started to chat about Korea. He showed me a sculpture of a teenage boy with three eyes, both arms in the air as he pushes the wall in front of him. Andrew said, "Do you know what the third eye represents? This is not the eye of wisdom but the eye of survival, giving him another way to cope with his feelings. The expression on his face shows that he has reached the point where he cannot cope with the fast changes in Korea. He feels left out and isolates himself, thinking of himself as—and then making himself—an outsider. He has a fearful face. He is up against the wall here. He doesn't know where to go anymore. There are a lot of artists in Korea trying to express this feeling of isolation, frustration and sometimes anger."

He continued, "It is commonly understood in Korea that a lot of people are not happy. We have many people saying that we have achieved so much, so why aren't we happier now? This is a huge subject."

Andrew was in Seoul when the disaster of the ferry Sewol happened in April 2014. "Everywhere people were talking about this accident, but then people weren't just talking about the accident. They were frustrated. They were angry, calling it the result of all the problems of Korea. The interesting thing is everybody was talking about the ills of society, and yet they were still part of society. They don't realize they are the problem."

I was very much struck by what he said, because I have thought that each of us, in our personal lives as well as our social roles, are part of the problem. Happiness is not something absolute. You cannot say this person or this country will be happier or less happy because of the climate, the economy, the religion, the government. All of those things will affect mood, but in the end, happiness is—not always, but more often than we think—a choice.

The 2011 documentary film *Happy,*[82] which was based on research studies, provides some interesting information. According to the studies, about fifty percent of our happiness comes from our genes, ten percent from our circumstances, and forty percent from what we do about our circumstances. This ought to be a huge relief and fantastic news for us. We can control forty percent of our happiness even if we are born into difficult circumstances with temperaments that incline us to depression or anxiety.

MONEY

You are so poor that the only thing you have is money.

—From *Libertador*, a film directed by Alberto Arvelo, 2013 (Venezuela).

I can't help but think that part of the general unhappiness in Korea is a result of our attitude toward money and success. My uncle used to own a vegetable shop at a market in Seoul. He worked every single day from five a.m. to six p.m., 365 days a year. I don't remember him ever taking any vacation or going out to enjoy himself. He was saving money and he managed to save quite a bit. One day he had a stroke and stayed in bed for a year before passing away. Thinking of my uncle's life reminds me what not to do. All he did was work. He lived to save money.

Jennifer Kim, a partner at two popular Chicago restaurants, Ruxbin and Mott Street, talked to me about the Korean focus on money. I told her my uncle's story. "That's very true with my family. I think they fit the mold. You are always so hard on yourself. You can go crazy that way. I'm older, so they're not as strict with me now, but they were very transparent with my upbringing. Their financial goals were my financial goals. Their unhappiness became my unhappiness. Probably there was a lot of inner turmoil. They will never fully acclimate. Happiness was neglected. Now they are older, they see that there is a different way to define 'happy life' or 'successful life.' It doesn't always have to come down to the bottom line. Maybe that was the way they were raised in Korea."

Undoubtedly, society measures our worth by how big our bank account is or what kind of car we drive, how beautiful we look, etc. We are endlessly searching for happiness in the external world by accumulating things or searching for approval from others. In turn, we limit our potential in life to these narrow and superficial goals and don't get to live authentically. There is only so much time and energy; if you are obsessively spending your life trying to get more things, you will miss opportunities for experiencing intimacy, surprise, and building lasting memories. Psychologists have found that what makes us happiest are things we are actively engaged in, that use our minds and emotions. The most exciting part of something like a new car is buying it. The things that make memories, on the other hand (trips, hobbies, friendships) remain valuable for a much longer time if not for a lifetime.

I remember one incident from my mom's seventieth birthday party in Chicago. My brother and sister-in-law invited some of their friends, whom I had never met before. We were sitting next to a couple and their son. The boy was about ten or twelve years old. Carlos was recording the party with his new video camera. I noticed that the boy kept looking at the camera that was placed on the table while we were eating. His mother also noticed and said loudly, "Do you want that camera? I'll buy you two!" I was very turned off by her words. Was she trying to tell us that she is rich? Does she normally spoil her child by buying him anything he wants? Giving your child an expensive camera just because he sees one in use and is interested is problematic enough. Also, imagine how overbearing and competitive she sounded, saying, essentially, "You have one camera; we are going to have two!"

I felt sorry for that child. Maybe he wanted to look through the camera and learn how it worked; maybe he wanted one so he could circle around the table like Carlos, being the "eye" of the party. But this mother had turned it into an airless pursuit of material goods. I suspect if she did buy him one, two or three cameras, he might lose interest in them quickly. She wasn't supporting his interest in video or in new technology by asking Carlos if the boy could look through the lens or see the footage. She wasn't suggesting buying him a starter camera and seeing what he did with it. She was treating the camera as just one more kind of "status."

WHERE DOES IT START?

It starts early in our society. A child comes home with a friend, and his mom asks, "Where does your friend live?" The son answers, "He lives in Backsamdong." Then the mom says, "Oh, small apartments.... " That is a seed for discrimination. So many grew up that way, basing everything on appearances without even being aware that it's discrimination, or that this might not be the only way of looking at things. Always comparing and competing, never making room for just being.

We look at everyday people, the laborers, factory workers, service people, who work very hard, and think they're not so important. We also think of ourselves as nobody until we get a certain title, status, or have a high-paying job. We live with the fear of ending up behind everyone else. Of course, we are not happy. How can you be happy when you are always compared to someone who is richer, prettier, or smarter? There's always someone who is ahead, no matter how lucky or hardworking you are. We are chasing a dream that is impossible to catch.

A friend told me once, "I always thought I would have a two-carat wedding ring." She sounded sad and depressed, thinking about the ring, not the marriage, not her husband, not the richness of her life. In that moment, she measured her happiness by the size of diamond on her hand.

When your cousin buys land, your stomach hurts.

— KOREAN PROVERB

Okay, we all understand the meaning of this proverb. Even if you are not a Korean, and you've never heard it before, I'm sure you lived some variant of it. Just go to Facebook and scroll through until you find a friend announcing some good news. If it happens to be the kind of news you long to have yourself, your stomach may well hurt. But what if you refuse to indulge this feeling, instead searching your heart for gladness that your friend or your cousin has had good fortune? What if you congratulate him sincerely! Jealousy and envy are a result of insecurity—the belief that you will never have what you want. You may think you don't deserve it or aren't smart or talented enough to get it. So, how do we reverse this mistaken thinking and achieve emotional maturity?

Try acting the way a confident person would act. Eventually, your feelings will catch up with your actions, and you will become that confident person. Maybe you won't get everything you want, but you will feel like you can make things happen, that good news will arrive for you as well as others. And then the next time another cousin buys land (or another friend gets a dream job or goes on a fabulous vacation), you won't feel jealous but happy. "Good for him! He worked hard for it."

When I was in my first year in interior design school, there was a Korean student who was one year ahead of me. We were not good friends, but we were friendly. One day I saw her work displayed on the gallery wall. For a couple of seconds, I was jealous, wishing that it were my work hanging on the wall instead. Then, right away I changed my thought, and I was happy for her. Returning to my classroom, I told my classmates, "Hey, guys, Hyunjoo's work is in the gallery hall, go check it out!" Hyunjoo happened to be in the room, and she was so happy that I was sharing her achievement with others. It also made me feel good to share her happiness at that moment.

One of our close friends became very successful with his company a few years ago. When I first heard about how quickly he was becoming rich, I have to say I was a little bit jealous. Probably that feeling was magnified due to the slow period we were having at the time in our business. After a few minutes of thought, I was happy that he was being rewarded for his talent and hard work. The funny part is that when you hear about someone's new success, you forget how much you have achieved yourself. You are just too busy focusing on what you *don't* have.

While you are working hard and improving your life, sometimes other people will get ahead of you. Sometimes you will get ahead of them. But often the person who is getting ahead financially doesn't mean he/she has a happy life. Not everything is how it appears to be. I have met many people who I thought, looking from the outside, had perfect lives. Then I got to know the person and found that wasn't true. Often life is not fair and outcomes are not equal. You don't know why some people have so much more than others, whether it's money, brains or good luck. This is something the world's thinkers have been struggling with for many thousands of years. Whatever the reality is, it's up to you how you will let it shape your thoughts and attitudes.

The happiest people don't have the best of everything; they just make the best of everything.

—UNKNOWN.

To many people, success means wealth or status. The emphasis is on money, not happiness. Of course, if you can't make ends meet, or if you have to work two or three jobs to do so, making money becomes very important in your life. I'm talking about those of us who work decent jobs and live fairly well—certainly by the standards of most of the world and history—but feel we haven't gotten where we want to. We haven't reached the level that will make us proud of ourselves, content with our surroundings: happy. You may say, I don't need a palace or to own half a dozen residences, but I'd really like a summer home on a lake like my sister has. Or, I'd like to get out of this apartment complex and into a nice, three-bedroom house in a good neighborhood with a deck and a yard, somewhere nice to raise kids. Someone else says, I'm not so young anymore; I just want an apartment that isn't a third-floor walk-up. And the person sleeping on the street says: I wish I had a room of my own.

It's all relative. If you don't see that, you will never be happy. And if you think money surely means happiness, why are there so many rich people who are not happy? And why are there so many much poorer people who are?

There is a certain level of income—what it is depends on time and place—that will remove the worst sources of financial stress: having a roof over your head, heat and electricity, food for your family, clothes and education, some cash for occasional small pleasures. You can be happy without reaching that level, but once you do reach it, if you are still not happy, or only very rarely, the chances are money has little to do with your discontent. In fact, studies have found that people feel rich or poor only in relation to others. The richest man in a poor village feels better than the poorest man in a rich village, even if the second man has more goods, a bigger house, and more security. It's not money that matters—after basic needs are met—but status. Status is about how you value yourself. It is human nature to value yourself according to what your culture sets out as important, but this is not unchangeable. People can learn to question their feelings. Our culture values money and position very highly—we are not the only culture that does, of course, but we have taken it to an extreme. But a culture is made up of individuals: you DO have a choice. One exercise that can help is to widen your field of reference—don't just think about yourself in relation to your friends or classmates, but in relation to people in the entire world and across history. If you are reading this book, I am sure that you have less than some but more than most.

What many people don't realize is how much of a cost there is to focusing so intently on money. Thinking about what you don't have gets in the way of living an authentic life, pursuing your own interests, expressing your own feelings. If you are always comparing yourself to others, how will you recognize the ways you are unique? It may be hard to believe that you are unique, but think of it this way. You are the only person whose thoughts and heart you can deeply know. This is a precious resource! Spending time paying attention to how you feel and what you think—with no concern about others' opinions or making yourself "better," just enjoying being yourself—can be very relaxing. It can make you feel steadier. Attempt to become more aware of yourself as an individual, with your own thoughts, experiences, likes and dislikes.

Let's pause once in a while to re-evaluate our state of mind and body to see how close or far away we are from feeling not only safe, not only content, but *ourselves,* so we can readjust our feelings as we go.

Another way we can cheat ourselves of happiness today is to think that the past was better—whether that past is a historical "golden age," our own childhood or youth, or just something from a few years ago that looks better now than it did at the time. Pascal, the French mathematician and philosopher, was quoted in the movie *Just a Sigh* as saying, "Happiness can't exist in the present. You either recall happiness or long for it. It's never in the present." I can relate to that thought. It reminds me of an exchange I had with Carlos many years ago while he was looking through a photo album with a big smile on his face. I asked him, "What are you smiling at?" He said, "I'm looking at the photos we took when we were in Europe the first time. What a great time that was. We should do it again soon."

The reality was he was unhappy from the very beginning of the trip. He doesn't like to fly so he couldn't get excited about the trip. You know how it is when you travel with someone who is not enjoying himself? You can't enjoy yourself either. The energy level of your traveling companion makes a huge difference in how the experience affects you. So here he was looking at the photos, looking back at the same trip, re-living the moments and he was happy. I was speechless at how his recollection was so far from what I remember as the truth! That made me think about how things look and feel sweeter when you are reminiscing about the past.

There's no harm in doing this occasionally. But there are some people who do it all the time, who focus on a past when they were happy or successful, and it doesn't matter if that was what was truly going on. As long as their thoughts are on days gone by, they won't appreciate what they have now. This is kind of like competing with yourself—judging your aging body against your young body, your actual success against a feeling of unlimited potential, the difficulties of everyday life against the photo-shopped sleekness of memory.

SELF-IMPOSED UNHAPPINESS

Jeric Park thinks that much of Koreans' unhappiness is self-created. "People want to live better. They want to drive a better car. They are feeling bad because they don't have all these things. People get upset when they drive a bad car. Wives say, 'Oh, I wish my husband had more money so we wouldn't be driving that piece of s*** around.' People get very depressed as a result of comparing themselves to each other. I think it's really caused by what our mothers teach us. They say things like, 'The daughter of our next-door neighbor is taller than you, oh my God! Her head is smaller than your head.'"

Hyemi Jung says, "Everyone criticizes their own culture to some degree, but nobody does it like Koreans. Nobody else says things like, 'I really don't like Korea. I want to leave Korea' when they talk about their own country. I don't like certain things about Korea, but fundamentally I love Korea. I think there are certain things that need to be changed, but it seems like many people say things without being able to support or articulate their reasons. People live stressfully, complaining every day, without changing anything. People don't take any initiative to make things better."

Korea is filled with overstressed and exhausted adults, students under ferocious academic pressure, and many elderly living in poverty, depressed and lonely. It's alarming, to put it mildly. Yet Koreans don't think much about psychological health. Many people believe that a positive outlook comes naturally with affluence, or that only seriously mentally ill people need a therapist. Seungchun Lim, the artist who created the sculpture with three eyes, thinks, "Because we were so poor, putting the food on the table was the most important thing in life. The sudden economic development made materialism appear to be the most important thing in life. We accepted and embraced a value system that has gone off the track. Maybe we were too busy and didn't have time to prioritize what is important in life. We think what's going on in our society is natural. We don't realize we are sick in our mind."

Koreans were living in survival mode for so long that we haven't had time yet to grasp the concept of a healthy mind. Thomas Kim shares his view on how we are: "I think the Korean culture puts a lot of pressure on people. It is a very ungracious culture that doesn't tolerate imperfection. This strong culture of perfectionism led to this judgmentalism and putting everything and everyone—how you look, where you went to school, your test scores, where you work—under the microscope all the time." Perfectionism is addictive. When we do, inevitably, fail at something, we blame and shame ourselves, causing ourselves such pain that we strive ever harder to be better and best, rather than questioning the faulty logic of perfectionism."

Brene Brown, the author of *The Gift of Imperfection* (2010), writes about cultivating the courage to be imperfect, exercising the compassion that comes from knowing that we are all made of strength and struggle, and believing that we are enough. When we become more loving and compassionate with ourselves, we can embrace our imperfections and be slower to judge ourselves and others.

Shame at our imperfections is one obstacle to happiness. Another is the sort of worry or self-criticism—the inner voice—that never shuts up. Guy Winch, author of *Emotional First Aid* (2014), says, "We sustain psychological injuries even more often than we do physical ones, injuries like failure or rejection or loneliness. Spending so much time focused on upsetting and negative thoughts—which is called 'rumination'— actually puts you at significant risk for developing clinical depression, alcoholism, eating disorders, and even cardiovascular disease." Simply put, when the mind hurts it affects us physically, so why don't we start taking care of our minds as we do our bodies?

We can work on shifting our burdensome thoughts, the ones that go around and around in circles: *Where am I going to get the money? What if he doesn't call? Why did she say that to me?* Studies show that even a two-minute distraction is sufficient to break the urge to ruminate. Each time I feel frustration, have a worry about something or any negative feeling, I force myself to think about something positive or visualize an image that makes me smile or calms me down. One of the images I use is a scene of a lake in Victoria, British Columbia, which we visited over twenty years ago. I don't even remember the name of the lake but I remember thinking, "It feels so peaceful that it's almost surreal." You will feel much better after you get accustomed to this mind-shifting exercise. It doesn't just make you feel soothed in the moment but helps you build emotional resilience to deal with life's challenges and hardships.

Anxiety is the result of constantly looking ahead and having negative thoughts and worries about the future.

There were many terrible things in my life and most of them never happened.

– MICHEL DE MONTAIGNE.

EMBRACING THE NOW

I have lost three friends to accidental death. I remember how odd and disjointed it felt when I heard the news of each of death. I was shocked by how quickly people can be taken away. What stayed with me is how important it is to appreciate each day. Since that time, I have noticed how many significant moments in people's lives occur when someone they love passes away. They have the same realization I did. We learn about life in the deepest way when a loved one dies.

Dr. Tim Suh, who practices acupuncture and Oriental medicine in Chicago, shares how his life changed when his mother passed away. "It was fifteen years ago when I understood what life is worth—how to value life. I realized I don't want to be catching up later. I want to do things now step by step, get to know what it is I care about. Before that, my life was always about following the American dream. My father also changed a lot. He actually softened after my mother passed away, when he realized 'Crap! I could have been nicer; I could have spent more time with her.' So he's nicer to my daughter. He is different with us since my mother passed."

Marjan, who lost her beloved boyfriend Puya in a surfing accident in Mexico, puts it eloquently, "My life's travels have unveiled to me happiness in the now, in the moment. It is not the past or the future. Even in my moments of deepest despair and sadness, flickers of momentary happiness have embraced my heart."

Each hardship redefines life. Marjan's story confirms to me that we should start working on our happiness now. Don't waste any more time. Don't let only tragic incidents teach you what is precious. Don't wait for the perfect conditions to be happy. They don't exist. What does exist, though—everything around you, everything you have—is fleeting. Someday you will look back and be nostalgic for some part of your daily life that right now you take completely for granted. Try to slow down your mind. Try to savor your life. If you wait to be happy, you may never be happy. There will always be something else that you think you need.

WHAT IS HAPPINESS EXACTLY?

We all know what joy is, what pleasure is, what contentment and "things are going pretty well" are. But happiness? It's hard to define since it's very subjective. I started asking people what it means to be happy. Here are a few of the answers.

- Having peace of mind.
- When life is in balance: excitement vs. boredom/idle time, work vs. family time vs. alone time. I am also happier when the sun shines ☺.
- A prerequisite for happiness is the absence of major worries. Everyone I love being healthy and safe, etc.
- Feeling authentic and that I have a purpose in everything I do in life.
- Learning new things, being productive with my work.
- Being loved for who you are.

These are all good answers. I can think about how each one of them has manifested in my life, and it seems that there's always been one or another of these feelings or circumstances at play, but it's not been what I focused on. Sometimes I took whatever was going well for granted; sometimes I thought it wasn't enough. I consider myself a fairly normal person and what I was surprised to find, as I researched the subject, is that "normal" people are precisely the ones current psychologists are studying.

POSITIVE PSYCHOLOGY

One day over dinner in Chicago, my designer friend Stefan Sagmeister introduced me to the field of positive psychology. Martin P. Seligman, a psychologist at the University of Pennsylvania, author of *Flourish: A Visionary New Understanding of Happiness and Well-Being* (2012), started the scientific study of human strength and positive traits based on the belief that people want to lead meaningful and fulfilling lives, cultivate what is best within themselves, and enhance their experiences of love, work, and play.

Psychologists had traditionally concerned themselves with mental illness and dysfunction, but Seligman was interested in the psychology of human resilience. Positive psychology is a relatively new field that examines how ordinary people can become happier and more fulfilled.

Seligman studied both happy people and unhappy people. The goal was to help people adjust negative styles of thinking *as they arise* as a way of changing their overall mood, developing cognitive habits—what you might think of as the familiar channels of thought that you fall into as easily as your car gets on the highway home—that lead to happiness. Seligman's ideas quickly caught on and are being practiced by many psychologists around the world.

Seligman found that happy people have the following habits in common.

- They pursue personal growth and intimacy.
- They surround themselves with family and friends.
- They judge themselves by their own yardstick, not by what others have.
- They engage in daily activities they truly enjoy.
- They don't worry.
- They forgive easily.

SEVENTY-FIVE YEARS OF STUDY

A recent survey of millennials asked participants what their most important life goals were. Over eighty percent said, "to get rich." Fifty percent of those same young adults said, "to become famous."

Robert Waldinger, American psychiatrist and professor at Harvard Medical School, is the fourth director of the Laboratory of Adult Development, overseeing a study that has tracked the health and mental well-being of a group of 724 American men for seventy-five years.[83] Two groups of men were tracked. One group consisted of sophomores at Harvard University, either privileged in their family background or present circumstances. The second was made up of young men from Boston's poorest and most troubled neighborhoods. Many of them lived without hot and cold running water.

They became factory workers, lawyers, bricklayers and doctors. One even became president of the United States (John F. Kennedy). Some developed alcoholism and schizophrenia. Some climbed the social ladder from the bottom all the way to the top, and some went in the opposite direction. As of 2015, about sixty of them were still alive and participating in the study. More than 2,000 children of these men are also participating.

What has been learned from the thousands of pages of information collected? "The clearest message that we get from this seventy-five-year study is this: Good relationships keep us happier and healthier. Period." says Dr. Waldinger in a TED presentation. [84] Protracted loneliness is toxic—it's literally a killer. Loneliness is not just related to how many friends you have or whether you are married. You can be lonely in a crowd. Some people's marriages are monuments to loneliness. You've seen those couples who never talk to each other, who barely even look at each other. Whatever interest or attraction brought them together is gone; they don't know how to bring it back, and they either don't believe in divorce, or it frightens them. So they stay together, but they are not together. They suffer, and so do their children.

It's the *quality* of your close relationships that counts. Honest conversations, activities together, trust and laughter—these are the building blocks of intimacy.

Another surprising thing is that the study showed, good relationships also protect our brains. People who feel that they have another person they can count on in times of need stay mentally sharper longer; their memories function better. Living in the midst of conflict, or in a marriage without affection or friendship is, in many ways, bad for our health.

As did the millennials in the recent survey I mentioned, many of the men in this study believed that fame, wealth, or high achievement were what they needed to have a good life. But again and again, over seventy-five years, this study has shown that the people who made the most of their lives, who were happiest, were those who cultivated relationships with family, friends, and community.

It's hard to maintain good relationships. They can be messy, complicated, and time-consuming. Relationships can conflict with your career at times—when your wife wants you to spend more time at home, for example, or when your kids need you. These are difficult choices, and there are no easy answers. But relationship work is necessary if you want to look back at the end of your life and feel that you made the most of what you were offered, that your life was truly lived, not wasted or simply endured. Rich or poor, it's the people you liked and loved, got to know deeply, even fought with, who matter in the end. So let's remember to nurture our relationships and treasure the people who share our lives. If you don't have good, close relationships yet, reach out and create some. It's never too late.

HAPPINESS: IT'S YOUR DECISION

Here are some things that I have found that make me happy and that have worked for many others as well: learning from books; wise friends;

interesting strangers and moments of self realization. Reminder: I'm not a psychologist or a therapist. I'm simply sharing from my personal experiences.

Living Authentically. This means knowing what it is that you most value, enjoy and appreciate, and arranging your life—career, leisure time, plans—to reflect that, rather than reflecting what society or your parents have told you that you should want. It means doing things for the fun or the challenge of it for yourself, rather than to boast that you got or did something that others may want. There's nothing wrong with going along with a friend or partner who asks you to do something you don't especially enjoy—but make sure that they also do this for you.

Women, especially, have a tendency to put others first, thinking that this is what they are supposed to do or that no one will like them if they don't. Yes, children often have to come first. And sometimes a friend or family member in trouble needs to come first. But if someone else is *always* coming first with you, you have a problem. If you let this go on too long, you will forget what actually gives you pleasure, what inspires and uplifts you. You will forget *yourself.* Don't let it happen.

Living authentically also means staying real and being no one but yourself. It means cultivating the courage to go against the mainstream if you believe in something. It's much harder to do when you live in a conformist society. But things are changing. We can be happier and grow fully as people only when we can face ourselves with honesty. Don't be ashamed about things you don't know. Don't feel small about things you don't have. Just own who you are now. There is a dignity in that. There is a pride in that. Most of all, it's real. It's worth a lot more than somebody who is pretending to be someone who he is not. When you are real, you can talk to anyone on an equal footing, one human to another without judging each other, with empathy and respect. We live with plenty of snobbery, pretension and presumption around us. When people are fake, I see emptiness. I'd much rather be myself than be empty.

In his art book *Things I Have Learned In My Life So Far* (2013), Stefan Sagmeister elaborated on one of the twenty things he learned in his life: "Trying to look good limits my life. Basically, this means I will be trying to appear as a nice guy. I tell myself: 'Do not be confrontational, do not tell somebody this is not right... appear as a nice guy.' It is actually something that fences me in. I would have a richer, probably fuller, more fulfilled life if I was willing and wanted to remove this attitude. I think it's a little bit because of where I come from in Western Austria, very close to Switzerland. This is sort of the normal case there. Trying to keep face. Keeping up appearances for the sake of not looking bad." Actually, this is the same or much more severe for Koreans and many other Asian cultures. We are often, if not always, doing or saying things that we don't want to do so we won't look bad to others. Yet it is possible to be truthful about your feelings without being rude or unnecessarily confrontational. People might initially think you are odd for being different. Eventually, they will accept you and even, in many cases, respect you more.

"Don't expect gratitude, you will never be disappointed." These were the words I found when I opened a fortune cookie one day at a Chinese restaurant. This has been one of the best sayings that I have kept in my lesson box. I still have the piece of paper with me. Sometimes we get disappointed or upset as a result of doing something for someone whom we feel has not shown adequate appreciation. That can create resentment and anger. To avoid negative emotion, when you do something for someone, do it because you want to do it regardless of whether you get anything back. Let yourself feel good for doing it, and if you don't get anything in return, you won't care since you weren't expecting anything in the first place. I was hoping to find more wisdom in fortune cookies but so far that one has been the best.

It's become a cliché, but it's worth repeating: **Life is a Journey, not a Destination.** The only destination we have is death. What if you have a big dream about how you will become very successful in your career, have a family, live in such and such a place—and then it happens. What's your destination then? Many people, at that point, start thinking about their earlier struggles and missing those days. It's kind of pointless to live that way. Why not enjoy the struggles as well as the success? And while you're at it, accept that none of us knows exactly what "success" will be for us—what we will believe, at the end, was the most important achievement of our lives. Our career? Our children? Our friendships? Or maybe just that we persevered through challenges and never gave up?

Forgiveness is Important. Hating someone takes a lot of energy. Already, we don't have enough energy to do things that we want to do. Why waste your limited store on something that gives you nothing back but only multiplies toxic energy inside of you? It's probably one of the most challenging things to learn—to just let resentments go, understanding that there is nothing to be gained. Once you do it, you will be much more at peace. Of course, if you are dealing with things that are a life and death matter, forgiveness becomes very hard. I'm not sure I could forgive in that situation. I haven't had that experience so I can't say (though I have read, as we all have, amazing stories of people forgiving those who murdered loved ones), but anything smaller than that, anything that doesn't affect your life in a fundamental way, you *can* let go of. It's a question of willingness and habit. I'm not saying it's easy, but you can minimize the harsh feelings you carry with you. They are not worth your attention.

Forgive Yourself. I think this is especially necessary for people who are driven and feel they must always be productive. I'm that person. I often blame or beat myself down for not-so-great results on something I was working on, for saying something not so intelligent to someone or making bad decisions. It's important to realize what you did and learn the lesson from it, but after that, feeling bad continually and blaming yourself doesn't change things. So work on not repeating your mistake, accept that you are human, and move on. Most of us feel better when someone who seems "perfect" shows her human side, so why do you want a perfect you? Why not find humor in the ways you are imperfect and use your own mistakes and flaws not only as lessons in what not to do next time but as a way of understanding and forgiving others' mistakes? I'm still working on this myself and doing much better now.

Wear Your Good Clothes! We all have good clothes or good dishes that we save for special occasions. What happens is that there aren't enough "special occasions" in our lives and most of these fancy outfits or fine china stay hidden in the closet and cabinets waiting to be used for years. Then we end up getting rid of them because they are no longer in fashion or we don't like them anymore. We deprive ourselves of little bits of happiness even when they are easily available. I watch my mom wearing her old clothes day in and day out when she has many good clothes in the closet. She uses mismatched plates when she has a whole set of dishes collecting dust. I was just like my mom for many years until I wondered: why am I not treating myself well? What am I saving things for? I have a friend who didn't know what to give her father-in-law for Christmas so every year she gave him special, expensive foods since she knew how much he loved to eat and how thrifty he was. When he died, she found all of the food that came in jars and bottles unopened. He was saving it! Each day is a special day. You are special. Enjoy what you have!

Practice Gratitude. Our last moving day three years ago was quite stressful, to say the least. While we were waiting for the movers to come, we started to disassemble the heavy entertainment unit we had in the living room. Carlos started banging one of the top shelves, and the next moment, I saw blood spattered on the wall and Carlos falling to the floor. The heavy shelf with its sharp corners had fallen on Carlos' leg. I screamed out loud and panicked, as you can imagine. I tried looking at his leg but had to turn my head instantly. Too late! I saw the white of bone through the blood! I called 911 and the fifteen minutes before the ambulance came felt like an eternity.

He was taken to the emergency room, but I couldn't go with him. I had to wait for the movers to arrive. Throughout the whole day, while I was conducting the move, I was worried, of course, but the move kept me busy and helped me from obsessing. Around seven p.m., Carlos returned with a large bandage on his leg. Doctors told him how lucky he was that the shelf didn't hit the artery; if it had, he could have bled to death. We were so grateful that day. We celebrated that he was alive and back home.

Gratitude puts any situation in a new light. You see that what you thought was "stress" was just an ordinary day—nothing like having a shelf fall on your husband, wounding or perhaps even killing him! This doesn't mean that you ignore stress or other difficulties, but you acknowledge that there are many good things happening, too. Gratitude is about appreciating what you have today while you are working towards whatever goal you may have. It's easy to forget about what you already have when you are focused on ambitious goals that require a lot of work and no small amount of luck. By practicing gratitude, our relationships with family and friends become stronger and more meaningful because we are consciously thinking about and appreciating them.

Surround Yourself with Positive People. Happiness is contagious. Just as an upbeat song can lift your spirits on a gloomy day, a smile, a laugh or optimistic remark from people around you can affect your mood. Over time, this effect is even more pronounced, as we fall into the habit of responding to things positively. By contrast, being with people who are unhappy or downbeat—people who always see the glass as half-empty rather than half-full—can drag down your mood and make everything look worse. Maybe you used to enjoy complaining with others—it was a way of being part of a group—but now you have a more positive attitude, and you can see that these old friends are holding you back. You can think about how much or little time you want to spend with people who harm your spirit or your integrity. If you know someone who complains all the time, you can say to him or her what Stefan Sagmeister says: "Complaining is silly. Either act or forget."

Exercise. I'm quite surprised when I encounter people who don't do any type of exercise. I feel that the benefit of exercise is just about infinite. I didn't think about exercising until about fifteen years ago when I started to feel real stress from managing a demanding account. I started yoga and regular exercise to handle my daily stress, but since then it has become a mandatory routine of basic mind and body care. After my yoga class or a tennis game, my head is clearer, and I feel more energized to carry on with my daily tasks.

Here are the scientific reasons why we feel better after exercising. When you exercise, as your heart rate accelerates, your brain assumes you are either fighting an enemy or fleeing from one. As a protective measure, your brain releases a protein called Brain-Derived Neurotrophic Factor (BDNF). BDNF both protects and repairs memory neurons and acts as a reset switch.[85] Other chemicals are released as well, such as endorphins (natural opiates that create euphoria) and other neurotransmitters that affect mood—the same ones that are stimulated by antidepressant medication. That's why we often feel so relaxed after exercising. Research has shown that people who exercise have much less age-related shrinkage in their brains, thus protecting against dementia, and a greatly reduced susceptibility to depression. Exercise also helps rid your body of stress hormones.[86]

A study conducted by Daniel Landers, from Arizona State University, suggests that exercise works better than relaxation, meditation, and music therapy for anxiety episodes.[87]

DEPRESSION

This chapter wouldn't be complete without some mention of depression. Depression is a special case, the underlying cause of the vast majority of suicides. Someone who is clinically depressed finds it difficult or impossible to do the things they know will make them feel better—calling a friend, going to a movie or the gym, practicing gratitude. They may know everything in this chapter ten times over but need more help to overcome their affliction. South Korea has the highest rate of suicide among developed countries. If you suspect you or a loved one may be depressed or suicidal, please get professional help immediately.

And always, remind yourself that you don't have to be perfect. If you feel inadequate or afraid of disappointing others, hopeless, you are not alone. That's a very human thing. Be kind to yourself. Don't let others determine your destiny. You are the driver of your life. You can survive this.

10

Think Outside The Box

How we choose to educate our children, make decisions about careers, and, in fact, how we make overall life choices depends on what we believe about the world—how and why things happen as they do, what influence individuals have, how much we can change, what we owe our parents and our society. You might call these The Big Questions. I don't claim any superior wisdom, but like everyone, I have opinions, and two that mean a lot to me are: a) whether or not there is an ordering force in the universe, we have more freedom, personal responsibility and ability to change than we think we do; and b) the more we learn about other cultures, other modes of thought, and other emotional perspectives, the more conscious our choices for our own lives can be. There are so many ideas and paths to knowledge out there—and without seeking them out, without experimenting, there's no way to know which ones might offer us tremendous opportunities.

We are born into a certain time and place with our own temperaments and family, and we can't just decide to be or do anything we want. In most cases, people limit themselves (and their children) as much as circumstances do. Just as your house cat doesn't know what it's like to be a wild animal, independent, catching her own dinner, most of us don't have any idea what we could be with more knowledge or experience. We have strengths and talents we don't know (and probably weaknesses, too). That's normal. What I encourage is to think about what this means: what more can we be?

It's not always easy to see this or to believe that we have power over our own lives. In many of the Eastern countries, we are guided by the Chinese zodiac for predictions of prosperity or warnings for the upcoming year, for planning important events like weddings, signing a contract, or what day to open a business. The belief is that your fate is defined—or at least strongly influenced—by your birthday, including the hour and minute of your birth.

Astrology is also popular in the West. While most people don't pay much attention or regard it as entertainment, many people diligently follow their horoscopes and believe in their astrological signs. From my personal experience, the descriptions are quite accurate for both Eastern and Western zodiac signs for many of us, and not so accurate for others.

It surprises me, in our modern Korean culture, how often we deeply believe in and fall back upon fate as an explanation. If someone fails: "Oh that's his fate." If someone succeeds: "That's his good fortune." Fate pretty much has decided our life path for us. We credit or blame fate for our successes and failures, ignoring an individual's hard or not-so-hard work, or whatever else may have affected the outcome. Moreover, our belief in fate—outside our control or the laws of science—makes it easier to believe in any number of superstitions, even to the point, in some cases, where they take over our lives. Rather than making our own plans and decisions, we consult and believe what others can tell us about our future. While this sounds fascinating—who isn't curious about the mysteries of the universe; who doesn't believe that there is much that is beyond our understanding?—I can't help thinking how limiting and even harmful this focus on astrology or advice from fortune tellers can be. Believing so strongly in fate undermines the strength of our will to create our own lives and removes accountability from us. It's not our fault. It's been decided already.

For example, my mom has lived her entire life believing certain things about herself. Every time somebody disappointed her, she would say, "I was born with no people luck." But when I look at those specific situations she was referring to, I realize luck had nothing to do with it. The result was either about how she handled the situation or people or had nothing to do with her at all. As we know, often things don't turn out the way we want them to. Of course, if I say what I see, she won't hear of it. She just defaults to her belief in fate and is convinced she can't change it. She abandons any possibility of making a future, similar situation turn out differently. What if she paid attention to what she contributed to the unhappy outcome and changed her thinking and behavior?

We are born with certain DNA that influences personality traits. Our early environment and upbringing—including such factors as the foods we eat and illnesses we endure, the presence or absence of siblings, our parents' happiness or unhappiness—also affect us. We can't control what we are born as, or born into, and so there are things we can't change about ourselves, but it's not true that we can't change ANYTHING. What I find interesting and helpful is to understand the four personality styles, a breakdown of personality types used in psychological testing today. This typology was developed and refined by a variety of psychologists building on the work of past thinkers. If you look at any branch of psychology—educational, business, self-help—you will find variations on this method of categorizing human difference.

These are basic characteristics or temperaments that we can notice in each individual. It is, inevitably, simplified, but it gives a pretty good picture of who you are and who the people around you are—co-workers, friends, spouses, whomever you have to deal with on a regular basis. Often we don't understand why other people think or behave the way they do. It makes no sense to us. We can't relate. But if you take the time to understand these distinct personality types—what motivates them and how they see the world—you will be better able to communicate and work with those who are different than you. As human beings are highly complex, no individual has only one of these styles. We are a mixture, but usually, you can spot a person's dominant type.

THE FOUR PERSONALITY TYPES

1. **Driver.** Extroverted and dominant, independent, candid, decisive, pragmatic, and efficient. This personality is active and needs challenges and values power and control, whatever station he holds in life. He or she is determined, strong-willed, and very competitive. The Driver is decisive, demanding at work and in personal life, sometimes visionary, usually optimistic. He or she has the weaknesses you would expect, often domineering and controlling, opinionated, insensitive, and inconsiderate of others' needs. The Driver can be hostile and unforgiving when things don't go his or her way.

2. **Expressive.** Charming, extroverted, outgoing, enthusiastic, persuasive, and spontaneous. This personality type is very good at influencing or persuading others, mostly because they enjoy it. Expressive personalities are most interested in other people, seek popularity and recognition, and prefer to be in the spotlight. Strengths include warmth, friendliness, responsiveness, compassion, and generosity. This type can also be

undisciplined, disorganized, dramatic/narcissistic, thoughtless and manipulative.

3. **Analytical.** Introverted, organized, detail oriented. This type may avoid unnecessary physical contact, has more subtle facial expressions, makes minimal eye contact in comparison to others, and often exhibits long pauses in conversation. The strength of Analytics is in their logic, their ability to drill down deep to understand a subject. They excel at abstract thinking, but their emotional intelligence is often undeveloped, making interactions with this personality type difficult. The analytical personality can focus intensely on minor details and may not consider others' feelings; their questions may seem critical and insensitive to others. When working with an Analytic, you should be prepared and thorough. You should try not to ask for quick decisions to be made, but rather allow them time to finish a careful review and discuss all pertinent details.

4. **Amiable.** Warm and stable. The kind of person you associate with comfort, reliability, safety. When communicating, the Amiable tends to use a calm and quiet tone, make eye contact and possibly gentle physical contact and to listen before responding in conversation. In general, the Amiable listens better than any other type and is sympathetic. On the more negative side, this personality type likes routine and may be slow to adapt to new situations. They tend to avoid rejection and risk, take difficulties personally, and may become stubborn if pushed to make a decision or beyond their comfort level. When working with an amiable, you should try to be patient and supportive and remember always to ask for their opinions.

REDEFINING SUCCESS

The Dalai Lama, when asked what surprised him most about humanity, answered "[A man] sacrifices his health in order to make money. Then he sacrifices money to recuperate his health. And then he is so anxious about the future that he does not enjoy the present; the result being that he does not live in the present or the future; he lives as if he is never going to die, and then dies having never really lived."

Most of the countries with the highest suicide rates are Third World countries, so Korea and Japan stand out. Outsiders wonder: what's going on in those countries? Korea and Japan have hyper-competitive societies. The main reason why young people lose hope and choose to end their lives is because of the pressure to succeed through the narrow path of college entrance exams.

Arianna Huffington, co-founder and editor-in-chief of *The Huffington Post*, tells a story from nine years ago. She woke up in a pool of blood in her office after collapsing from exhaustion. She described the incident as a "wake-up call."

"And that's what started me to redefine success, to go beyond the first two metrics that our culture basically has reduced success to: money and power slash recognition, fame, etc...to include a third metric which includes well-being, wisdom, wonder and giving.

"Our current notion of success, in which we drive ourselves into the ground if not the grave—in which working to exhaustion, to burn out, is considered a badge of honor—was put in place by men...in a workplace culture dominated by men."[88] She notes that this culture doesn't work for men either. "We need to redesign workplaces, redesign the way we approach work, redefine what success is. So while, even a few years ago, things like meditation and sleep and pauses were seen as new-agey, you know, now we see them as performance enhancement tools. It's important for us as we are climbing the ladder, accomplishing our dreams or striving to put food on the table, we don't forget all these other things that make our lives full and worth living."

You can easily get obsessed with making money as your life goal and define yourself as a success—as my uncle and many others have done—and then pass away never knowing the real meaning of living life. How heartbreaking is that? How empty it feels, wasteful of the unique gift of life. When you are addicted to money, you lose soulfulness. You perceive, connect, and associate everything and everyone with money and treat them in such a way both consciously and unconsciously.

Miriam Kim was raised in Argentina. She left Argentina for L.A. after intense disagreements with her mother.

"It was very confusing for me as a child. On the outside, my mom was very Argentinian, but inside she had very different expectations for me. Because I was the first daughter, she had an image of me traveling the world. She told me I needed to be international because that's how you become an open-minded person and learn to accept more people and be socially adept. She loved that aspect of being an immigrant. But at the same time, she couldn't let go of her traditional Korean side. My mom was very strict with me. That's why I left.

"She always dictated which school I had to attend. I've been very rebellious since I was a little girl. She told me I needed to think for myself and be strong, but then she wouldn't give me any power. I really wanted to be a psychologist. That was one of my dreams. She rejected that and told me I was going to go to business school because that's what makes money. So I went to business school for six months. That didn't work out. I decided that I just had to get out of there, so I left. We didn't see each other for the next ten years. My mom changed during my absence. She realized a lot of things that she had done. So she started to write me letters and we got closer. Now she's the coolest woman. I invited her to come and live with me in America. Now, I love my mom. She changed a lot. She is more open-minded. The mother I knew before would be dictating to me, telling me how to raise my children, getting involved in my relationship with my husband. Now, she doesn't get involved at all. How I raise my children, she doesn't care. She says, 'They are your children.' She made a completely 180-degree change. The turning point was when I left Argentina. She was heartbroken. That was the moment she realized what she had done."

Bill Chi, my nephew, shared the story of one of his best friends, Danny Kwak. "Danny is a brilliant musician. He's really gifted. He pursued music for one year and then his father basically forced him to become a lawyer. Luckily for him, he likes law, but it's not his true passion. I believe that you should go after your dreams but have a backup plan. Your parents should encourage you to go for what you love, what you are passionate about because that's what you are going to be best at. Korean parents don't do that. They're completely fixated on status and titles; they're very limited that way.

"In the musical TV show *Glee*, you know how they have stereotyped Asians? They had an episode about oppressive Asian parents—how the parents crushed their children's dreams. They're basically making fun of Asians. It makes me feel sad because it's true. They think it's a joke, but it's not flattering at all. That's how Americans see Asians."

Many Koreans, when they hear how people feel/do/think about certain things in the West, laugh and say, "They are saying that because they don't live in Korea." Maybe this makes them feel better or justifies their thoughts and beliefs. Many Koreans living overseas think and do the same thing as they would in Korea, though. For example, forcing their hopes on their children is one of them.

CHOOSING A PROFESSION

Everybody has different strengths and weaknesses. You can force people to choose things that don't fit their personality, but you can't force them to be happy that way. Of course being a doctor, dentist, lawyer, or engineer is not a tragedy, and many people are fulfilled and at their best doing that work, but Bill was describing a mindset of desperation where an entire society believes that only certain professions are desirable. They force these work choices upon their children because they offer financial security and social respect.

He clarified his feelings by saying, "Super-smart Korean people end up being corporate vice presidents or something like that because they just listen to their parents who don't know the true range of possibilities for their sons and daughters. They could be millionaires or innovators or bigger contributors to the world."

Maybe it's too late for older generation parents to grasp their children's true potential (or maybe not), but our young parents can do it differently. They can boldly encourage and support their children's interests and passions. Help them think and dream things that are outside the box, outside of conventional thinking. They can explore ways to discover and maximize the potential of their children. Let them do things they enjoy and love, let them follow where it takes them rather than working just to make money. Even Confucius said something that's right on the mark for our modern career considerations.

Choose a job that you like, and you will never have to work a day in your life.

— CONFUCIUS.

Korean parents consider the legal profession one of the most desirable for their children. Getting into a good law school is very competitive and it takes a lot of work and sacrifice to graduate and pass the bar. It is a considerable investment. Yet I have met many lawyers, some quite successful, who have chosen to leave the profession. They didn't enjoy being lawyers; some actually hated it. Megyn Kelly, an American journalist on the Fox News Channel, is one of those people. Ms. Kelly was a well known TV journalist. She became news herself when she boldly asked presidential candidate Donald Trump questions concerning his insulting remarks about women. His response was very crude—proving her point—and it seemed for a while that it might mean the end of his candidacy. Many American women were proud of Megyn Kelly for speaking out.

At the age of fifteen, Ms. Kelly lost her father to a heart attack. He was forty-five years old. She told Charlie Rose, "But there was a silver lining to that tragedy. I thought a lot about it over the years. I believe that it's made me keenly aware of my own mortality. And it has led me to make different and better choices for myself in the thirty years since his death.

"I don't think I would have made the switch out of my legal job had it not been for that awareness that, you know, time is passing me by. And it will end. And you really need to make the best choices for yourself while you're here—as hard as that may be. And what I realized after eight or nine years of practicing law is that just because you're good at something doesn't mean you are happy."[89]

229

Joe Tan put it this way, "Previous generations were raised to believe that work is work…if it was supposed to be fun, they'd call it something else. Fortunately, today the tides seem to be shifting, perhaps because the need is so great for passionate and creative minds to solve some pretty important challenges in our world."

LOSERS OR WINNERS?
Let's take a look at some of the super-achievers in the West.

"This guy's parents give him up for adoption. He never finishes college. He job-hops quite a bit, goes on a sojourn to India for a year, and to top it off, he has dyslexia. Would you hire this guy? His name is Steve Jobs." (Regina Hartley, Human Resources Manager at UPS.)[90]

Richard Branson, English business magnate, founder of Virgin Group, which comprises more than 400 companies, was a high-school dropout. Branson also has dyslexia, which often leads to poor academic performance and has caused many kids to drop out of schools that don't understand their disability (This is changing now.). The headmaster of his high school, who obviously saw something in him, predicted that he would either end up in prison or become a millionaire. It's important to note that Branson's parents always encouraged their son's interests and activities.

Bill Gates, co-founder of Microsoft, was fascinated by computers since his early teens. Gates dropped out of Harvard in 1974, seeing an opportunity to start his own software company. He had talked this decision over with his parents, who were supportive of him after seeing how much Gates wanted to start a company.

Mark Zuckerberg dropped out of Harvard in his sophomore year to complete his project, Facebook.

Margaret Mitchell, author of the famous novel *Gone with the Wind*, didn't do well in school. She didn't fit in with the other girls in college but she was an avid reader and had a childhood full of imagination.

Walt Disney, cartoonist, animator, film producer, creator of Disneyland, had many jobs since he was a little boy, ranging from delivering newspapers to being an ambulance driver in France working for the Red Cross. He dropped out of high school at the age of sixteen. His first cartoon studio made no money. His second company ended up in bankruptcy. Eventually, the Walt Disney Company was set up and Disney built his state-of-the-art studio in Burbank, California. He wanted to create a place where artists could explore, fail and try again without being fearful. "It's kind of fun to do the impossible," he said.

Einstein is regarded as one of the smartest men of all time, but his background isn't entirely stellar. Einstein's parents were always worried about his development. Apparently, he had some odd tendencies, like pronouncing words to himself silently before saying them to others and speaking more slowly than others his age. "His slow development was combined with a cheeky rebelliousness toward authority, which led one schoolmaster to send him packing and another to declare that he would never amount to much," Einstein's younger sister recalled.[91]

Oprah Winfrey was born into poverty in rural Mississippi to a single teenage mother and raised in an inner-city Milwaukee neighborhood. She has said that she was molested during her childhood and early teens and became pregnant at fourteen. Her son died in infancy. She became a world-renowned talk show host and philanthropist.

All these people, and many more who are considered the best in their field, either had a learning disability, dropped out of high school or college, or were born into poverty. By Korean standards, these people would have been failures, losers and shamed sons and daughters. Just imagine how their parents would have treated them if they'd been born Korean! They would have been thrown out of the house or disowned!

This says many things about how we as individuals develop and grow at different speeds and in different environments. As we each have distinctive personalities, the driven ones and curious ones will find their way. It's rarely easy. You just have to keep searching, following, or creating opportunities for yourself.

Hartley added, "In a study of the world's most highly successful entrepreneurs, it turns out a disproportionate number have dyslexia. In the U.S., thirty-five percent of the entrepreneurs studied had dyslexia. What's remarkable [is that] among those entrepreneurs who experience post-traumatic growth, [many] now view their learning disability as a desirable difficulty, which provided them an advantage because they became better listeners and paid greater attention to detail. They don't think they are who they are in spite of adversity; they know they are who they are because of adversity. They embrace their trauma and hardships as key elements of who they've become and know that without those experiences, they might not have developed the muscle and grit required to become successful."

I'm not saying to young people: drop out of school if you don't like to study. If you don't want to go to college, you can still be successful. It may happen, but it's a long shot. Not everyone is a Bill Gates or Mark Zuckerberg. A college degree is still the best predictor of adult income. My message is that if you are in a situation where you are not doing well, if you feel like you are learning the wrong skills or are in an environment that doesn't encourage or support you, don't give up! Don't think of yourself as a loser. Your talent and opportunities may lie elsewhere. As long as you have curiosity, interest and a passion for knowledge in any field, keep pursuing it. We live in an online world. You can learn a limitless amount on the Internet. You can learn at your own pace and as much as you want to. The world of knowledge is at your finger tips.

Our traditional definitions of success have been very narrow. Success was defined either monetarily or by having a high-status profession like lawyer, doctor, accountant. We live in a different world now. There are so many fields and professions where you can explore your potential. There are so many industries that are in need of creative and challenging minds. In the design field alone there are opportunities in graphic design, product design, interior design, and numerous positions in web design. For example, UI/UX designer (user interface/user experience in computer-human interaction on websites, mobile apps, products) is one of them. There are also challenging careers in architecture, advertising, marketing…. You can achieve a lot more through some of these professions than through conventional professions—both monetarily and emotionally, depending on your priorities, talents and efforts.

The new and evolving definition of success includes doing work that gives you joy and offers interesting challenges and a certain higher level of satisfaction. Most importantly, individuals can decide for themselves what success means. I asked Melissa Kim: How do you measure success? She said, "If I am not bored and making a living, I think I am successful."

COACH JOHN

In Korea, the focus is so much on scores that we grow up thinking nothing can matter more than that. A friend in Korea once told me that we

Koreans don't work hard unless it's a competition. That leaves out all the internal pleasures of working towards a goal, the pleasure of being "in the zone." This is when our ideas are flowing smoothly and we lose track of time. There is also the pleasure of cooperating and enjoying each other's talents. No wonder we get stressed out and get discouraged about our lives. As you can see from the different personality types, not everyone is born competitive. Some thrive in that kind of environment and some thrive in a more relaxed atmosphere. We need to stop putting everyone in the same category and expecting them to win.

Our parents want our children to be number one in everything— from the best motives— but there can be only so many number ones. What about the rest of us who are not number one? Oh well, that's most of us! Should we feel bad, depressed, put our head down and live our lives like we are nobody? I definitely think not.

John Wooden was a basketball player and coach. As head coach at UCLA (1948-1975), he won ten national championships in a twelve-year period. The record is still unmatched in the world of basketball. He shares the values and life lessons he passed on to his players, emphasizing success is about much more than winning.

"The accumulation of material possessions or the attainment of a position of power or prestige, or something of that sort, are worthy accomplishments perhaps, but in my opinion not necessarily indicative of success. So I wanted to come up with something of my own.

"I coined my own definition of success, which is: Peace of mind attained through self-satisfaction in knowing you made the effort to do the best of which you're capable. I believe that's true. If you make the effort to do the best of which you're capable, trying to improve the situation that exists for you, I think that's success, and I don't think others can judge that. It's like character and reputation—your reputation is what you're perceived to be; your character is what you really are. And I think that character is much more important than what you are perceived to be. You'd hope they'd both be good, but they won't necessarily be the same. Well, that was my idea that I was going to try to get across to the youngsters.

"Giving all, it seems to me, is not so far from victory. Don't whine. Don't complain. Don't make excuses. Just get out there, and whatever you're doing, do it to the best of your ability. And no one can do more than that. I tried to get across, too, that—and my opponents will tell you—you never heard me mention winning. Never mention winning. When a game is over, and you see somebody that didn't know the outcome, I hope they couldn't tell by your actions whether you outscored an opponent or the opponent outscored you."

This takes true character. I know this from my heart because I'm a tennis player myself. My tennis games are not for big stakes like national basketball games, but I completely understand how hard it is to win and how equally hard it is to lose.

EDUCATION AND CREATIVITY

Of course, life does not begin when one gets that first job or makes a decision as to which field to pursue. We are shaped by our education—not only what we learn, but how we learn. In terms of how our brains develop, adolescence is a special time, setting up the structure for the years to come. In our grandparents' time, before we had the kind of exposure we have today, what the elders of your family and village taught you was what you most needed to know. It's not quite as simple now. There are many more sources of information: family and community, books, magazines, web, movies and television. But our brains still prioritize what's learned when we're young, within our immediate environment. This means that while lifelong education is necessary and desirable, what you learn when you're young—and what you don't learn—has great influence. Because the world is changing so rapidly, many people stress the importance of learning how to learn, of critical thinking, flexibility and, most of all, imagination.

> *Logic will get you from A to B. Imagination will take you everywhere. Imagination is more important than knowledge. For knowledge is limited to all we now know and understand, while imagination embraces the entire world, and all there ever will be to know and understand.*
>
> — ALBERT EINSTEIN

Leeah Joo is a Korean American painter, lecturer, and a teacher at Westover Girls High School in Middlebury, Connecticut. She was at her art exhibition opening reception at Andrew Bae Gallery in Chicago when I met her. With sadness, Leeah shared her experiences relating to the Korean students in her classes. "One of my joys of working at Westover is that there is always a handful of Korean students. It's really nice to get to know and have a relationship with these teenagers from Korea. Their English is very rough, and most of the time their parents are in Korea. I often have parent-teacher conferences via email or phone with an uncle who is a second generation Korean American. It is very sad, I think, because the girls are far away from their homes. They come here when they are maybe fourteen years old. The whole purpose of them being in this country is so they can marry the right person, but I just can't imagine sending my son away even for a week. The four years of their most vulnerable and precious time as teenagers?

"When I have these conferences, I'm an art teacher so we are focusing on art, and all they want to know is, 'What are you going to do to get her in to RISD (Rhode Island School of Design)? She's got to get in to RISD.' And I say, 'Well, we are going to try hard.' They are asking what can I do as a teacher to help the girls get into an Ivy League school. They are fourteen years old. They work around the clock. Their English is really rough. There is often no possibility of going to an Ivy League school with their lack of English fluency, but you can't tell them that. You can't tell them, 'Well, think about the well-being of your child.' The other things are more important, but basically, that's what they want. And that to me points to unhappiness. The students work so hard. They are so stressed out to get perfect scores, but then what's going to happen? I ask them, 'Are you planning on staying here for college or are you going to go back to Korea?' They say, 'The plan is to go to college here then go back to Korea.' Because that's the only way to guarantee that they are eligible to marry somebody who is well educated and well off. Without these badges of foreign school education and the Ivy League tag, they are not going to get good matches."

The next part is where we have to pay attention. This is the part that tells us why we need to change the education system in Korea in the most urgent way. "Korean girls coming to my class are extremely talented. They literally have perfect scores in all their math and science classes. Because they work so hard and that is expected of them. Even though they are not the most talented artists, they work their butts off. They will stay up all night to finish something. They compensate for whatever they lack in quality by quantity, by the hours they put into it. But in the more advanced classes where the drawing projects or painting projects are more conceptually driven, where the focus is thinking on your own, coming up with your own ideas, they can't do it. They can't. In the end, it's something you see all the time. I've had that conversation with other teachers there.

It's the same thing. They are unable to self-motivate, to think outside the box. You know just the general spirit of seventeen- and eighteen-year-olds in high school in the U.S.—usually they have crazy ideas with absolutely no quantitative ability to support their ideas. They are usually not smart enough to actually see it through. It is so opposite for the Korean girls. They have been driven so hard and they are born into a society where it is like you just do do do and don't reflect at all on what's actually happening. You're on the fast track of now. Now you are thirteen, now you are at boarding school or trying to get into the best high school, best tutoring program, and you never have time to think on your own. They really suffer in the end. Even if you work with them to prepare the portfolio to get into an awesome school, college or whatever, at some point, they have to have some ideas of their own. Artists have to think on their own and be creative. And they really can't. That's the most damaging, handicapping thing, and it's the way they have been raised."

Many of the goose parents say their children are also in American schools to get away from Korean schools. "Although the academics in Korea are more rigorous, there's no creative mind there," says Jiyun Lee, a Korean mother with children in school in America, quoted on NPR. "Everything's rote memorization, and it's purely academic — there's no individual thought in their teaching."[92]

My friend Valeria, an architect, shared a new trend she sees in American schools. "It seems like in Korea there is a strong focus on intellect, on the developing of intellect. In America now, even the public schools are trying to be more whole. They're trying to develop something like 'think with your hands' so you start to be an inventor and they're starting to bring back more arts and music. The activities are a little bit more integrated. There is a little bit less focus on academics. Where Matteo [Valeria's son] goes to school, it's less about putting content in and more about drawing potential out."

Ken Robinson, author and educator, thinks we need to radically rethink our view of intelligence. "We know three things about intelligence. One, it's diverse. We think about the world in all the ways that we experience it. We think visually; we think in sound; we think kinesthetically. We think in abstract terms; we think in movement.

"Secondly, intelligence is dynamic. If you look at the interactions of a human brain, intelligence is wonderfully interactive. The brain isn't divided into compartments. In fact, creativity, which I define as the process of having original ideas that have value, more often than not comes about through the interaction of different disciplinary ways of seeing things.

"And the third thing about intelligence is, it's distinct. I'm doing a new book at the moment called *Epiphany* (The final title is *The Element: How Finding Your Passion Changes Everything.*) which is based on a series of interviews with people about how they discovered their talent. I'm fascinated by how people got to be there."

Ken had a lunch with Gillian Lynne, British ballerina, choreographer of *Phantom of the Opera* and *Cats*, the longest running and second longest running shows in Broadway history. Ken asked her, "How did you get to be a dancer?" She told him that, when she was at school, she was hopeless. The school, in the '30s, wrote to her parents and said, "We think Gillian has a learning disorder." She couldn't concentrate; she was fidgeting.

Here is another great talent who didn't do well in school to the point that her mother took her to a doctor to see what was wrong with her. After hearing Gillian's problems, the doctor left Gillian in the room with the radio on, music playing, while he talked with her mother outside the room. Then the doctor asked the mother to look—Gillian was dancing to the radio. He noted that she was a dancer and encouraged Gillian's mother to send her to dance school.[93]

Diverse, dynamic, distinct. This is how you could describe a great design—a great school—a great city. It's a description of something complicated enough and energetic enough to thrive. It's exciting to think that this is what we all have inside our skulls—not the same intelligence but intelligence itself: powerful and adaptable, capable of much more than rote learning or predigested answers.

It seems clear that the challenges facing Korean educators now involve how can we expose our young people to new experiences, sensations, and states of mind. We should be very proud that South Korea ranks as one of the top three in math and science in the world. We should be proud of all the hard work that went into this. But when Western journalists look deeper into how we got where we are, they write about it with sympathy for Korean students, but expressing doubt about the Korean education system. Many foreigners who are familiar with our educational conditions tell us how they see Korean education. Their observations are nothing less than the truth.

Dave Hazzan has been living in Korea for fourteen years and taught English for ten years. He offered his honest opinions on Korean education. "Koreans don't study in an effective manner. They spend a lot of money for inefficient education. The Korean education system is poor, with very little critical thinking required. They put a lot of money in the hagwon (cram school), but they still speak poor English. You learn a language to speak, to communicate, not just to pass a test."

There was a *Washington Post* article in 2012 about Korea's educational system. Jasper Kim, a professor at the Graduate School of International

Studies at Ewha Woman's University in Seoul was quoted as saying, "A lot of employers make English fluency a criterion for whether to hire or not hire." She added, "And more on a social or cultural level, English is viewed as a superficial language. Not necessarily needed, but kind of viewed as an academic luxury handbag. If you can speak English, it means you've had the resources, which means—in the Korean mind-set—that you come from a so-called 'right family.' And this is what companies are looking for."

LEARNING FROM THE FINNS

While Asian countries, Hong Kong, Singapore, and South Korea are topping the math and science world rankings, Finland always appears on top among Western countries.

We mostly know this county as home of the Nokia phones. This small Nordic country shares a few major similarities with Korea. They are both small, with a homogeneous population and a lack of natural resources. Also, interestingly, Finland has the title of the least corrupt country in the world on the Corruption Perception Index. (Somalia and North Korea share the title of most corrupt).[94]

What else? In 2010, Finland was picked as number one by Newsweek's global survey of quality of life.[95] But most noteworthy is the newfound fame of their educational reform. The Finns are attracting the attention of the world. One of the leading Finnish authorities on education reform, director of the Finnish Ministry of Education's Center for International Mobility, Pasi Sahlberg, has a written a book, *Finnish Lessons: What Can the World Learn from Educational Change in Finland?*

He hosts about a hundred visits a year by foreign educators who want to know the secret of Finland's success. His book answers many of the questions he is frequently asked.

There are no private schools in the Finnish school system, nor private universities. From pre-K to the Ph.D. level, all Finnish students attend public institutions. Meanwhile, affluent parents in America can spend more than $35,000 for one year of private secondary education.

Sahlberg stresses that what matters in Finland is that educators are respected, with pay and prestige commensurate with that respect. They also have more responsibility for the curriculum and teaching methods than in America. In Finland, the teacher-training programs are among the most selective professional schools in the country. And principals are expected to notice any lapse in teaching and deal with it promptly and effectively.

So far, this sounds like what Korean and American parents alike could easily support. The most profound difference is that, as Sahlberg points out, Finns do not think competition is a useful motivator. The very idea makes them uncomfortable. Sahlberg quotes a line from Finnish writer Samuli Paronen: "Real winners do not compete." Students don't compete against each other, and schools don't compete against each other for the "best" students. Even if your initial response is to think that this will never work, it's hard to argue with Finnish success.

This all started decades ago when the Finnish school system was badly in need of reform. The changes that were made then were not in the name of excellence, but equity. Since the 1980s, the idea that all children should have the same opportunities to learn, regardless of family background, income, or geographic location, has been the core value of the education system. Education is seen as a way to create a harmonious society—without sacrificing quality. Of course, all countries are different, and I don't expect either America or Korea is able and equipped to adopt 100% of the Finnish model. But it's one worth looking into.

CONFORMISM VS. INDIVIDUALISM

When all think alike, then no one is thinking.

— WALTER LIPPMAN

One blogger, a Western English teacher, describes Koreans, "People dress the same around here, they like the same food, they listen to the same music, and they even drive the same cars. In Western countries, there are different forms of beauty; here, it's one ideal. Back home, cities have different forms of character; here it seems like there's one simple design. We tend to find common ground between right and wrong, black and white; here it's one thin path of normality. Once again, it doesn't affect the expats that are teaching English in Korea directly. Koreans are actually quite understanding about cultural differences, but it's so damn boring to look at."

If you come from North America or Europe, it's easy to see us this way. Korea suffers from a lack of natural resources and a high population density, with seventy percent of the land uninhabitable. In size, South Korea is comparable to the Midwestern state of Indiana. We are stuck between the giants China and Japan, who also have conformist cultures. It would be surprising if we had anything but a conformist culture.

The loudest duck gets shot. – Chinese proverb.
The nail that sticks out gets hammered down. – Japanese proverb
Sharp stones get hammered flat – Korean proverb

Our culture is group oriented. A person's identity is fundamentally linked to the groups to which he/she belongs—family, regional origin,

243

education—and people's behavior reflects this. In Korean companies, until very recently, individual initiative was not encouraged. Anyone standing out from the crowd was seen as arrogant or a showoff. The group would ensure that person knows his place.

We assume the individual cannot survive outside the group. In a larger sense, this is true of course—human society is deeply connected, and this provides us with necessary material and emotional security. But there is a spectrum of possible relationships between the individual and the group—very close/identified on one end and extreme self-sufficiency on the other—and in Korea, we have gone farther than we need to toward the identification end. If we move away from this, we are nobody (emotionally at least) is the fear that rules us. How about we think in a different way? We can still bond, respect, and hang out with our groups while retaining our individual thoughts, styles and dreams—and acting on them without being ridiculed or threatened. There's more room for difference than most of us imagine—and not only room for it but a great demand for it. Korea needs all the new ideas we can generate. Companies and the schools that prepare us should create and encourage safe environments for people to think and express freely because there is no other way to compete and sustain success in this global economy. This aspect of culture is changing fast in twenty first-century Korea, thanks to the Internet and the global spread of culture. Young people are being asked to show much more initiative and, reluctantly in some cases, older people are accepting the change in relative status and power.

Adam Grant talks about 'originals' in his TED talk. "I've been studying people that I have come to call 'originals.' Originals are nonconformists, people who not only have new ideas but take action to champion them. They are people who stand out and speak up. Originals drive creativity and change in the world.

"What about fear? Originals feel fear, too. They're afraid of failing, but what sets them apart from the rest of us is that they're even more afraid of failing to try. They know you can fail either by starting a business that goes bankrupt or by failing to start a business at all. They know that in the long run, our biggest regrets are not our actions but our inactions."[96]

TOASTMASTERS

Education is part of the story. Another important component is communication. We are an intelligent people. But, somehow, many foreigners see us in a not so favorable way when it comes to communications. Here are some relevant opinions.

"Koreans lack the ability to discuss or present their opinions in a logical and reasonable manner but are good at insisting without the ability to communicate intelligently."

"Korean people are weak at expressing their own opinions."

"I see the lack of conflict within Korean families, the workplace, and in Korean society in general to be an aspect of the culture that is flawed and could do with some change. Honest discussion—and the intellectual and verbal conflict that arises from it—is how we all move forward. To not be able to speak openly and honestly with someone without fear of reprisal and dire consequences is something that I cannot respect, accept, adapt to, or feel comfortable with. In Korea, I am uncomfortable that the right to disagree, argue, and debate honestly seems to be taken away from many people. The frustrating thing is that to notice this and complain about it in writing or even to friends is often seen as something worthy of shame, stubbornness, laziness, and sometimes even bigotry and racism."[97]

I read and hear this type of comment quite a bit in foreigners' books and talks about Koreans. Even many Koreans say we Koreans are lacking in critical thinking and are not able to articulate our thoughts. I think people get this impression because we don't normally get opportunities to express our thoughts in logical ways. It's not taught in school or at home. Many of us, if we choose to communicate when there is a conflict, express our thoughts in more emotional ways (which makes sense if we have to fight an internal battle before we even open our mouths). We get angry, cry, whine, scream, insisting on what we say in a quick outburst. Also, our culture is all about *ppalli-ppalli* (hurry, hurry) with very little patience. Our emotions move our lips faster than our brains. We are a highly emotional people.

I'm still a ppali-ppali person even after living in America for thirty-six years. I remind myself constantly to take it easy whenever I get impatient. But I want to share something that helped me become a better communicator, to evolve from being a passive observer to an instigator of conversation, socially and at work.

I am a relatively outgoing person. I remember raising my hand to sing in front of my classmates during lunchtime in junior high school. I also remember making a presentation in Korean history class and raising my hand again to play piano for the annual class choir contest even though I knew there was a better piano player in our class. Now, I look back and have no idea where I got the courage to do it. It's not that I felt confident that I was good at singing or piano playing, but I just kind of had this blind faith that I could do it even though it was nerve-wracking.

The whole courage thing pretty much disappeared when I came to the U.S., mainly because I thought my English wasn't good enough. I became a quiet person.

One day I was with my classmates at Northwestern University working on a group assignment. We were preparing a presentation and I said, "I really get nervous speaking in front of people, especially since English is not my native language." One student said, "You should go to Toastmasters! I went for a couple of years, and I'm so much better now." I asked, "What is Toastmasters?" "It's an organization where you practice public speaking and leadership skills." The very next day, I joined a Toastmasters club near Michigan Avenue, and I was a member for five years.

I can't say enough good things about Toastmasters. The way it works is that you give speeches that last five to seven minutes. You write the speeches on any subjects you like. You practice and give the speech, and then you receive evaluation on your delivery, tone, body language, content, structure of the speech, etc.... It's not easy the first time, but you keep doing it, and it gets easier. You build more confidence each time. You play different roles, not just giving speeches but evaluating other people's speeches. This helps you develop listening skills. Each meeting also includes Table Topics before the main speech part begins. One of the members will ask you a question about anything he/she wants to. It can be about current events, what's your favorite movie and why, what would you do if, etc., and you have two minutes to answer. For a long time, this part was the most difficult for me because you don't know what the questions will be about and you may be clueless about what to say, but you still have to say something. It keeps you on your toes. Fun!

Most of the people in my club were professionals who had to make presentations regularly at work. However, everybody can benefit from joining TM. Communication skills are the most important skills we can have. Clear and effective communication helps any relationship at work or at home. In America, people say the biggest fear they have is the fear of public speaking. Toastmasters is not just about overcoming the fear of speaking in front of people. You learn from each other by giving speeches and the evaluations you receive from the audience. Practicing helps you build confidence—how to speak clearly so your audience can listen without effort, and how to make your points with logic, economy and persuasive language so that people will be convinced by your message.

TM is an international organization. I was very happy to know that there are several TM clubs in Korea now. If you haven't heard about it, I highly encourage you to join one. If there isn't one in your area, you can start one yourself. Start raising your hand even if you feel shy or uncomfortable! The more you do it, the easier it gets. Remember, it's all about practice. And everyone can benefit regardless of what you do for a living or how old you are. What makes it so much fun is listening to others' speeches while improving your own.

ONE DEGREE SHIFT

Megan Bhatia was my fellow Toastmaster in Chicago. She is one of the best speakers I have known in the Toastmaster clubs. One day during the meeting break, she told me about the seminar she and her husband Marty attended in LA called High Performance Academy, which was lead by Brandon Burchard, an American author/speaker on motivation. She briefly shared what the seminar was about and instantly I was pulled in. There are four pillars—physiology, psychology, productivity, persuasion—as they relate to high performing people. All four are important, but I specifically was interested in the psychology part.

Megan summarized the key points of the seminar. "One of the basic ideas that is coming out of modern psychology now is the idea of a growth mindset and a fixed mindset. As the words imply, with the growth mindset, you see that there is an alternate possibility for yourself and you believe you can achieve that. The fixed mindset is that it's always been like this, so it's always going to be like this. With the fixed mindset, you are not going to take the actions that you need to take to change your life. Having a growth mindset is something that you can foster. If you turn the tractor one degree, where would you end up over time? You will end up at a different location! You will be different. So it's all about the small changes."

A very interesting talk on this subject is by Rory Sutherland. He talks about the power of reframing—of looking at a situation or problem in a slightly different light. You should read or listen to his whole presentation, but I will quote one of the examples he uses of how taking psychology into account matters. "Here's a beautiful example of a psychological solution deployed in Korea. Red traffic lights have a countdown delay. It's proven to reduce the accident rate in experiments. Why? Because road rage, impatience and general irritation are massively reduced when you can actually see the time you have to wait."[98]

We can be our best selves at any given point if we have the right tools. It's all about creating habits that work for you.

START A BOOK CLUB!

I also started a book club with some of the friends at the TM. It lasted for twelve years.

Book clubs are an excellent way to socialize and spend time with your friends. We had six to ten members. We decided to keep it small; otherwise, it would become an organizing nightmare and not everybody would get an opportunity to speak. We read both fiction and non-fiction books, but mostly fiction. We met once a month or every six weeks for Sunday brunch at a restaurant or at someone's home, taking turns. Stimulating conversations made the two hours fully enjoyable. We talked about the characters, different interpretations of the story, and disagreed with each other. It's fun to disagree. You get an opportunity to convince others to see your side and vice versa. I remember leaving each book club meeting feeling satisfied and productive. It sure felt like my world had gotten a little broader each time as a result of talking about the characters, their situations and emotions, and the lessons every book offers.

We didn't have a lot of time to read since everybody worked full time. But somehow we did it. Also, having the book club forced us to read more than we would have otherwise. You can have a book club for the rest of your life, regardless of your age. You get wiser since you get to read lots of books. Your communication skills improve, too, since you get to discuss a variety of topics. Finally, it's always fun to have meaningful conversations with your friends. I stopped my book club because I wanted to dedicate my time to writing this book, but as soon as I'm done writing, I'll be picking it up again.

TED TALKS
"Ideas worth spreading"

I have mentioned TED talks several times in this book because I find them so illuminating. I started listening to them about five years ago. TED stands for technology, entertainment, and design. But it's much more than that. The talks are about topics of human interest, offered in a hundred languages. You get to hear from leading innovators, educators, entertainers, business leaders, scientists, people with inspirational stories, and the thought leaders of today on a huge range of subject matter.

So why should we listen to TED talks? When you are consumed with your daily life and your own environment, it's easy to forget that you are part of this big world. We are all connected—in more ways than we realize. If you don't have an awareness of the world, you have a smaller perspective and a narrower view of who you are as a person, or who you could be. We have parts of ourselves that need encouragement, ideas we have forgotten or put aside because they seemed too different. Nothing can make you more aware of yourself than listening to others—especially across cultures, age, gender, ethnicity—and finding a spark of commonality.

Once you sign up on the TED website, you will get an email every day with a different speaker. If the topic doesn't interest you, skip it, but try listening at least for the first one or two minutes. You never know what you might learn. The presentations are short, anywhere from three to fifteen minutes. TED is all about life inspirations. Perhaps you will realize you are not alone regarding a certain experience or feeling, or perhaps you will change your views on things you've never thought about deeply before. I have used several quotes from TED talks' speakers throughout this book. I hope you've enjoyed them, and I hope you become a regular listener as I am. One of the first talks I listened to and was inspired by was the one I have previously quoted from, "The Politics of Fiction," given by Elif Shafak. It touches the very fabric of what I want to accomplish in this book. She said, "Imaginative literature is not necessarily about writing who we are or what we know or what our identity is about. We should teach young people and ourselves to expand our hearts and write what we can feel. We should get out of our cultural ghetto and go visit the next one and the next. In the end, stories move like whirling dervishes, drawing circles beyond circles. They connect all humanity."[99]

THINKING FOR YOURSELF

Thinking on your own may sound risky. I understand the social pressures; they are real and you will have to deal with other people's disapproval from time to time. Hopefully, that will be offset by the freedom and happiness you find in forging your own path. There are ways to make it easier on yourself.[100]

1. Use social media less often. I know it is tempting, but restrict your usage so that you're not constantly checking what other people think. Counting how many 'likes' or retweets you get is not only an addictive pastime, it doesn't take into account what something actually means to you.
2. Critique mass media messages. Popular television shows, magazines, music, video games, and other media are major forces in shaping expectations. Always keep a critical eye open. Consider what the creators are trying to "sell" you—I don't mean the advertisements, I mean the stories, songs, etc. What emotions and attitudes are they asking you to agree with?
3. Examine your own actions. After each social, family or work encounter, look at your own behavior—or at least make a point of doing this regularly—at least several times a week. Think about what you did, what you were thinking, and what resulted. If your actions or decisions were made to please someone else, to get along or avoid conflict, recognize that these were reactions to pressure. Is that how you want to live your life?

4. Expose yourself to different viewpoints. The more educated you are about diverse perspectives, the more new ideas—and the more nuanced ideas—will come naturally to you. Talk to people you wouldn't normally talk to, even online. Reach out. Travel if you can. Read a lot of books, not necessarily the newest ones. Fiction, nonfiction, history, popular science, the arts—whatever interests you. But read widely.

5. List your priorities. Think about what would make you most happy, if social pressures didn't exist. List the activities you enjoy, or ones that you would like to try out. Don't worry if none of your friends likes the same things. Explore on your own.

6. Examine your inspirations. What excites you? What makes you think? I'm not talking about copying something that you appreciate, but letting it bring new ideas and possibilities to mind. Use others' imaginations as a jumping-off point.

7. Let others run their own lives. It's not your job to tell people how to live. Your judgments of others may not take into account what they have been through or what they are hoping for. Don't give up your standards but be compassionate and remember: when it comes to other people's lives, we know less than we think we do.

8. Talk about your perspective. If anyone wants to talk to you about your attitudes or behavior, be as open and honest as you can, given the situation. (Obviously, sometimes it's better to be discreet.) There's a reason you make the decisions you do, and talking about them can help reinforce your confidence, and maybe even encourage others to think for themselves.

9. Understand Consequences. Being comfortable with your behavior does not make you free from consequences. Change is risky—this is why we fear it—and learning to embrace it does not mean the risk goes away. Think about what you say and do

carefully and make sure you are prepared to face negative reactions. Certain kinds of "backlash" can be empowering, teaching you that people's opinions won't destroy you.

One of the greatest discoveries a man makes, one of his great surprises, is to find he can do what he was afraid he couldn't do.

– HENRY FORD

On the other hand, there are times when something you can't afford to risk is at stake. Think it through and realize that you don't have to do everything all at once. Try one or two suggestions a week, read it again once a month as a reminder. Before you know it, you may be a whole different person inside and out!

11

Work

We spend most of the productive part of our lives at work. Work is our livelihood and one of our primary identities. Where we work, whom we work with and for, and how we work as a group affects the work result as well as our personal satisfaction. When you have a healthy and productive work environment, your satisfaction level increases. When it's the opposite, your daily life can be unhappy and unproductive. It can drain all your energy just to endure another day. Of course, if the latter is your situation, you will hope to find another job elsewhere, but in Korea, changing a job is not as easy as it can be in the West. So many of us just stick it out even if we are miserable. We follow the rules, try and get along to go along, and manage as best we can. Some of us are just floating in the ocean, not knowing or able to decide which way to swim. We just go where the waves take us and try not to drown.

For people trapped in a job, work is about making a living. That's why we work, period: to eat, pay the rent and other bills, survive. If you are trying not to drown, you don't expect words and phrases like meaningful, enjoyment, satisfaction, stimulation, inspiring challenges, being your best, to be attached to work. But what if that weren't the case? What if those words could be attached to work and make it much more than just a living?

Jason Fried is a co-founder of Basecamp (previously 37 Signals), a co-author of *Rework,* and a long-time friend. He told me why he works. "I enjoy making something. I enjoy building and creating something. That's very creatively and intellectually fulfilling. Software is what I know how to build. I don't know how to build a house or a car or furniture. So I build this. The fact that I can make money doing it is a bonus."

Wouldn't it be awesome if we all could describe our work as Jason does?

Since Guus Hiddink led the Korean soccer team to the semi-finals of the 2002 World Cup held in Korea and Japan, "The Hiddink Syndrome"[101] has become a common phrase in Korea. The interesting thing is, what Hiddink did with the Korean soccer team, organizing the team around the best players rather than seniority, education, family or personal connections, isn't super revolutionary in the West, although it sure was in Korea. Many books on Hiddink's method became bestsellers, and corporations wanted to adopt his leadership style. So after fourteen years, I'm wondering how much of the Hiddink Syndrome is at work now in Korean society and corporations? Regrettably, not much. It's clear that some changes are on the way. A few companies have implemented initiatives, but the majority of organizations still follow the same old path, continuing familiar methods. Why should we charge into unfamiliar territory despite the success we witnessed with Hiddink?

Making fundamental changes that affect ingrained habits and attitudes in an organization is not easy. Habit and familiarity are powerful. But it may be a necessity, not only for the growth of our economy but to sustain our competitive edge in the global market. I understand too well that sometimes we need a few reminders or a little push to make big changes. Certainly, I do! Here are a few reasons why I believe we need to be reminded of the Hiddink method in our workplaces.

HIGH TOLERANCE FOR INEFFICIENCY

Many people say that they love how Korean cities are run so efficiently. Ppali-ppali is one of the words that describes this Korean characteristic. We have no patience. Everything has to be done fast and right the first time. That's why I have a big question mark about how companies work in Korea. A rigid, vertical, hierarchical structure based on age and seniority has many downsides when it comes to efficiency. Before discussing this more, I want to mention and acknowledge that each company has a different culture. The majority of this chapter is based on interviews with people who have worked and consulted for large Korean corporations in Seoul.

One observer, let's call him Tom, shared his views on how Koreans work. "Every society has contradictions and paradoxes. Koreans have a remarkable capacity for torture. They don't complain if they're working very inefficiently or if things are inconvenient. Individuals will put their heads down and just push through all the bureaucracy. They just accept it. That's just the way it is. They do ppali-ppali with all the bureaucracy without recognizing the overall inefficiency of the plan. If they do complain, they are going to be in trouble. So that doesn't even cross their minds. Americans would say, 'What is this? This is bullshit!' Koreans will not do that. Koreans are real team players in that regard. They just do it."

The company where Tom worked had an email system that was extremely inefficient. You couldn't even save an email. There were ways around it, but basically, it was very inefficient. Millions of hours were wasted because of this email system, which was designed by the company. In his five years working at the company, there was never a single update to the program. People just worked around it. So there is the incredible Korean capacity to suffer. If you complain, it raises suspicion, and your life will be very difficult. As long as the software could be worked with in some manner, everybody went along with it. You can complain about small things, but if you complain about fundamental issues, you will probably be out of a job. It's an unwritten rule, and it's not just the big companies.

Tom continued, "Group activity gets in the way of innovation. Suffering stifles innovation. When you are used to a certain inefficient situation, and you believe it's necessary not to complain, you forget how to notice inefficiency. The part of your brain that might look for solutions goes to sleep. A lot of innovation is based on making ordinary products or processes work better. You have to be ready to change the system—and you do not do that in Korea. If you try, you'll be considered to be against the group, and you'll be severely punished. I understand that there are situations and industries where too much questioning can lead to chaos; and in any business, there has to be a balance. You can't have everyone wanting to change whatever they don't like or understand. But that's not what I'm talking about. I'm talking about a fundamental fear of rocking the boat, of standing out as the person who says: it can be done better."

REPORTING

When we were asked to create a detailed report for a project we had just finished for a Korean company, I was a little puzzled. We had never been asked to make such a report by any client before. In the West, it's not customary for creative companies to describe and justify their work in massive detail in a reporting format. Creating this type of report can take as much time as doing the actual work. Then I learned that this is required practice in Korean companies. So I started asking some of my interviewees about their thoughts on this reporting system.

Jeric Park says, "The most challenging thing working with Korean companies is inefficiency. Let's say I'm working for a German company, and I say, 'Here is a ninety-page report.' They will say, 'Oh, that's too long. Can you summarize it in thirty pages? You are the expert. We trust you. You don't need to prove anything to us. Just give us a summary.' In Korea, it's different. The youngest employee will start breathing down my neck. Then, if I give them a ninety-page report, they will say, 'It should be 300 pages.'"

Sometimes when the report is submitted to the boss with a recommendation for the best path to take, the boss wants other options to be included so he can compare them and see the evidence leading to the conclusion that this is the best decision. The problem is that when the employee who created the report has already found the best option for the project, now he/she has to spend several hours or days coming up with other options just so the boss can justify his decision, in case the best recommendation fails. The boss doesn't trust the worker to do the job right, and as a result, time is wasted, and frustration mounts.

Reporting doesn't only happen at the end of a project. It is part of daily life in a Korean company—whenever a senior person wants to know what's going on in a certain area, he asks for a report rather than simply talking to the people who've been working on it.

Ron Ezsak, a software industry veteran, used to consult for Korean companies. His take on the reporting issue is, "If a senior executive were able to talk to any employee, he would learn all the things about the business he should know, not what the sanitized reports tell him. Massive reports are a way for low-level people to demonstrate their competence and depth. They exhaust all their resources and produce an absolute mountain of data. So it proves that they are working. But, as I told them, 'All these things are great, but it's the worst possible place to start because if your answer is buried in there somewhere, [the reader] has to go through all of it and hope that [he/she] doesn't miss it. You are much better off summarizing what the data provides, making that actionable and then referencing the data that supports it for anyone who wants to investigate it further.'"

I mentioned to Ron that I was told that one of the reasons for the reports is for the benefit of people who come after them on a certain project or area of the business. They can learn from the reports.

Ron answered, "Business is not static. Reports from six months ago don't tell you about today. If someone has to learn part of the business, the reports might be useful, but if someone is operating in the business, I don't think it's helpful. That's my opinion. I think large, detailed reports are there to prove that someone can produce large, data-rich reports. In fact, the more details that are in the report, the less actionable the report is. In other words, a twenty-page report really should be just one page. It should say, the data says this; we should do that. If anyone wants to go to the data and prove that's correct, here is the data. That's why businesses now have graphs and business intelligence dashboards that say: this is up; this is down. This is good; this is bad. You can act on that."

It's hard to believe, but Koreans have been listed as having the worst productivity in the OECD. Michael Kocken, former Global Human Resources Officer of Donghwa Holdings, wrote an article giving seven reasons why Korean workers are not productive. This is what he wrote on reporting. "During my time at a Korean company, one of the observations that I made was that co-workers would spend two to three days adding in an array of fancy-looking shapes, images, flow charts, and graphs to a PowerPoint presentation that contained roughly half a day of research. That is the power of perception in the Korean office, and it forces workers to spend ridiculous amounts of time 'beautifying' simple reports that would take 10 minutes to present in an informal meeting or chat." [102]

SHARP STONES GET HAMMERED FLAT

We might be sitting next to the future Steve Jobs, but we would never know it because he is young, and we don't want him to shine. We don't respect younger people. We don't respect new people. They have to pay their dues. They have to suffer. That's our culture.

Hyunjin Kim worked for eight years as a project manager in Seoul for big corporations before coming to Chicago in 2015 to continue her education at Northwestern University. "You can't be smarter than your boss. If your boss thinks you are smarter than him, and you stand out, all the bosses are going to spot you as a threat, one who might take their place, and eventually they will make you quit. So if you want to keep your job, you have to make sure not to stand out. You need to do just okay work and make sure you keep your boss happy."

Incompetent employees aren't easily fired. They may get a salary freeze, be transferred or demoted, but to be fired is unlikely. Many of them stay on as long as they can at their same position, often because they feel they have no other choice. Meanwhile, young, capable employees need to move ahead, but the positions don't open up.

Major corporations like Samsung, LG, and Hyundai are very competitive. These young and brilliant people work so hard to get hired by these companies, but once they start working there, they soon find out that some of their bosses are not very confident or capable. Sung H. Kim* works at Samsung Corp. To not stand out, he pretends he doesn't know things. To have any chance of promotion, you need your boss' recommendation. Of course, this is the case at any company. And in any country, personal relationships matter. What is more pronounced in Korea is that the way of getting that recommendation is not by doing your best work but by making sure your boss likes you. In America, that might mean that your boss thinks you are a decent person, courteous, reliable, considerate of others—someone most people would be comfortable working with—but the relationship usually isn't very personal. It won't translate into social life outside the office. In Korea, on the other hand, it doesn't matter how much you don't like drinking, if your boss likes it and wants to go out every night, you need to go with him whenever you are asked if you want to get that promotion.

Many employees consider leaving these companies within one to two years. Some search for foreign companies in Korea to work for but many decide to stay at the Korean companies if they are able to endure it. Why? Because the Korean companies pay better salaries. Hyunjin worked at a Korean company for five years and a Korean Canadian-owned company for three years. The contrast of working environments in these two companies was like night and day.

In the Canadian-owned company, an employee is promoted by his or her capabilities, regardless of age, but in Korean companies, it doesn't matter how someone excels at his/her job; promotion is uncertain and slow. Here is an example of what was said during a work evaluation with a young employee who deserved a promotion.

Evaluator: "You are more talented and a much better worker, but Shin has a family and is older than you. So let's promote Shin this time."

Lisa Oh echoed Hyunjin's experience. "They cut out all the people with super talents because they think they are threats to the existing authority and hierarchy system. Young people leave the company because they want to work efficiently and in the most productive way, but the company doesn't allow it. When you start at a Korean corporation, you go in as a smart person, but working there for many years, you gradually become dumb. In the meetings, generally nobody speaks up or disagrees. You don't question seniors' decisions. Korean companies don't want efficiency; they prefer harmony. They don't want individual stars. That's why really smart workers leave the company."

Ron says, "I have seen very talented people turn into statues because a senior executive was nearby. This inhibits creativity. Very talented people are artificially suppressed. It's an encumbrance. The way Asian kids are brought up—to make a generalization—reverence for elders and being reserved are considered desirable. What that translates to in business is they don't speak up about frustrations at work. They are trained to accept it, make the best of it, ignore it, and move on."

Imagine you are on a team competing with another team. One team, the A team, utilizes everyone's best ideas and has the fewest decision-making layers. On the B team, a few senior people decide what the best ideas are from reports that went through multiple edits, being massaged and sanitized. If you're on the B team, you are surrounded by coworkers who are maybe politically savvy, but are either not talented in other ways or are people who have learned to use their talents very cautiously. The A team, on the other hand, is encouraged to use all of their talents. Which team do you think would come up with more innovative and better results and continue on that path in the future? Not only that; which team would you like to work for?

Do you want a team where you are challenged, stimulated, and excited at the workplace? Or a team that ties you down because you are young, where the only way to express your ideas is by knowing the right person or by making the right person like you (which can take a lot of energy and time)?

I think it's fairly obvious which team most of us would like to work on and would thrive.

PROS AND CONS OF TOP-DOWN STRUCTURE

Dave Hazzan told me, "Communication is a huge problem anywhere in Korea. You can't say anything to your boss. You can't run a company that way. The top-down approach doesn't work." Obviously, it has worked for Korea so far. We all acknowledge the new Korean economic power was achieved through sheer hard work, pure tenacity. But now it's about working smarter. Working fewer hours and getting more done. You don't have to be working long hours to make up for the inefficiency. Hazzan also reminds us about the public relations problem. "Attempts at branding are very poor—like the poor videos promoting tourism. It's probably [the fault of] old Korean men at the top making decisions. The hierarchy system stifles innovation. Koreans do so well when they move to other places."

Hazzan and the others I spoke to made good points about the downsides of the hierarchical organizational structure: inefficiency, waste, delay in the approval process, lack of collaboration, and lack of innovation. But I was still thinking about Korean successes when I asked Thomas Kim, "How do we have the number one technology company in the world with such an inefficient system in place?"

He remarked that democracy has never been the most efficient form of government. Many ancient and modern thinkers address this tradeoff:

the messiness and accountability of democracy versus the speed and efficiency of autocracy. He said, "In Korea, some companies are really effective. It can be inefficient when they have someone incompetent in charge, but when they have someone good, it is impressive how quickly they get work done. And how they move as a unit. They can move in the wrong direction, but when the direction is right, I don't know that many companies in America that can move like Samsung does."

So, as in many areas in life, there is not one right answer, but it is important to ask the questions, and specifically to ask the questions that matter to YOU. What kind of work structure will work for what you need or will play to your talents? This is a question not only for individuals but for companies and countries.

I came across an employee review of a design company with a flat structure that speaks to the pros and cons of a democratic work environment.

"Pros: I've been at ABS* for about one year now. The people I work with on a day-to-day basis are some of the smartest and nicest people. I'm able to collaborate with a wide range of folks—from younger talent all the way up to executive leadership.

Cons: Because it's such a collaborative space and people are so passionate, sometimes you have a lot of opinions. It can cause work to slow down, but it's all coming from a good place."

In a patriarchal/hierarchal organization, subordinates always defer to their superiors. Confucius' teaching is that the subordinate owes obedience and honor to his superior. This begins in the home, where the father is the absolute ruler. In Korean history, the rule of the father echoed

265

the rule of the chief and, later, the king. Today, we don't have a king, but we still have fathers and bosses. Also, military service is mandatory and the army is anything but democratic. Future corporate leaders learn to reemphasize that culture during their service, and it may not serve them well in world business. Add to this the Korean focus on relationship—which I discuss below—and the practice of blind obedience based on status can lead to everything taking on a personal tone.

Jeric Park says, "I'm not concerned about the formality. I'm concerned about the result. I'm concerned about what is right and wrong. I don't humiliate people. I criticize ideas but never people. In Korea, when you criticize people's ideas, they think you are criticizing them. We need to distinguish between critiquing the work and criticizing the person." As hard as it sounds, this is another important part of being professional.

I asked Jason Fried, "What do you think about young employees not being allowed to speak in front of seniors at work?

"I think it's important for anybody who has an idea to be able to share with anybody else. So the Korean or Asian model wouldn't be my preferred one. I understand where it came from, and I think it's probably changing. It's an extremely traditional setup. Ultimately, you are doing yourself a disservice if you only allow ideas to come from a couple of people instead of from anybody. Anyone at Basecamp who has questions about what we're doing or has a suggestion, idea or disagreement, can talk to me, David (Hansson, Jason's business partner and creator of Ruby on Rails.) or anybody else about it anytime. There is no hierarchy. It doesn't make sense to talk to me if the fridge is broken. There's someone better to talk about that, obviously. But if it's an idea for the business or a concept or something that we should be considering, I'm all yours."

Jason's company is an unconventional off-site/on-site work arrangement with new ways of looking at collaboration and productivity. Jason and David have published several books on these subjects. They have fifty employees, thirty-six of them working off-site in thirty-two different cities around the world, and fourteen people working on-site in the Chicago office. I visited his brand-new office some time ago. It's a beautiful modern, open office where he has a desk that's the same as everyone else's. I asked how the open office structure was working out. "We have an open office, but we also have private rooms where you can go when you need privacy. If you don't have that, it doesn't work very well. A lot of open office situations are pretty bad because people are very distracted. They find it very hard to focus, hard to think, hard not to be bothered by somebody else. So I think it's typically a really bad setup, but if you do have private rooms or private spaces where people can go when they need to, then I think it works great. I like the combination of open and closed."[103]

There is no doubt that this new idea of young people speaking up will meet with strong resistance from the older generation at many companies. One day you wake up, and someone tells you that the things you were taught and believed were right all your life have to change—that has to be a huge shock, beyond confusing, and very upsetting for many people, especially those who hold an upper-level position.

The necessary core changes in the current system are not about disrespecting or disobeying superiors. It's not about young people showing off their talents or intelligence. It's about collaborating, everyone working smarter, more efficiently together, and giving opportunities to young people who can contribute in much bigger and impactful ways under experienced and capable leaders. Wouldn't it be thrilling to work at a place where you could express your opinions and ideas freely, where your talents were supported and encouraged? How fulfilling would it be to see your hard work and efforts recognized without your superior getting upset or feeling threatened? We need everyone and anyone participating in innovation. Creating an environment where young and old can open up and exchange ideas and be creative—that sounds invigorating and energizing to me. Any other way just holds us back from moving forward and being competitive in this forever changing, fast-paced global marketplace.

I learn a lot from different people just in general daily life. Everyone has different experiences and different stories; they have information I don't have. Good ideas can come from anywhere. When creative minds are confined and oppressed in a rigid, structured environment, eventually they end up feeling like robots with a severely diminished ability to think beyond their immediate tasks and needs.

RELATIONSHIP. RELATIONSHIP. RELATIONSHIP.

> *One of the great problems of our age is that we are governed by people who care more about feelings than they do about thoughts and ideas.*[104]

–MARGARET THATCHER

Western principles emphasize individual choice and rights while Confucian principles emphasize the good of the group or community over the rights of the individual. When you are used to working in a rules-based system, as in the West, it's hard to understand the relationship-based work culture. Good working relationships are required at any workplace. But relationships solely based on connection, gift, and favoritism, can be experienced as corrupt, inefficient, or unfair. [105]

George Harrison* shared his experiences and observations working at one of the major corporations in Korea for several years. "Korean business culture is strongly relationship-driven. This is not necessarily bad, but if you're talking about global business, it's a problem. For example, in the 1990s, Samsung was the best company in Korea. At the time, people at Samsung thought the only thing that mattered was that they were the best in Korea. People around them respected them. That's all that mattered. Making everyone around you happy is what's important. That's why, for the Koreans, certain rules and regulations, laws, and global business practices are not actually important. That's why innovation is so difficult. The goal is not to innovate; the goal is to satisfy the relationship. You want to make your boss happy; you want to satisfy that relationship with the boss. You know *noonchi* [a Korean concept signifying the subtle art and ability to listen and gauge others' mood] is very important.

"One way to impress people around you is working very hard, long hours… Koreans work very hard in a group context where everyone is working together. That's their motivation. Koreans don't need to know why they are doing something. They just need to know they are all doing it.

"Koreans are extremely smart, extremely capable people—and I'm not just saying that to be polite—but their cognitive capacity is almost completely devoted to other people. Everybody is thinking of other people. Noonchi on steroids."

WORKING HARD?

Lisa Oh is a competent, intelligent, and decisive person. I asked her, "People say Koreans are the hardest-working people on earth. What do you think?"

She said, "What does working hard mean? Based on my experience, spending the most time at work is 'working hard.' I don't know; maybe

I only worked at bad companies. The way I work, if it's something I can finish in two hours, I finish it in two hours. The others work leisurely. A meeting may start at eight-thirty a.m. and last two or three hours, while it could have been over in thirty minutes. After six p.m., overtime pay starts. The work an employee could've finished during the day, he purposely doesn't do. He stretches it out to the evening. Then the worker goes to a dinner that the company pays for. He returns to work and goes to sleep. In the morning, he tells his boss, 'I worked all night.' There are so many people who do this. Higher-ranking people do this more often.

"There are many university professors who don't work hard either. They arrive to class thirty minutes late, or they arrive on time, then say, 'Oh, I forgot to bring something' and go to their office and back, which normally takes thirty minutes. They don't respect students' time. People who have been earning money this way don't want things to change. They are unhappy when they have a co-worker who is a female, (really) hard-working, who doesn't work overnight, doesn't go to the spa, yet her work result is so much higher."

Jungah Kim* says that on her team, once a person reaches a certain high position, he hardly does any work. The actual work is done by the lower-ranking employees. Her team had eight managers doing almost nothing, with two workers doing the actual work. It appears that the cultural norm is "I have paid my dues, and now it's time to coast."

Jeric Park adds, "There's a difference between the people who spend the most hours at work and the hardest-working people. I ran a design center for eight years in Korea. I had about forty-five employees, engineers, designers, colorists, UX, research. Koreans are much more passive. It's not like in the U.S. where people come to work even when nobody's watching. If you are an early bird, you come to work at seven a.m. You work through lunch, eating a turkey sandwich, then you go home around four p.m. or five p.m. You look after your kids. You get back to your email again, then you go to sleep. It's not like that in Korea. People have to be watched. That's how they grow up. Koreans spend a lot of time at work, but Americans are much more efficient in terms of outcome and productivity. "

THE PETER PRINCIPLE

> *In a hierarchy, every employee tends to rise to his level of incompetence.*
>
> - LAURENCE J. PETER

The Peter Principle refers to an observation about hierarchical structure described in the 1969 book *The Peter Principle* by Laurence Peter. The idea is that when you are good at something, you are awarded a promotion. You may not be good at the job to which you are promoted (management, usually). But once you have the job, it is unlikely you will be demoted; people just work around you. So, who gets the work done? People who haven't yet reached their level of incompetence. This makes it harder for people on the lower levels. If you are a bad manager, you just create extra work for subordinates by not organizing or planning properly, not getting resources in place. Things have to be done hastily at the last minute. It's not so great for the promoted person either. David Burkus, author of several books on leadership, innovation, and strategy, wrote, "Newly promoted team members often find themselves over-extended and their performance suffers. Moreover, when the new workload calls for managing projects instead of contributing to them, the newly promoted spend less and less time working on tasks that drew them to the firm in the first place…The Peter Principle is more than just a satirical comment on large bureaucracies or a strange organizational phenomenon. It's a symptom of a culture that overvalues titles and undervalues being connected to the work you're best at."[106]

Ron downplays the importance of the Peter Principle. "It's not that I disagree with it, but people don't become incompetent on their own. I think some organizations let people run as far as they can. When they can't run any further, they begin to dispose of them; they put them back down somewhere. They can play, but they won't get hurt. I think the best organizations help people grow personally and professionally into additional levels of competency."

Peter's book was written about American companies, and as we have explored in this chapter, Korean companies function differently. Yet my sense is that the Peter Principle still applies, though it may take different forms in different cultures. What interests me most is how this situation can be avoided.

"Not only should your organization understand the basics of training and development, but you must integrate it with the company's talent practices (career progression and leadership) and also create a culture of learning," said Josh Bersin, corporate HR analyzer, talent management and leadership, in a *Forbes* article. "As Peter Senge and many others have uncovered, a learning culture is perhaps the most important asset a company can build."[107]

Bersin's team found the most important elements of capability building to be "creating a management culture that's open to mistakes, building trust, giving people time to reflect, and creating a value system around learning."

I second the hiring criteria of Michelle Lee, Editor in Chief, *Allure* magazine.

"I like hiring people who have a love of learning. It all boils down to attitude: Are you someone who's cool with maintaining the status quo, or are you someone who wants to grow and will keep pushing? Second, there are no divas allowed. I want direct, opinionated people who will speak their minds freely, but collaboration and creativity can be crushed easily when there's someone on the team who's toxic and just wants to cause drama. No, thank you. Other qualities I value: being an outside-the-box thinker (it's okay to be a little weird—I'm into it), having references say that you're both hardworking and easy to work with, and having the ability to and interest in wearing multiple hats without getting too stressed out."[108]

Every individual has a different energy level and energy tends to fade as one gets older. The more curious you are, however, the more desire you have to learn continuously and inspire/teach others along the way. If you are like this, there are fewer chances then of becoming one of the Peter Principle's incompetent employees, no matter how old you grow. The company you work for may not be alert to this problem, but you can be. More than that, you can choose to turn down a promotion, if it is not to a position where you will thrive. You can discuss with your employer other ways your success can be rewarded and expanded—perhaps a lateral move or a redesign of your job title and duties so that you do more, instead of less, of what you are best at.

HIERARCHICAL CULTURE CAN BE DEADLY

Our rigid, hierarchical culture was the reason for losing on the soccer field and for hundreds of people being killed in plane crashes in the late 90s.

Malcolm Gladwell is the author of *Outliers: The Story of Success.* One of the book chapters is titled "The Ethnic Theory of Plane Crashes." Gladwell spoke to CNN money in 2008. "Korean Air had more plane crashes than almost any other airline in the world for a period at the end of the 1990s. When we think of airline crashes, we think, 'Oh, they must have had old planes. They must have had badly trained pilots.' No. What they were struggling with was a cultural legacy, that Korean culture is hierarchical. You are obliged to be deferential toward your elders and superiors in a way that would be unimaginable in the U.S."[109]

A *New York Times* article claimed, "According to an investigation by a team of Delta executives in 1999, many of Korean Air's woes were rooted in the airline's rapid expansion in the 1980s, when pressure to hire pilots quickly brought in many with minimal qualifications. Making matters worse, most of its pilots were Korean Air Force veterans with a strong authoritarian streak. Senior pilots tended to ignore warnings or advice from copilots, especially those who had been their subordinates in the air force, and junior pilots were discouraged from speaking up. The harm done by this dynamic was made clear in a 1997 crash in Guam that killed 228 people. An inquiry found that the co-pilot had failed to warn the pilot that the plane was descending onto a ridge as it approached the airport."[110]

The United States Department of Defense banned its employees from flying on Korean Air planes. South Korean air safety was rated in a lower category. Neither Korean Air nor its smaller rival, Asiana, could expand service to the United States or share codes with American carriers.

Korean Air hired David Greenberg, a retired Delta Air Lines vice president, to save the airline. He instituted American training and testing standards, far more exacting than what the 1,700 Korean Air pilots were used to, and demanded changes in the "cockpit culture."[111]

"On the ground, Mr. Greenberg began basing promotions and transfers in the company's ranks on merit rather than connections and friendships."

"What's necessary is to keep the focus, keep the concentration, whether times are good or bad," Mr. Greenberg said. "It takes years to build recognition, and one slip can destroy that. There's this tendency to become complacent, to say, 'We've perfected this thing, let's coast.'"

One way to prevent 'coasting' is to break up patterns and assumptions, especially those that have to do with hierarchy. For example, some Korean Americans make a strategic decision about which language to use to get the best results when working in Korea.

"When I go to Korea for business meetings, I don't speak any Korean. Because if I speak Korean, if I *insa* (Korean greeting), now we are going to relate on their terms; and on their terms, I'm a child. They are right. I'm wrong. But if we speak English, if they look at me as American, now we are communicating on my terms. There is no honorific language." Thomas Kim took this approach after learning about the reasons for the Korean Airline crashes. "They would speak indirectly, using honorific terms, saying, 'It appears as if we are approaching....' as opposed to 'What are you doing!?' and taking over. So the prescription was that Korean-based airlines cannot use Korean in the cockpit. They have to speak English."

Vicki Lee, who worked as a consultant for Deloitte consulting firm in LA, made a conscious choice that she is only going to speak in English when she is working with Korean clients. If she speaks in Korean, then they will treat her within their hierarchy. She says that she would feel so burdened that she thinks she couldn't do the work.

The first non-Korean president of Hyundai-Kia Motor Group, Peter Schreyer, a German automobile designer known for the design of Audi TT, talks about his young designers in an interview with *Car and Driver*, an American automotive enthusiast magazine.[112]

In response to C/D's question on how hands-on designer he is, he speaks to how unimportant the hierarchy is when he is working as a designer with people. "You cannot do it by [issuing an] order." He goes to the models and has direct dialogues with the designers showing and guiding them on what he wants and doesn't want, not as the executive to keep them in line but as a designer sharing his vision and directing the course.

He tries to spend as much time as possible in Seoul. He felt he needed to make the effort to meet more people within Hyundai and Kia, because due to the hierarchical workplace culture, young employees found it difficult to approach seniors if they were not their direct superiors. "Having a glass of wine and talking with them whenever I could was my way of reaching out," Schreyer said. To fellow and younger designers, Schreyer's message was never to be afraid to take on challenges because, without them, it's impossible to achieve anything.

In a Q&A with *The Wall Street Journal*, Schreyer was asked about his new responsibilities as the first foreign president.

"It's mainly in design. People think, 'Oh, now that he's president, he's got to go to this meeting or that meeting,' but it's not so much the case… Design is in the middle of all developments – marketing, IT, finance. It's connected to all those places…I have a growing influence on the culture of the company and the design teams. I think there is also maybe a different understanding of hierarchy and how to express opinions here than there is in Europe. The door is open to anybody to come to me if there is something they'd like to know or if there is another opinion."[113]

Don't push growth, remove the factors limiting growth.

– PETER SENGE, *THE FIFTH DISCIPLINE.*

We may not see the urgency of reviewing and restructuring the existing top-down system in our organizations. But as Ron explained, "[There is a growing] opportunity for talented young people who aspire to do great things in business, whether domestically or internationally, with less constraint by the hierarchical culture" The truth is we simply do business differently. We certainly can continue with how things are now. But how about looking at the loss of billions of dollars from the years of inefficient work routines and habits? What about the wasted talents of unfulfilled employees who could have been contributing to the company and the world? What we have lost—and are still losing—is beyond price.

EMPOWERMENT AT WORK

Ron continued, "They play the game and follow the rules. Drinking, working late, just being part of the team. Hong Kong, Japan, Taipei, they are all the same. They work a little differently now. I think what has changed is empowerment. In business cultures where middle-level people are not empowered, they're very stressed. They put in long hours. They are on the train going home at midnight, after drinks and everything else. But when they are empowered, when they are allowed to innovate, they don't do that as much. You see that all over the world where the new model of working is more about what you can create than what you produce. The technology industry has done a lot to expand that. It's true in many parts of the auto industry as well, in many parts of the world. People are empowered to solve problems or create opportunities where before they were glorified clerks."

When I was thinking the problem lay in the organizational system, Ron directed me to see it from another perspective. He pointed out that the system is not the problem. The problem is how the system is implemented. The boss may be the most important person, but everyone else can't be there just to serve the boss. That's a lack of leadership. Good leaders manage goals while they lead people. They support the success of all those people who work for them. It's a very different exercise requiring a very different approach. When people in an organization share a common appreciation for the goal, there tends to be more job satisfaction, more enthusiasm and more motivation.

Ron explains the main reason why you must extend the opportunity to take risks when you allow an emerging level of empowerment. Because if they don't want to take any risks, if they only want to be safe, what does that do? People will take the least innovative way. It suppresses the very thing that creates a competitive advantage. Ron is a big fan of Peter Senge who has written extensively on the concept of creating a durable competitive advantage. "It's not always safe. You want to be safe as it relates to your clients or customers' tolerance for challenges. You want to be safe as it relates to understanding what the market's tolerance for risk and challenge is. But inside your organization where things are reasonably contained, where you have the opportunity to control things, that's where risk should be embraced."

Jason Fried talks about the way he empowers his employees. "We pretty much give everybody a lot of autonomy to run their work however they want to run it. Which means we might tell them this sort of thing needs to get done, but however you decide to do it, however you want to implement it, is fine. It's largely up to them. The longer they've been here and the more success they have had, the more freedom they get. So I'm a big believer in empowerment." He starts everybody at fifty percent of his trust and as they do better and better things, they get more trust and more freedom and more leeway to do things on their own without having to be directed. So people start in the middle, and they can either earn more freedom or they can lose a little bit if they try to do a few things on their own that don't pan out. Maybe they need more help doing some stuff for a while. Maybe then they can learn again and then they can do better. He thinks the important thing is to give people a little leeway, give them autonomy and let them prove to you they are capable of handling things on their own. Then they get more and more opportunities to do stuff. So, everyone has an opportunity to get there. They just have to show Jason and his partner, David Hansson, a few times so they can see what they are really capable of doing.

Thinking about what Thomas Kim said about democracy in relation to hierarchical structures, I asked Ron, "You would imagine people work more efficiently in a company with a flatter structure?"

He talked about the military comparison and how in the army, the objective is clear and it is broken down into clearly defined tasks. Except at the very top, where generals discuss strategy, there is no innovation desired or accepted. Companies with clear objectives can also work that way. But most companies today need to be more open and aware of changing market forces, changing demands, and their greatest resource is the minds and imaginations of their employees.

"So often in these large companies, the answers are hiding in plain sight, but because [the bosses] are looking for what they want, not what they need, they don't become visible…

[The companies] find themselves in those situations where you create multiple versions of the truth, and that's the problem. Everything becomes sanitized."

He thinks flat or metrics-based organizational structures can be very effective for certain things. Some types of organizations in certain industry segments thrive because their structure is organized in a flat and metrics-based way, with shared resources, shared services, etc. There are not a lot of layers of insulation or leadership. A lot of companies do very well like that, but the current hierarchy is the patriarchy of Korean business organization. Culturally, there's an emphasis on respect: you honor the elder members of your family. Of course if it's a family business that turns into a business culture—and all the large Korean multinationals began as a family business at one point—then your respect for your elders and the family directly translates into those who are seniors in the business getting the same kind of respect.

"So you can't just say, 'Hey! Let's pull this thread and unwind the garment all at once.' But what you can do is you can have some organizations within the hierarchy go flat where they need to move fast, where they need to find or create something innovative, where they need to remedy problems quickly. The kind of things where people with different perspectives and different skills come together and collaborate to address something in the rapid environment. So then, within the hierarchy, you can have flat structures. Then, after a while, you might see a transformation. More organizations will transition because it can be more effective."

Sun: "Basically, start small and experiment."
Ron: "You can't eat an elephant in one bite."

WILL IT CHANGE?

The changes seem to be coming whether we push back or resist, whether or not we agree on how or where they are coming from. "I think it's starting to change because countries are way more connected," Thomas Kim says. "For example, one of my friends works at Google interfacing with a Korean version of Google. People are getting a taste of some of the more

Western flattened work structures and meritocracies. The best ideas win, not the highest person. It is happening before people realize—oh, wow, I enjoy working in that kind of culture. So one thing I'm very hopeful about and that is happening more and more is that companies are going to Korea to poach talent from Korean companies because it's easy to do... You are selling quality of life—the idea that your job doesn't need to be miserable, that you can work with dignity and be respected."

I asked, "That's benefiting foreign companies, though, not Korean companies, isn't it?"

"To me, it's lesser of two evils. To see people working like they do and unhappy as they are? I care more about that changing than about Samsung doing well. People don't enjoy working there. I'm hearing a very different tone now. Maybe five years ago if you worked at Samsung, you were just really proud, and it was prestigious. Nowadays, people who worked at Samsung, they look back on it as a miserable time in their lives. So I feel like it is changing."

Our connected world makes it impossible for any country or company to remain in the past. It's more a question of how quickly it changes and how much it benefits—or costs—Korea. Brilliant young engineers and designers can go anywhere, and many might. Keeping these employees by offering careers in dynamic companies where employees are empowered and productive with working conditions comparable to what is in the global marketplace may be the crucial next step for Korean companies.

PROFESSIONALISM

While I was listening to all the interview recordings related to the workplace, it occurred to me that we lack professionalism in several aspects. The definition of professionalism is "the skill, good judgment, and polite behavior that is expected from a person who is trained to do a job well."

Showing professionalism is highly important, and not just for people in leadership positions. It directly relates to the company's reputation, morale and success. One of the key requirements of being professional is respecting everyone you are working with at all times. If you only show professional behavior to your bosses or clients and don't respect or display inappropriate behavior to your coworkers or your vendors, you won't gain sincere respect from them and have a supportive team on your side.

I was asked to be on a conference call with the Seoul office when we were working on a project for a Korean company. This project came through another agency that was facilitating the call.

The call was scheduled for eight p.m. Chicago time, which is ten a.m. Seoul time. I called the conference call number. The agency account manager and I were on the phone, but there was only silence on the Seoul office side. After a few minutes, I asked the account manager, "Are we still having the meeting or did the client forget that we are on the phone?" He said, "No, this is very typical." I was thinking, "Wow, this is pretty rude. Not being considerate of other people's time, especially in the middle of the evening... just because she is the client?"

Eventually, the client came to the phone. It had been maybe twenty minutes. I was expecting some kind of apology, but none came. The account manager introduced me, saying that we are working on the current project, and Sun is Korean also. And I said, "Hello!" in Korean. The next thing I heard sounded like a nose fart. The meeting was brief, and we were just confirming a few minor things. It was several years ago, but I still remember that call. I'm sure this was an isolated case, but I started to question people at different agencies about Korean professionalism. Here are some of the comments I received from American agency people working with Korean clients.

"They only want big names. It doesn't matter if the style fits the project. The name is the most important thing."

"They don't say what they mean at the meeting but later come back with insults or complete opposite feedback from what was given at the meeting."

"The initial stage is lack of trust. Preserving perception is most important to the senior people."

"Very demanding, inhumane at times. The manager had to go to a funeral, and the client demanded that he be at the meeting."

"Tons of emails, must be done, has to be perfect, very demanding, can be offensive."

"Putting instant blame on the agency even though it's their fault. They lack courage for truth."

"Korean people are raised in a specific way. They never question their bosses. Here, people can challenge authority."

"The marketing people had no experience, no marketing background or qualifications in marketing. They worked in engineering in the air-conditioning division. It's like I was teaching them Chinese or calculus."

"When you want feedback, instead, you get decisions. Decisions are made behind closed doors. No conversations, very different working process, limited dialog, spec changes without much feedback. It's very frustrating."

"We wished they were more straightforward. They were just too polite."

Some things that are considered unprofessional are asking personal questions or making presumptuous comments during interviews or meetings, not getting the maximum work result due to insufficient communications with your vendors, putting unqualified people on the job, and drinking to the point that it affects work performance. Being professional also means putting your personal feelings aside or not taking things personally, being open to receiving feedback without being emotional. It's about the work, not about you. Giving constructive feedback without blaming or attacking the people who are doing the work. Simply put, being professional means it's all about work—doing it well and respecting everyone while doing it.

CANDOR AND CLARITY

"In the 1980s, when I started to go to Korea, it was a clumsier place. People were aggressive and not very polished. People were angrier. There was a lot of stupid arguing," Ron said. "Now, Korean people have more confidence. They are still aggressive and assertive, yet a little more polished and refined. Confidence tends to do that. They have to keep wanting it. They have to commit to it. Traditional business culture exists everywhere in Asia. Candor and clarity must be present. Business executives in the U.S. demand candor and clarity. You go to large Korean meetings, and people don't speak their minds."

Clarity has to do with all the employees knowing what the goals of the organization are, what the short and long-term goals of their department are, and what is expected of them in particular. It sounds obvious, yet while some of it is clearly obvious to most employees, a lot isn't. Better products, higher profits—and getting that report out on time—yes, most people know that much. But Ron thinks that they may not be able to articulate how their work and the work of their colleagues contributes to the company's goals, what is more and less important, what are natural learning mistakes or problems that can be smoothed out and what are disasters. There is a great deal that could be said about this in terms of specifics, but these would be different for every company.

In any company or organization, some things need to be known only by a few people, and certainly, discretion is important in company-client and employee relationships. Yet in many companies, there's a lot of secrecy just for the sake of secrecy, to make people feel important, or to muddy the waters about whether goals are being advanced or not. The more people have a sense of what is expected of them and what the company hopes to achieve in a given year or given area, the better they can contribute and the better they can see what problems are developing. The idea is to move people away from thinking only of their own short-term security in an organization—how not to be criticized or have their pay reduced—and toward a vision where the long-term security of both employee and company are entwined.

To achieve this level of candor and clarity will be a huge cultural change for the Korean work environment. It's like trying to change the DNA of who we are. But once we start going in the new direction, there will be less confusion, less frustration, greater competence and higher productivity. Particularly when it comes to working with partners from around the world, with all the natural confusion that arises from cultural and language differences, candor and clarity are paramount. If you've ever found yourself in a strange country where you don't know the language, you will be aware of how candor and clarity help: candor in admitting to yourself and others what you don't understand; clarity about just what information you absolutely need to receive or impart, and in what order (how much is the bill; where do I pay; which direction is my hotel). With the tools of candor and clarity, you have reduced the problem to its smallest dimension, and you can go about trying to communicate further.

CONFUCIANISM AND CAPITALISM: NECESSARY CLASH?

As we look around our Korean society, we see tension and conflict everywhere at home and work. We are standing between two ideologies, Confucianism and Capitalism. Conformity, hierarchy, frugality, and group harmony are the core foundations of Confucian values. But the capitalist success that we are chasing depends on principles that go against many of these values. Our standards of success are capitalist ones: material abundance, improved lifestyle, profit. We emulate not only Western business practices but Western culture as a whole. People are studying abroad, traveling, emigrating and bringing new perspectives into Korean society. Tension and conflict are not surprising in this meeting and merging of cultures. What's coming next for Korea will be a blend of East and West—but what the exact proportions of that blend depend on the arguments, ambition, resistance and compromises that are now taking place.

Some people wonder: can these two ideologies coexist? Are we living in a society with too many contradictions?

Alfredo Park, partner at FITC, producer of design- and technology-focused events worldwide, thinks that this puts us in a good position.

"The fact that Neo-Confucianism and Christianity have coexisted together for the past 130-plus years is pretty amazing. There are more Christians now in Korea than any other religion, but they still have a very *Yugyo* (Confucian) way of thinking. And they also like to buy a Mercedes if they can. I don't think the identities are mutually exclusive. I think what you need to do is harness the good from these different perspectives and make it all work together."

CREATING LEADERS

Management is about arranging and telling. Leadership is about nurturing and enhancing.

—TOM PETERS, AMERICAN WRITER ON BUSINESS MANAGEMENT PRACTICES, AUTHOR OF *IN SEARCH OF EXCELLENCE.*

We have heard so much about making the bosses happy and how important relationships are in the workplace. I started to think about what kind of bosses we have in our organizations. What kind of leaders are we working for? Do we have good leaders? How easy or hard is it to become an effective leader in a rigid hierarchical organization?

Ron shares his take on what makes better leaders. "A very large technology services company out of India with twelve-hundred people, as brilliant as they are, with layer upon layer of PhDs and master's degrees, still didn't have real business acumen. It's something different in the U.S. The way we raise our kids, the way we teach our kids. We may not score the highest in math and science but we problem-solve much better. In consequence, we are better leaders. It is just because of the way we are taught to perceive things.

"In most emerging economies, the first thing they do is crank out talented and highly-skilled engineers. The mind of the engineer is linear, not abstract. Engineers are taught to disassemble things, evaluate each component, then reassemble it. Commerce isn't linear or direct. People are making decisions and evaluating risks. The ability to think abstractly and experience a variety of environments are what make you more effective. So those kinds of things matter as well as the cultural hierarchy and the reverence for seniors that is demanded in many Asian countries."

Sun: "Many people want to be in the leadership position, but how many of them are willing to be a bold leader?"

Ron responded, "First, you need to empower people; where that happens, leaders will emerge. Not everybody is going to be a leader. Not everyone is a leader, but everyone can be a manager. What's required in a manager is different than what's required in a leader. You can look at a group of teenage boys. Maybe they're playing soccer or something. Leaders emerge. They step forward on their own. The problem with a lot of organizations, particularly in East Asia, is that there is not an opportunity for those who have leadership qualities to step up. They appear later in their career because then they are at a point where they have enough autonomy to bring that forward. A lot of organizations will do much better if, in the lower ranks, those leaders emerge."

When I mentioned Ron's view to Thomas (that Western culture makes better leaders), he strongly rebutted it, citing Korea's dominance in Internet speed and connectivity, mobile devices and cost-efficient automobiles. "Korea and Koreans are world leaders. You can't dispute that. And what's even more amazing is that all this happened in the last thirty years. Korea is a force to be reckoned with. Now, when they say a leader—outspoken, talkative, extroverted, a person who commands attention—that type of person we have maybe not so many of, but that's not synonymous with leadership. Leadership is about results. I think Koreans are not as talkative. I would say Koreans tend to be more introverted.

"Koreans are more internal processors then external processors. External processors need to talk to sort their thoughts out. As they talk, it becomes clear to them. A lot of Korean people are not as much like that. And a big part of it is culture. You think by yourself. You use fewer words to say something more important. You use a lot of indirect communications and when there are older people in the room you defer to them. You're very conscious of what you are saying. You have to pay attention to social dynamics, and you have to use noonchi when you talk. In Western culture, there are no rules. I say whatever I think, but that has nothing to do with leadership.

"Leadership is about influence. One of the forms of influence is speaking. But speaking can be done in many different ways too. I think the Western thinking is that the more words you use, the more air time you take, the more weight you have in the room. I don't think that's always true. Sometimes just a few important words will make a difference. I think internal processors are more effective. In fact, they have done some studies. A larger percentage of Fortune 500 companies' CEOs are introverts, not extroverts. Their finding is that extroverted CEOs tend to be a little more egotistical and make the company about them and their pride. The introverted ones are very thoughtful. They don't need to have the last word… So the person who says Koreans are not leaders—I would challenge that person's understanding of leadership. Now, if they say we are quieter, I would agree with that."

Jason Fried describes the qualities of a good leader in a way that I think sums up the best of both Ron's and Thomas' arguments. It's not about style but substance.

"If everyone is thinking about what's next, the leadership should be thinking about what's next after that. You need to be able to step away from the work, let other people do it; otherwise, you become a micromanager. You need to inspire people to do great work. Good leaders I have run into are able to see things from different perspectives. They can step into someone else's shoes and see the situation in another way. They're not one-sided. They are multifaceted thinkers. And then honesty and integrity have to be there. If people don't trust you, they don't believe you. If you say something, and people don't believe it, then you're not a leader. I think that it is critical that you stand for what you say. You keep your word. Sometimes you are human, and you make mistakes, but when you say something, people believe you. That's very important."

In the end, it seems that we have been set up to be followers, at least in the early stages of our lives. We were raised and accustomed to suppressing ourselves as opposed to expressing ourselves. I think we Koreans are naturally aggressive people and resilient people. Look at Korean azummas. We survived our harsh history and that marked us for a while. But now we are more than just survivors. We are creating something different. We are working and playing on the global stage, and that is an adjustment. It's not surprising that it is taking time and that there are so many ideas about what is wrong, what is right and where to go next. We are disadvantaged in some areas because of some of the qualities that we were brought up with while other qualities have helped us leap ahead.

We have come this far with the tools of our traditional culture. Just imagine how far we can go when we let ourselves learn from the cultures around us, using what we have as a foundation, not a ceiling. Nobody can empower us—we must empower ourselves. We have our share of leaders and creative geniuses. We just need to learn to nurture them and let them emerge.

Work is not meant to be easy, and nobody gets up every morning wanting to do it, but it should be rewarding in more ways than just financially. Humanity could have stayed on the level of hunters and gatherers, working only for food, shelter, safety and reproduction, as animals do, but we were restless. We were curious. We kept inventing, experimenting and building more complex societies. Today there are thousands of kinds of work, each contributing to human welfare and each requiring a different set of skills and talents. It is an amazing tapestry, the world of work. I encourage everyone to be excited about finding his or her best place in it and to fight for the rights of everyone to think, express, create, and learn.

12

Design

I studied interior design and had been working in the field for two years when I met Carlos, who was at that time an art director at BBDO ad agency in Chicago. We used to go to Rizzoli, a bookstore in Chicago's Water Tower Place on Michigan Avenue. On every visit, Carlos would buy a full bag of books on graphic design, photography, and typography from all over the world, especially from Japan and England. He used to tell me how much he had been influenced by and admired the creative work coming from those countries.

We decided to get married two weeks after we met. We may be holding the record as the couple with the quickest path to marriage. To this day, we haven't met anyone who got engaged in a shorter time than we did. We married one year later and started the honeymoon stage of our lives. A few months into our peaceful daily life, Carlos came home from work and said, "I'm quitting the agency. Let's start our own design business!" I wasn't too excited about the projects I was working on at that time and my reliable intuition responded to him, saying, "Yes!"

Carlos handled the creative side, while I handled the business side. He already knew a lot of people from the Chicago agency world, and we started receiving one project after another, without much quiet time in between. I learned about graphic design and advertising. Carlos' work started to win awards and was published in design magazines and books around the world. We moved to a bigger studio and started hiring more designers. Carlos was invited to speak at design conferences around the world, especially in the U.S. and Europe. I traveled with him, introducing our company before Carlos started his presentation. Throughout the years, our studio's work has earned a lot of recognition, and we worked very hard to create the best design out there. I feel very blessed to be in the creative world and to be around so many people with so much talent and creativity.

There are upsides and downsides to the creative design business. For me, the upside is that we graphic designers can create visual images and words to help audiences understand, be interested in and attracted to a product, idea, service, or message. The job utilizes our intelligence and imagination, pushing our creative minds in all directions. It is exciting to be part of this process on each assignment, facing different challenges and delivering the final creations to meet the client's objective.

BAD DESIGN. BAD BUSINESS.

The downside is that once I started to develop an appreciation and eye for good design and realized its importance, I also started to notice and be bothered by the many bad designs surrounding us. One of these experiences happened with the Korean restaurants in the Chicago area. We go to Korean restaurants quite often. Dining out at Asian restaurants is one of my favorite things to do. I love Korean food, as well as Japanese food, Chinese seafood and Vietnamese food. I'm a foodie. I even have a food blog called savorychicks.com with three other friends from Bern, Switzerland, L. A., and San Diego. It's interesting to see how many restaurants come and go. While food is the most important part of a restaurant's appeal and sustainability, the atmosphere is critical as well. Of course restaurants with both elements are much more likely to succeed. While I am grateful that there are good Korean restaurants in Chicago, I dread going to these restaurants with my friends, who are mostly non-Koreans. Most Korean restaurants in Chicago have decor, bathrooms, or services that are way below what people are used to. I know that most of these mom-and-pop restaurants were opened by first-generation Korean Americans who don't have any concept of design. Why should they know? They were never exposed to what good design is. I probably wouldn't have known either if I wasn't in a creative industry. I tried to help one of the restaurants in our neighborhood, Bucktown, with my friend Valeria Cardoso. She is a very talented architect and was working at IDEO (one of the most innovative design consulting firms in the U.S.).

This place was called Akai Japanese restaurant and was owned by Jennifer and Paul, a middle-aged Korean husband and wife team. The restaurant was only a few blocks away from our house. It was quite large, and the main dining room was crowded with too many tables and chairs and decorated with many tacky items randomly placed. The atmosphere was such that when you walked into the room, you kind of felt like just turning around and walking out. I wanted to help. I felt so bad for the owners, who were sweet and good people. We offered to volunteer some time and effort to improve the ambience. We gave the owners advice on what they could remove and how to de-clutter the room. We spent a day with them at IKEA, getting some lighting fixtures to soften and enhance the atmosphere. But it was extremely hard to make them understand why their current design was bad for their business. They implemented some of the suggestions, but when I returned a few days later, they had put back some of the items that we had suggested that they remove. The place went out of business after struggling for a couple more years.

I have seen a few Korean restaurants go out of business even though they had good food. They had been my regular K-food destinations for many years, and I was disheartened to see them go.

Another example of a Korean business in Chicago that could hugely benefit from improved design—even though they are doing fine financially—is King Spa. Korean spas are a rarity in Chicago, unlike in L.A. King Spa opened in 2010 in a suburb close to Chicago's downtown. The main room looks like it was designed by our parents. The owners had other spas in other cities that were profitable, so they probably didn't see any point in investing money improving the atmosphere, even though they could surely afford it. Since the Korean bath/spa was a unique concept to Americans and there wasn't any competition, through Groupon promotions (a global e-commerce company, connecting subscribers with local merchants), King Spa started to become popular. As long as the business makes money, many owners don't care how their place looks. The truth is the places look good to the owners. They did their best and don't see the need for or importance of professional design. Design is a whole new concept to the older generation and many Koreans. What most first-generation Korean American business owners don't realize is that if you invest just a little more and think through the presentation of your business, your business will have a much higher probability of succeeding. This is true especially over time and if competition increases. Customers are greatly impacted by how your business looks and feels, and those feelings directly speak to your pocket.

WABI-SABI: ZEN PHILOSOPHY[114]

While every country can offer its own unique aesthetic to the world, the Japanese aesthetic stands out and has earned high esteem from designers around the world for many decades. The core principles are still relevant today, although many designers are not even aware of their existence.

So what are Japanese aesthetics—specifically Zen aesthetics? What makes them so inspiring?

"Wabi-sabi" refers to an aesthetic influenced and formed by Buddhism, which celebrates the beauty of things "imperfect, impermanent, and incomplete." There are seven design-related principles that govern the aesthetics of the Japanese garden and other Japanese art forms to achieve Wabi-sabi. These principles encompass more than just designs; they are equally applicable to life. Wabi-sabi is a philosophy and is seen in Japan as an integral part of one's inner and outer life— one's outlook as well as one's surroundings.

Kanso (簡素) Simplicity or elimination of clutter. Things are expressed in a plain, simple, natural manner. This reminds us to think not in terms of decoration but in terms of clarity, a kind of clarity that may be achieved through omission or exclusion of the non-essential.

Fukinsei (不均整) Asymmetry or irregularity. The idea of controlling balance in a composition via irregularity and asymmetry is a central tenet of the Zen aesthetic. The enso ("Zen circle") in brush painting, for example, is often drawn as an incomplete circle, symbolizing the imperfection that is part of existence. In graphic design, too, asymmetrical balance is a dynamic, beautiful thing. Try looking for (or creating) beauty in balanced asymmetry. Nature itself is full of beauty and harmonious relationships that are asymmetrical yet balanced. This is a dynamic beauty that attracts and engages.

Shibui/Shibumi (渋味) Beautiful by being understated, or by being precisely what it was meant to be and not elaborated upon. Direct and simple, without being flashy. Elegant simplicity, articulate brevity. The term is sometimes used today to describe something cool but beautifully minimalist, including technology and some consumer products. (Shibui literally means "bitter-tasting.")

Shizen (自然) Naturalness. Absence of pretense or artificiality, full, unforced creative intention. Ironically, the spontaneous nature of the Japanese garden that the viewer perceives is not accidental. This is a re- minder that design is not an accident, even when we are trying to create a natural-feeling environment. It is not raw nature as such but shaped nature that achieves the charm of the spontaneous without suffering from clutter or imbalance.

Yugen (幽玄) Suggestion rather than revelation. A Japanese garden, for example, can be said to be a collection of subtleties and symbolic elements. Photographers and designers can surely think of many ways to visually imply more by not showing the whole; that is, showing more by showing less.

Datsuzoku (脱俗) Freedom from habit or formula. Escape from daily routine or the ordinary. Unworldly. Transcending the convention- al. This principle describes the feeling of surprise and wonder when one realizes one can escape the conventional.

Seijaku (静寂) Tranquility or an energized calm (quiet), stillness, solitude. This is related to the feeling you may have when in a Japanese garden. The opposite feeling to the one expressed by seijaku would be noise and disturbance. How might we bring a feeling of "active calm" and stillness to feverish designs outside the Zen arts?

WHAT DOES HE DO FOR A LIVING?

When I first told my mom about Carlos, she asked me, "What does he do for a living?" I said, "He works in advertising. He is an art director and a graphic designer." She asked, "What is graphic design?" I answered, "He creates corporate identities, develops brands and creates promotional materials for companies, etc…." Mom said, "I don't understand…." Then I would say, "Mom, just remember, he is a designer."

Carlos tried to explain what he does to his parents for many years, but they have never quite understood. They are just proud and happy that he is doing well with his profession. His parents escaped Cuba in 1965 with three sons and settled in Miami. In the beginning, they worked two and sometimes three jobs to support their family.

Our parent's generation was busy putting food on the table. How certain things around them looked weren't that important. Since then, however, the value and contribution of design have been critical to the quality and enjoyment of our more affluent lives. The wealthier Korea became, the more aware we were and the more we preferred things that were innovative and well designed. This is especially true for the younger generation. Whether it's fashion design, graphic design, architecture, interior design, industrial design, product design, automotive design, packaging design, motion-graphic design, or textile design, design distinguishes and defines each decade and who we are as users of particular products. Most people look at products, choose which of many options to buy, use them and love them, but don't ever think that behind every product, there are designers who put countless hours, sweat, vision, and their own heart and soul into their creation.

DESIGN AND THE ECONOMY

Do people understand the importance of design in general? I guess not. Graphic design, for example, is another word for visual communication. When you look at posters, brochures, product packaging, movie posters, websites, or company logos, the design allows you to understand what things are and how they work, what they stand for, what they offer. You can relate, identify, be inspired, or entertained. Good design brings clarity and aesthetic pleasure. Bad design can create confusion, aesthetic depression, and indifference for the users and viewers.

I interviewed Joe Tan and Markus Diebel, well respected industrial designers in the U.S. They both came from Germany and started their careers at IDEO.

Joe always had an itch to start his own thing. Three years after being at IDEO, he co-founded a company called Incase, which has a big following in Korea. Incase designs and produces popular accessory products around the Apple platform. He sold the company after fifteen years and started a consulting firm, Moreless, having Google as one of their main clients.

Markus Diebel worked at IDEO for twelve years as a design director before joining Incase. They have been a team ever since. They both joined Apple in 2015. Together, Joe and Markus have designed and manufactured over 1,000 products.

I asked Markus about the importance of design.

"Design understands. Design bridges. Design fills the space between the user and the product. It invites you in and makes the product understandable. It makes the product emotionally valuable. It makes the product functional. It creates value around the product. Without design, this wouldn't exist. There wouldn't be a relationship between the consumer and the product. Only design can achieve that. Without design, there would be no brands, because products are the tangible manifestation of the brand. Without products, there would be no brand, without brands there would be no economy. So design is very important. Design is the touchpoint, the interface of the brand and their consumers. It is very important that these touchpoints be thought through. Completely thought through with passion, love and dedication. These people who call themselves designers, they have to understand the position that they are in. The designer is not only there to produce beautiful things. It's a responsible position. Products are here in this world and are supposed to be sustainable. They are supposed to have a certain value. They have a certain lifespan, and then they get dumped. What happens to these products afterwards? You have to be responsible for this. That's how I see it. We are making a good life and making beautiful products, and creating and helping people to understand the world better and making it more functional."

My friend Valeria, the architect of Brazilian origin with whom I tried to help the Korean restaurant owners, is married to Joe. I asked her, "How does design help human life?" She responded, "This is a big question I've been trying to answer for myself. I'm a person addicted to beauty. I want to know what is my value. Because I'm not doing projects that make a social impact. Not really affecting anything in the world. Sometimes I feel a little bit crappy about it. What is it that I can leave behind? What is my legacy? I have a fascination for beauty. There is a Brazilian architect who says, 'Beauty is for everyone. Beauty is democratic.' That's why he will build a beautiful building that is for poor and for rich. It's for everyone. So if my ability can bring to life a moment of contemplation, a moment of relaxation, a moment of beauty, that's sweet to me. If now I can bring that to families, if I can bring that to my work group.… I spent a whole year designing a workspace for people who work so hard. They didn't have any time for themselves. They didn't even have a space to sit and eat. They were sitting in front of a computer to eat. I wanted to give them a minute of sun, a minute of sitting in a nice place and looking at something beautiful. That could be a small little piece of happiness. I don't know yet. It doesn't really feel grand, but it is pure.

"In my life, every apartment I moved into, every crappy, cheap apartment, I tried to make beautiful. There is not a place that I moved into that I didn't make an effort to make beautiful. There's no price for that, and you can bring that sensation to anything.

"My son, Matteo, lies down with me and says, 'This house is so beautiful.' He is six years old. He has a very strong sense of aesthetics."

Joe and Valeria live in San Francisco where they have built my favorite house. I've seen lots of nice houses in my life, but theirs is something special. Valeria shared the intention and effort that went into building their house. My first question to her was where she gets her inspiration as an architect and a designer.

"From everything. I get it from people. I do so many intellectual things. I am not like a visual artist who can just come up with art on the canvas. I research a lot. I do really long interviews. I look at how people live. I look at the history of the neighborhood. I find a bunch of little pieces that are kind of like a puzzle. I find myself, as a designer, kind of orchestrating all these little pieces and putting them together. I don't ever feel that I come up with something completely fresh out of my own self. I piece things together. My projects are always for people, right? For someone. It's not like I'm doing a piece of art for myself. I've never been able to do that.

"Even for our house, Joe and I did a lot of research. A lot of sustainability research and a little bit for just us. This is a Victorian house. I didn't want to make it completely modern. I like the idea of an old house. It makes me sad when I go to a house where everything has been stripped away, and it's fully modern inside. So I wanted to bring the history back to this house. We did a lot of research on proportions, openings and moldings to bring some of the flavors back. Then, after that, the principle of the house is to-getherness. We wanted a house where people are together. We are together. So we created a kind of a big layout of opening and connecting. And then in terms of taste—how I grew up in Brazil, things are a little bit more rustic. We wanted the house to be warm, even though we wanted minimal and modern. So it's a little bit of me and a little bit of him. For the objects, I wanted something elegant, and I didn't want clutter. Also, we like white.

"It's an international design. You see a little bit of Brazil, Japan, a little bit of Europe. What I like about design is the things that have spoken to me in life. What's mine here is the ability to balance."

I asked her, "What did you learn at IDEO that you didn't know before?

"They taught me how to design for people. In architecture school, we are trained to design through our own lens of how we think things are. At IDEO I learned how to look at the simplicity of people, and that is huge. They don't teach that in school. Architecture is a very egocentric discipline. Nobody teaches you to be a channel. They teach you to have your own expression that sometimes can be very autocratic. It's all about authorship and control. At IDEO, design is all about people."

"What does it mean that it is all about people?"

"It means that maybe what I design for you is not exactly how I would have designed it for myself. It's the best of what I can do for you. It's very different. What I've designed at IDEO, if I didn't have this process behind me, probably I would have done completely differently. But they are in-sightful. They were tailoring design to the customer, and they were right. It is taking the ego out of design and filling that space with the person or people we are designing for. It is really an egoless process. Very beautiful."

A designer's job can be very powerful. People respond to good design instantly. It makes people's lives easier, better, even special. How serious of a responsibility is that? People want to surround themselves with well-designed things and places, whether they are clothes, houses, restaurants, products, or cars. It makes them feel good in many different ways. Design evokes strong emotions. We get excited around good designs, and we think about or remember things that we wouldn't otherwise. We are trans-ported, the way we are in beautiful landscapes. Certain visual proportions and relationships are just pleasing to the human brain and are connected to feelings of peace, safety, happiness, aliveness, and anticipation. Good design doesn't necessarily require lots of money spent on materials. It's more about the creativity of the maker. Any good designer could take the home of a poor person and make it more appealing without spending a dime. Money helps, of course, but the eye of the designer comes first.

COPY VS. ORIGINAL DESIGN

Quality is more important than quantity. One home run is much better than two doubles.

—STEVE JOBS

As I mentioned before, I discovered new Korea in 2008 when we did a proj-ect for a Korean company. After the presentation in Seoul, they invited us to have lunch, and several people from the project team came. During the casual talk while eating, I asked, "How come Korean car companies copy other existing car designs? It seems like all the Korean cars we see in the U.S. are comprised of a blend of design details, all mixed on the same vehicle, almost in an effort to capture the recognizable aspects of what makes a particular car unique. For example, I saw the trunk from a BMW, combined with the front headlights of a Mercedes Benz, together with the hood of a Jaguar." One person answered, "I think the idea is that making the design similar to what people are used to will generate familiarity and friendliness towards the product; therefore, people will be more welcoming to the similar design." I was very surprised by that answer. I wasn't expecting it, but it gave me insight into what might be one of Hyundai's reasons to take that direction. And no doubt, being a Korean person, he was trying to find a good excuse for the lack of originality for Hyundai.

I was kind of depressed about seeing copycat designs coming from my home country. I remember trying to ignore the fact that it bothered me. In the West, copying is looked down upon. A me-too product doesn't get respect as a brand. I remember having a moment of shock when I first saw a Hyundai car with this mixed design approach. Some people may not care as long as the price is right, but a lot more people react negatively to copied products. I was reading several blogs about this issue here in the U.S. Many people were flabbergasted by how similar the car designs were. People were questioning, "Is this legitimate and tolerated by the industry?" "Is this a case of convergent design, or is it outright copying?"

The main goal of Hyundai at that time was selling as many cars as possible—the goal of every company—but they missed the most important strategic mark: the brand image. When you put out a product in the world, even automobiles, where reliability and safety, engine power and gas mileage may be the most important metrics, design is crucial. It's the same with the clothes we wear. We care about the fabric, texture, color, and quality of the sewing, but the first thing we notice is the design of the clothes. Our fashion choices tell people how we see ourselves as individuals and in society (personality and status) and to some degree, what we value. The products we choose define us to others.

I asked Carlos, who is a car fanatic (he even has a car blog, cartype.com) what his impressions were when he first saw those cars.

"My first impression was that they were ugly. It was clear what they were doing, copying. But they were not even copying right. So they looked cheap. They were destroying the brand in every way. There was no character. They didn't put any value on themselves, so they took the cheap route. It just set a bad precedent for everything they do. If I see that they are copying the design, which is the most visible thing, then I jump to the conclusion that everything else is bad. If you are willing to show me something that's dismissing the value of creativity, brand position, obviously you are trying to cut corners in other areas. That doesn't make me want to buy a car from you."

Since then things have progressed for Hyundai in terms of quality and design. By 2012, Carlos was quite impressed with Hyundai and Kia cars. He started telling others about how much he likes some of the Korean cars, especially Kia Optima Turbo. "Things they are doing with the warranty offers, their designs, use of materials, feature sets, etc.... I haven't seen that quick of an advancement in the automotive industry in a long time."

SO WHY DO WE COPY?

If people have to choose between freedom or sandwiches, they will take sandwiches.

–Lord John Boyd Orr

In desperate times you don't think about the future, you think about today. Today it is cheaper and much easier to copy someone's product and make a living by selling it than to spend research and development time coming up with new products with their own design.

Valeria says, "You learn by copying. I think Korea is in the early stage of understanding design. In Brazil, we didn't have a strong culture of design either, so what we did with that is we tried to bring it from another culture that does it well. So it's kind of copying. Then you start to find your voice. Then you start to copy less.

"So for me, copying is not necessarily a bad thing but more like the early stage of learning. I feel that, at some point, if you keep practicing and practicing, you can close the books and start doing your own thing. But I think that comes with maturity. In a way, it's a process. Copying is a tool to start."

Joe shares his thoughts on this subject. "Why is it important to innovate? It's basically to be ahead of the game. When you copy something, you are already two steps behind. You may be able to replicate something really well, and maybe that's awesome, but you are already behind the market because, by the time you copy something, your competitor is already on to the next or next-next product, so you are not only a step behind, you are two steps behind. So by the time you come out, you make a wrap, maybe you get a little bit of market share, maybe your product is cheaper, but it's never original. Over time, over the long term, you don't gain the trust of the customers who care about originality or care about a really high-quality product."

Inger Klixbull, Group Creative Director at Ogilvy & Mather Chicago, says, "When you look at a copied product, it doesn't give you that Wow! It doesn't give you the smart insight. You don't fall in love with it in the same way. You fall in love with something that really entertains you, enlightens you, makes you look at things in a different way. I think that's what great design can do. Good designs have good ideas behind them. Good design is way more than just making things pretty." She adds, "Original ideas move us forward. If we kept copying, mankind wouldn't be where we are today. When you take one idea and combine it with something else, you make something new. That's the way the world works. That makes us move forward. In order to keep progressing, you have to come up with new ideas."

RISK AND INNOVATION

If I had asked people what they wanted, they would have said faster horses.

—HENRY FORD

"Asking people what they want doesn't necessarily mean they can tell you about the next big thing. It just tells you what they already know about what they want. So if you do focus groups and marketing things and all this, it doesn't mean that you get a new product. You will just copy what's out there. So you have to have guts, and you have to risk as a company. We have to explore and sometimes ignore people's opinions," Markus says.

I asked Joe more questions about inspirations and innovation process.

"I get inspired by many different things, maybe within the design field but also outside of the design field. It has a lot to do with, I guess, different creative industries, such as art, fashion, music, film. I draw inspiration from different fields even more so than from my own field.

Everything I see in my own field, it's kind of already been done. So you look for inspiration elsewhere. For me it's also a lot about materials, exploring things that haven't been done before, maybe not so much for the sake of being different, but for the sake of making it better. If a material is better, let's explore that. Sometimes it's about functionality but also making things that people need rather than thinking what is trendy or what sells right now. For my partner and me, it's much more about let's do fewer products with higher quality, fewer products but better products. That's always been our motto.

"You asked about students before. For students, it is always important to say that you can't be afraid; you have to take risks. I think risk-taking is something really, really important. You have to jump over your own shadow. Be willing to take risks. There isn't much to lose except to try, and it's okay to fail. It's okay to try and fail and try and fail over and over again until you find the right thing. In industrial design, failing is not something to avoid—it's something to embrace. Through this process of elimination and experimentation, we come to the answer. So you can't be afraid of failing.

"It's interesting because sometimes some of the phone companies put out so many different phone models, just to see what sticks. This is similar to what the Japanese have been doing. They are okay with trying things. Here in the U.S., try your own things but within your own walls. You try and try and you make prototypes and find the right thing, but in the end, you just put out one thing that will work. Hopefully, for everyone. That seems to be more successful and efficient. You are still trying and failing a lot, but you are only putting out what you think will be successful. You create a language that's consistent over time. I think this is the weakness of some companies—they put too much out there, and they don't have much of a focus.

"Having taken all these risks and having a lot of options, you then have to filter things and bring them to their essence. The product can have so many different features and so many things that are interesting, but it gets confusing. There are such complexities. You have to be able to distill the complexity down to something very simple, at least in product design." Joe concludes.

Risk-taking is a relatively new concept in Korea. There are good reasons why we don't want to embrace risk-taking but also why we should. "It's a very difficult thing because there needs to be a lot of money behind it, which will be risked. It can be only done with a great mission, a design mission. If something is risky, that means it hasn't been done before, or it's something new that you don't know about. That's the definition of risk. Not many people are taking risks. Because their careers are at risk, the money is at risk, whatever it is at risk. Apple always takes a risk. I'm not sure how to describe to you the makeup of Apple's formula. Why we are doing things differently than the rest of the companies. We are the richest company in the world, so somehow we do it right. Whenever we develop a product, we really think things through. It's not about creating hundreds of products. We design one product, and we do it right. Absolutely right. And it can be very risky, too. I don't know how else to describe it to you, Sun." Markus says.

"What prevents a company from being innovative? How does a company cross that line from playing it safe to taking the risks and being innovative and a leader?" I asked Markus.

"I think finding alignment and consent is integral to Korean culture. So when you make a decision, everybody has to agree. Then the boss says yes. If everybody agrees, and they do the focus groups and research, and everybody likes this one concept, they decide that this will sell the most.

That's the mistake they make. It's not about what everybody agrees on. It is not about what makes money. This is not how design can be done. Because then this design is already old and doesn't mean anything. Because you cannot design what everybody likes. When the iPhone came out, that was revolution. It was an evolution of the smartphone. There were touch screens out there already, but it created a new type of UI (user interface) that wasn't out there before. You have to have balls. You have to take risks in order to be innovative and create new markets, to create excitement in the market. You can't just water it down to what everybody likes because that's what's going to sell. Nobody's going to be excited about this. Maybe a lot of people will buy it, but nobody's going to be excited about your brand. Decisions are made by many, many people trying to find consensus within the company and get the blessing of the big bosses. But that's part of Korean culture. Nobody says, 'Let's do something new. We are going to revolutionize this. Let's do something else.'"

> *To me consensus seems to be: the process of abandoning all beliefs, principles, values, and policies in search of something in which no one believes, but to which no one objects; the process of avoiding the very issues that need to be solved, merely because you cannot get agreement on the way ahead. What great cause would have been fought and won under the banner "I stand for consensus?"*

— MARGARET THATCHER

THREE DESIGN PRINCIPLES

Markus created these design principles in 2005 while he was working at IDEO. The way he describes them, "They have to work in accordance. They have to be in balance with each other. We don't think you can do anything if you are missing one of these principles. They all have to be engaged. They all have to be activated. We also think that these principles apply to life, to the way you lead your life. It's about sharing, collaborating, and opening up to other people who are better at something that you can't do."

1. **Humanize.** Make things according to the users' needs. Make things friendly. Make things approachable. Humanize the product. Understand the emotional parts of the product. Create a passion between the user and the product. The product has to have levels of wowing the users. Whether it's a tactile experience or inside of the product.
2. **Think beyond.** Think outside the box. Jump over your own shadow, over boundaries, to see what's possible. Make it different. It needs to have or do things that other products don't have or do. Users should be proud to own the product. It's crazy different even though it's familiar. It's humanized but in a new way.
3. **Zero in.** Focus. Make it essential for the user's life. Make it integrate so easily that the user doesn't even feel it. When you design something, get rid of the redundancy. Filter things out. Find the essence of things. When you design something, you don't add all this superficial stuff. When Steve Jobs designed the Apple iPhone, they said, "One home button is enough. On and off switch is enough. You don't want to have all these features. Make it as a simple as possible for everybody to understand."

It's interesting to realize that these design philosophies and principles are very similar in their nature, regardless of how old they are, where they are from, who articulated them. They all call for "simplicity."

Less is more.

— Mies van der Rohe, one of the pioneers of modern architecture.

IMPOSSIBLE INNOVATION PROCESS

Jeric Park shed some light on Samsung's process. "Designers are high quality nowadays in Korea. If you look at Samsung, they do have very strong stuff. It's just that they have to deal with the bureaucracy. If they do something new and creative, if they innovate something that's never been done before, there is no way to back it up. They cannot defend it. It's not defensible. In order to defend it, the only way is to have a reference. But it's a huge dilemma. The upper leadership says, 'I want innovation with proof.' And if it has proof it is not an innovation. The only way to get through that senior leadership approval is to actually say, 'Apple does this.' It comes from the ignorance of upper management.

"So the next step toward innovation is to say, 'We will do something like Apple but much faster, much cheaper and with higher specifications. We will add more features than ever.' That was a way to compete. The market still accepts that. It is embarrassing for designers. On the other hand, there are designers who are not aware of ethics in design. There is a big generation gap, but it is changing company by company. The upper management, they don't understand it. They don't get it. Most of them, they got there not through right qualifications but through line. Line is like a branch/line of 'personal' connection within an organization. When you meet Samsung people, they talk about line all the time. Whose line are you? Basically how you line up changes your life. It has been that way for a long time now. It is changing a lot, but it's not going to go away until there is a complete transition from the old generation to the new."

THE DESIGN TALENTS

One of the many tasks of running a design firm is interviewing graphic designers. Over the past twenty years, I have interviewed perhaps several hundred, yet if you asked me to name the five best, I would have a hard time. Not because there are more than five, but because there aren't five that stand out. Its hard to find a great designer—a true visionary who reshapes how we see the world around us. Maybe because great designers approach problem-solving in a different way than most people. They push boundaries and find unexpected answers and even unexpected questions. We were and are very fortunate to have many excellent designers working with us; they were not easy to find.

Most of the reputable design studios in the West are small shops. The reason for this is many creative people don't want to deal with corporate politics or climb the ladder within the structure of big companies. Designers who have revolutionary ideas that are not familiar to a mainstream audience will find it hard to implement their vision within a rigid work environment. It doesn't take a lot of capital to start a design business, so many venture out and set up their own shops, like Carlos. This is very common in the West across many industries—some big companies have great reputations, but very often the best work is found at a "boutique" company.

I'm hearing that there are a lot of good small design shops in Korea as well. Now I'm curious about young designers in Korea. What are they interested in? What is their future in the world of design?

FEELINGS VERSUS WORDS

Markus did several design workshops in Seoul a few years ago. One of them was at SADI (Samsung Art and Design Institute). He also did the same workshop in San Francisco and Bangkok. I asked him to share his experience of the workshop in each place.

The task was to design a product in three days using his three design principles that were mentioned previously. It was interesting how students from different parts of the world reacted to this task.

"The Korean students did something I liked a lot. Their approach was very poetic. The idea was to design an alarm clock. The principle 'Humanize' seemed to resonate a lot with the students. So, for example, instead of showing the digits on the watch, they liked to see the projection of the moon and sun coming up. This kind of more metaphorical design—more emotional, metaphorical design. That's what they liked a lot. For example, for an iPhone, you have a lot of gestures with swiping or pinching with your fingers. It's more like behavioral stuff. That's what they liked a lot. Your alarm clock, instead of using a button to switch it off, you will make a gesture—you will throw it against the wall, or stand up, or smell the coffee, then you will wake up. That's what they were into. You know what I mean. It's this kind of humanized approach that I liked a lot. They had a lot of ideas like this. I wondered where this came from.

"Americans didn't have that. For them, it's was more like 'Okay, let's design a really cool watch with a projection.' It was very technical. But the Koreans were very emotional about it. I worked for Coway. I did an air cleaner for them that won many prizes and awards. In Korea, now, it is one of the best selling air cleaners. It has a hole in it that symbolizes air: the air travels through a hole. They really liked this metaphor that we're traveling through the hole that was symbolized by that design, you know. Samsung uses flowers in their design. Colors symbolize certain things. There are symbols everywhere, metaphors—in your advertisements, everywhere—there are symbols. Pick up these symbols, put them into a design but make the design super simple."

I had been wondering about why Korean dramas are so popular in many countries with different cultures. When I was chatting with young K-pop fans in Miami, they told me that they watch Korean dramas also. Several of them repeatedly mentioned that Korean people seem to have 'pure emotions'. Initially, I was taken aback by those words describing Korean people. So I asked them to elaborate more on their meaning of 'pure emotions'. Brad Batstone answered, "The [actors] we do see on TV, in movies, and music videos are often expressing extreme emotions. For example, while the characters can be over the top sometimes, we see how different these shows are from American dramas, and we associate Koreans with having stronger emotions. At least some of us believe that Koreans are capable of expressing emotions to a greater degree than others."

Henry Lau, a Taiwanese Canadian singer, former member of Super Junior M (a K-pop band) and, a composer, was on Yu Huiyeol's Sketchbook, a Korean pop music program. Henry said that he is a foreigner, that Korean people can tell he is a foreigner by his music; they say it sounds too much like foreign pop. So he asked Yu Huiyeol how he could obtain that "Korean" vibe? And Yu Huiyeol told him, "It [the music] needs to be sad, but romantic at the same time. You need to melt the hearts of those listening."

I watched some K-dramas myself for research purposes and then got hooked too. They do a really good job of catching the human moments in very tender and sweet ways and revealing raw emotions in sad or devastating situations.

Brad articulated K-drama's attributes well by saying, "I guess if we had to put it into words, I think that Western culture, especially

American culture and music, cares more about getting to the point. The focus is on the words and what you say, whereas in Korean culture, the focus is on how you feel, the emotions that the melody and moment bring you. So while these may not be perfectly accurate, they do shape how we see Koreans, and thus some people might believe that Koreans have purer emotions or are better at sharing them."

SIMPLICITY AND METAPHOR = KOREAN DESIGN?

In our conversation about Korean versus American design, Markus continued, "If you combine these two, simplicity and metaphor, you have a Korean design. That's what I saw. Samsung does that very well. This is where the power could be. If they see these ideas as their roots, this is what Koreans could be in UI (User Interface) or in many designs. They should not saturate it too much, though. If they put too many flowers in their designs or too much symbolism, then Westerners won't like it. So that was the feedback I got from that workshop, more specifically from SADI.

"The other thing was the amazing amount of ambition. They were very eager to come up with the best thing in the least amount of the time. Here in the U.S., students don't have that kind of ambition or desire to put out their best work. They're lazy, the American students. They don't have this striving to change the world. They kind of think design is a cool thing. The Japanese have ambition too. Germans have it with all their hearts. They are passionate about it. I didn't feel that Americans in the schools where I taught had that passion. Koreans were very passionate. I don't know where that comes from. Maybe the teachers are strict. 'If you don't do it by tomorrow you are out?' I know that Samsung is very strict in general. If you don't make it in school, your future is kind of doomed. It's part of the system. In Germany, too. You have a free school system; however, you have this innate struggle, innate ambition to change, to be the very best in everything you do. Look at the German car manufacturers. In America, we don't have that many examples except Apple, where I work. We want to be the best in everything we do. We have this ambition. Not many companies have that. Japanese companies have that. Samsung has that. Not many companies or people have that. I felt that in Korean culture, it's there."

DESIGNER'S PASSION

On top of having a good portfolio, one of the things I look for in designers is: Is this person passionate about design? What does that mean? That means being a designer is not just a job, but it is a much bigger part of their lives. When you are passionate about something, you are more curious, more alert, more observant, more motivated. You enjoy what you do and that makes you a better designer.

Markus elaborated on why it's important to have a passion. "Otherwise, why would you do anything? With everything you do in life, why would you do what you do? Design is a very competitive market. You have to have a passion in order to distinguish yourself. Only with a passion and love for your profession can you distinguish yourself. Only passion helps you to stand up again when you fall. Only passion gives you that power to move on and move up. Design is not easy. Design involves understanding business and manufacturing. It's not just designing shapes, it's understanding the business. You have to have the passion for the business. I think also as a designer you have to be passionate about all kinds of designs. I draw my inspirations from everything, from architecture to cars to fashion. I'm very much into fashion; all the fabrics they come up with are very important. I design backpacks as well as chargers, headphones and humidifiers. I design almost everything, whether it is soft or hard, and these materials come from everywhere. Right now, everything is connected. Technology and lifestyle nowadays are connected, so you have to be interested in all these things."

Joe added, "Being passionate allows us to endure our failures and push on until we achieve our goals. I believe that passion is what gives us the willpower to stick with something, to not give up, to explore, and to ultimately succeed."

"Some people live their passion each and every day, while others search for it throughout their lives. The key is first to identify what makes you happy, inspired, fulfilled, excited, purposeful—or even outraged. In other words, find something that moves you to be your best self, to take on a cause or a challenge that deserves your time, attention and intention."

DESIGN STUDENTS. HIGH HEELS AND BEAMERS...

Markus shared something he noticed at the Arts Center in L.A., where he studied. "There are a lot of Koreans now, and they come from rich families. LA has a history of Koreatown, and there are a lot of rich Koreans in LA. The Arts Center became a place where a lot of rich Asians go. Many of them are not very talented. So these girls, they come to school with their big Beamers and high heels. They walk around in high heels in the shop. In my time, there were a lot of talented people there. They were poor and had no money, but they were very talented. Now it has shifted. I don't see a lot of talent there. You find that they don't work as hard as some other designers from other nations. In Korea SADI, they look for the best students they can find. In Korea, I didn't see issues like this as far as good designers, but here I'm not sure how that works. I haven't seen many Korean American students with the same attitudes that the Korean Korean students I saw in my workshop in Seoul had."

Hungry students work harder, as their life depends on it. That's what Markus saw at the SADI design workshop: young, passionate future designers. Design is a serious business. It requires talent and hard work. Many young people choose design because they like fashion or cool products, or because they think it's an easy profession. For those who come to school in high heels, I would say, "Let's learn to show your creativity, not your superficiality or how rich your parents are. Plz. leave your heels at home."

CAPTURING THE SPIRIT

Korea is at the forefront of technology and has developed a strong manufacturing and distribution base. Our next challenge is to rediscover our Korean heritage within a design language that speaks to the world and better represents who we are as a culture. We have noteworthy and substantial arts, styles, and expressions. We have so much to build upon.

One of my main discoveries in Korea in 2008 was seeing the many streets and neighborhoods with lots of great places to go, eat, and see things that got me excited and would be interesting and enjoyable for foreigners as well. How grateful I was to see the Samchungdong neighborhood with its old houses and the old structures converted to shops, galleries, and restaurants. These are the jewels of Korea. These are the places where people can get a glimpse at our past and appreciate our culture. As familiar as they are to Koreans, they are refreshing and very interesting to outsiders. Right now, the major cities are being transformed and beautified and redeveloped. The planner/visionaries of Korea, whether they are government officials, organizations, or influential individuals, must work hard together to protect and treasure whatever old remains—whatever represents the history of people and culture. Any place can have modern buildings and modern things, but no other place has your history and culture. That's precious.

The world still doesn't know much about Korea. We have so much to highlight what is Korean. It has become a habit for us to believe that anything from the West is better than what we have. The world is starting to notice that many things from Korea are cool, different, and desirable. The Western market is always hungry and ready for things that are different and innovative—and so is our own next generation.

FINDING THE KOREAN VOICE

Joe got to know more young creative Koreans. "They were already in a sort of creative, independent, and happy environment. Some of them used to work for Samsung, and they couldn't stand it. They went outside and found their passion. They found their own thing. So the people I know over there are much more into the creative culture already. They talked about how they grew up in a very strict environment. How it is customary to go out with coworkers at night, and you have to go drinking, you have to do all this etiquette stuff and still show up the next morning, even if you are drunk or even if you have a hangover."

Melissa Kim says, "The Korean government and also companies don't realize how much Korea can influence and play a bigger role in global governmental relations or economics. They still are not confident enough to step up to where Korea needs to be. They are very afraid and still like to follow orders or copy what other advanced nations do instead of coming up with new and original thinking and policies that could benefit Korea as well as many other nations and people."

Markus liked the potential of the young designers he saw at SADI workshop several years ago, and he sees things are definitely changing. "They (Samsung) are developing their own UI. They have good designers there, and the technologies they use, their housings, the quality of the phones is really good. You have to maintain this quality somehow. It's not just Samsung; there are whole other companies like Coway. The designs Coway put out are really good. I worked with Coway designers. They are pretty good designers."

Yet he doesn't believe Korea can become a strong global driver in design. I asked, "Why not?"

"Because of the setup of the industry there. It can only become a country that does well in the design field. It'll never have its own voice. This is the fabric of how the industry is built. It's too hierarchical.

"Look at Samsung. They don't usually do the risky things. They don't do the emotional things, or they don't do the simple things. They always leave out one of those three principles. I'm not sure. It might be up to Samsung to decide what design will be in the future. Maybe the design culture within Samsung will change.

"GS is one of the biggest companies in Korea. They invited us to design products for them. These guys were pretty cool. They have other designers working for them already, international designers. If you go to GS shops, they have really cool brands. Many sub-brands are created within the big brands in order to relate to young Koreans. Because young Koreans, they get tired of all this mass commercialism."

Jeric Park says, "The most important thing is understanding good design and making the educated design decisions. We don't have that yet."

Park gave an example. "The middle manager will say to you, 'Sun, I love your design.' Then he takes it to the top executive, who says, 'I don't like it,' without giving any reason. Then the middle manager would say, 'I don't like it either. That looks pretty bad.' People are very influenced by those in power. They are very afraid of being decisive. The top executives are the problem."

I asked Park about his level of confidence in Korean designers' abilities.

"It's very high. I would say A-minus, or four out of five. In terms of leadership or dealing with the committees, I would say about two." I asked, "What do we lack the most in our own design ability?" Park responds, "Creativity. Accommodating and supporting innovation is our biggest enemy. I do a lot of lectures, and I've seen a lot of designers doing the same thing. They try to get accepted by others by showing what they are already familiar with. Let's say you are doing a cafe. They show a cafe in London, and then you show a cafe that is different and new in Korea but looks a lot like a London one. People would say, 'Oh, it's a good cafe because it looks like a London one.'"

OUR TURN

Let's hope Markus' assumption that Korean design will never have its own voice is misguided. If we're aware of the obstacles to originality—such as rigid hierarchical structures—we can try to modify or eliminate them so our imaginations can run away from the familiar and toward original ideas.

Korea is at a turning point. The young are ready to develop their visions, using our country's unique strengths and traditions as well as global ideas. We are all shaped by our cultures and though that has its limitations—as I have written about extensively in this book—it also has great benefits. The specifics of culture—the ideas, images and experiences you grow up with and know in your bones—are the raw material of innovation in the arts and sciences, as in business and politics. They are what have emotional resonance for you. Culture gives you a perspective that's different from those who grew up elsewhere. You can let yourself be blinded by it (seeing only what you grew up seeing), or you can use it to reveal new aspects of the world to a larger audience. Korea is on the verge of doing this. Everything that may seem old-fashioned or limiting can also be refreshing, exotic, fascinating. It's a question of how it is framed. I am not only talking about how Korea and Korean culture looks to foreigners, but how Korea can look to its young creative thinkers, those who can take different pieces of the puzzle—Korea, Europe, America, and other parts of Asia—and create something new.

The downsides to Korean culture that I have explored in this book—conformity, rigidity, too much focus on status, money and looks, lack of family intimacy—are all things that can work against creativity. Is it possible that some of them can also serve creativity? The Western ideal of the creative person is one who is most of all an individual, which is opposite of conformism. Can we find the strength of our weakness; that is, use our conformity and focus on social cohesion and agreement to work on unlocking creative potential in the most explosive way? Cultural qualities, like personal qualities, develop for a reason. When these qualities dominate too much, it can be tempting to go to the other extreme, but the wiser course is to look for the value in what you have and trim away the parts that aren't working, that belong to the past. Conformity avoids conflict—often at too great a price—but conflict for its own sake isn't good either. Imagine if we could have social cohesion without stifling freedom and imagination.

I believe Korean creativity can exist without giving up the desire to aid society as a whole; we can have a creativity that actively seeks to include and honor the contributions of others. This is not a new idea; the West is coming toward it from its own direction (crowdsourcing—the process of raising funds or soliciting ideas or content from a large group of people, especially an online community—is a good example of this). Korea is a society of smart, striving workers with a tradition of respecting the needs of society as a whole. If we can remove the stigma from risk-taking, we can encourage our young innovators without becoming a people addicted to adrenaline and the individual above all. We can realize that life is change and change is exciting without becoming a throwaway culture. We can soften our focus on looks and money without denying the importance of aesthetic pleasure and material security. We can realize that creativity is the recognition and exploration of what is different in every person, country, or era. It is everywhere.

Let's stop the culture of automatic copying and start creating our own things. Korean things. The world will appreciate and value Korea's own designs. They are just waiting for them to arrive. Young Koreans are much more exposed and eager. Their global curiosity is the highest from all the Asian cultures. It's like saying we want our turn. Ready to take charge.

The Invitation

It doesn't interest me what you do for a living. I want to know what you ache for and if you dare to dream of meeting your heart's longing.

It doesn't interest me how old you are. I want to know if you will risk looking like a fool for love for your dream for the adventure of being alive.

It doesn't interest me what planets are squaring your moon...
I want to know if you have touched the centre of your own sorrow if you have been opened by life's betrayals or have become shriveled and closed from fear of further pain.

I want to know if you can sit with pain mine or your own without moving to hide it or fade it or fix it.

I want to know if you can be with joy mine or your own if you can dance with wildness and let the ecstasy fill you to the tips of your fingers and toes without cautioning us to be careful to be realistic to remember the limitations of being human.

It doesn't interest me if the story you are telling me is true. I want to know if you can disappoint another to be true to yourself. If you can bear the accusation of betrayal and not betray your own soul. If you can be faithless and therefore trustworthy.

I want to know if you can see Beauty even when it is not pretty every day. And if you can source your own life from its presence.

I want to know if you can live with failure yours and mine and still stand at the edge of the lake and shout to the silver of the full moon, "Yes."

It doesn't interest me to know where you live or how much money you have. I want to know if you can get up after the night of grief and despair weary and bruised to the bone and do what needs to be done to feed the children.

It doesn't interest me who you know or how you came to be here. I want to know if you will stand in the centre of the fire with me and not shrink back.

It doesn't interest me where or what or with whom you have studied. I want to know what sustains you from the inside when all else falls away. I want to know if you can be alone with yourself and if you truly like the company you keep in the empty moments.

—ORIAH MOUNTAIN DREAMING

References

1   Kaste, Martin. (2012, July 11). Korean families chase their dreams in the U.S. *NPR.* http://www.npr.org/2012/07/11/156377938/korean-families-chase-their-dreams-in-the-u-s

2. Israel, Ronald C. (2012, Spring Summer). What does it mean to be a global citizen? *Kosmos.* http://www.kosmosjournal.org/article/what-does-it-mean-to-be-a-global-citizen/. "A global citizen is someone who identifies with being part of an emerging world community and whose actions contribute to building this community's values and practices."

3. Shafak, Elif. (2010, July). The politics of fiction. *TED.* https://www.ted.com/talks/elif_shafak_the_politics_of_fiction/transcript?language=en

4. Landphair, Ted. (2012, March 29.) Remembering at the Korean war memorial. *Voice of America.* http://blogs.voanews.com/tedlandphairsamerica/2012/03/29/remembering-at-the-korean-war-memorial/   http://www.cbsnews.com/news/how-many-americans-died-in-korea/

5. M*A*S*H*. CBS. 1972-1983. https://en.wikipedia.org/wiki/M*A*S*H_(TV_series)

6. O'Dea, Terri. (2013, March 20). My happy place: Seoul, South Korea. HVBIZ. com. http://www.hvbiz.com/profiles/blogs/my-happy-place-seoul-south-korea

7. World Economic Forum. The Travel & Tourism Competitiveness Report 2015. http://www3.weforum.org/docs/TT15/WEF_Global_Travel&Tourism_Report_2015.pdf

8. Breen, Michael. (2004). *The Koreans.* (New York: St. Martin's Griffin).

9. Ibid.

10. Quote attributed to many people over the years. The closest early match is a Texas newspaper article in 1977 citing Frank Outlaw, the owner of a chain of supermarkets.

11. Marx, Patricia (2015, March 23) About face. *The New Yorker.* http://www.newyorker.com/magazine/2015/03/23/about-face

12. Ibid

13. Ibid

14. Ehrenfeld, Temma. Plastic surgery doesn't build self-esteem. (2012, December 12). *Psychology Today.* https://www.psychologytoday.com/blog/open-gently/201212/plastic-surgery-doesnt-boost-self-esteem

15. Ramsey, Meaghan. (2014, September.) Why thinking you're ugly is bad for you. *TED.* https://www.ted.com/talks/meaghan_ramsey_why_thinking_you_re_ugly_is_bad_for_you?language=en

16. Marx, Patricia (2015, March 23) About face. *The New Yorker.* http://www.newyorker.com/magazine/2015/03/23/about-face

17. Ibid.

18. http://blog.naver.com/tokitoc/20198530544

19. Greenberg, Alissa. (2015, June 2). 'Helicopter Parenting' hurts kids Regardless of love or support, study says. Time. http://time.com/3904527/helicopter-parent-study-controlling-students-kids-children/

20. Everett-Haynes, La Monica. (2013, March 19). The dangers of 'overparenting.' The University of Arizona News. https://uanews.arizona.edu/story/the-dangers-of-overparenting

21. Kamenetz, Anya. (2015, August 29). How schools are handling an overparenting crisis. NPR. http://www.npr.org/sections/ed/2015/08/28/434350484/how-schools-are-handling-an-overparenting-crisis

22. 12 ways to raise a competent, confident child with grit. (2015, May 28). AHA! parenting.com. http://www.ahaparenting.com/blog/10_Ways_to_Raise_a_Competent_Confident_Child

23. Skolnik, Deborah. n.d. How to stop helicopter parenting. Parenting.

http://time.com/3904527/helicopter-parent-study-controlling-students-kids-children.

24. Murcko, Tom. n.d. Focus on process, not outcome. *How to Live.* http://www.howtolive.com/focus-on-process-not-outcome/#.VnLoAWAVcqY, by Tom Murcko

25. Henrich, Joseph. (2015). Princeton: Princeton University Press.

26. Mendes, E., Saad, L., & McGeeley, K. (2012, May 18). Stay-at-home moms report more depression, sadness and anger. *Gallup.* http://www.gallup.com/

poll/154685/Stay-Home-Moms-Report-Depression-Sadness Anger.aspx?utm_source=alert&utm_medium=email&utm_campaign=syndication&utm_content=morelink&utm_term=All%20Gallup%20Headlines

27. Kolata, Gina. (2005, Nov. 29). Is there a link between stress and cancer? *The New York Times.* http://www.nytimes.com/2005/11/29/health/is-there-a-link-between-stress-and-cancer.html?_r=0

28. Wingert, Pat. (2009, July 9). 5 Biggest Mistakes of Mothers- in-Law. *Newsweek.* http://www.newsweek.com/5-biggest-mistakes-mothers-law-81797

29. Chua, Amy. (2011, Jan 8). Why Chinese Mothers are Superior. *The Wall Street Journal.* http://www.wsj.com/articles/SB10001424052748704111504576059713528698754

30. Yon, Hwangbo. (2015, October 20). In South Korea, fathers are strangers. *The Hankyoreh.* http://english.hani.co.kr/arti/english_edition/e_national/713641.html

31. Yogman, M., Garfield, C.F. Fathers' role in the care and development of their children: The role of pediatricians. (2016, July). *Pediatrics. 2016, 138*(1):e20161128. https://pediatrics.aappublications.org/content/pediatrics/early/2016/06/10/peds.2016-1128.full.pdf

32. Esther, Lee; Da-hye, Kim. (2015, October 2). Studies show involved fathers have positive effect. *Korean JoongAng Daily.* http://koreajoongangdaily.joins.com/news/article/article.aspx?aid=3009792&ref=mobile

33. PRI. (2015, August 10). Could a Korean reality show really make men be better fathers—and husbands? http://www.pri.org/stories/2015-08-10/could-korean-reality-show-make-men-better-fathers-and-husbands

34.   LaPorte, Nicole. (2011, May 6). The Korean dads 12-Step program. *The New York Times.* http://www.nytimes.com/2011/05/08/magazine/mag-08Here-t.html

35.   Esther, Lee; Da-hye, Kim. (2015, October 2). Studies show involved fathers have positive effect. *Korean JoongAng Daily.* http://koreajoongangdaily.joins.com/news/article/article.aspx?aid=3009792&ref=mobile

36.   Kreger, Randi (2013, August 22). The invisible power of childhood emotional neglect. *Psychology Today.* https://www.psychologytoday.com/blog/stop-walking-eggshells/201308/the-invisible-power-childhood-emotional-neglect.

37.   Society for Personality and Social Psychology. (2012, June 12). A father's love is one of the greatest influences on personality development. *Science Daily.* Web. http://www.sciencedaily.com/releases/2012/06/120612101338.htm

38.   Blake, Matt. (2014, February 3). South Koreans drink TWICE as much the Russians and more than five times as much as the Brits. *Daily Mail.* http://www.dailymail.co.uk/news/article-2551059/South-Koreans-drink-TWICE-Russians-five-times-Brits.html#ixzz3umtGcRBq

39.   Cha, Christopher. (2015, April 23). How to survive a drinking session in Korea. *CNN.com.* Web. http://www.cnn.com/2015/04/23/travel/parts-unknown-bourdain-korea-drinking/ CNN how to survive a Korean drinking Frenzy

40.   Ornishi, Norimitsu (2008, June 8.) For English studies, Korean students say goodbye to Dad. *The New York Times.* http://www.nytimes.com/2008/06/08/world/asia/08geese.html?_r=0

41.   Goh-Grapes, Agnes. (2009, February 22.) Phenomenon of wild goose fathers in South Korea. *The Korea Times.* http://www.koreatimes.co.kr/www/news/nation/2009/02/117_40060.html

42. Reed, Bronwen. (2015, June 15.) 'Wild geese families': Stress, loneliness for South Korean families heading overseas to gain edge in 'brutal' education system. *ABC News*. http://www.abc.net.au/news/2015-06-16/thousands-of-south-korea-families-apart-for-australian-education/6547604

43. This American Life. (2015, September 18). What's going on in there? *WBEZ*. http://www.thisamericanlife.org/radio-archives/episode/567/whats-going-on-in-there, 9.18.2015

44. Sang-Huan, Choe. (2009, November 1). South Koreans struggle with race. *The New York Times*. http://www.nytimes.com/2009/11/02/world/asia/02race.html?ref=southkorea

45. https://www.youtube.com/watch?v=sNq9j_lg5Pk

46. Izawaru. n/d. Multicultural Korea: 'Dirty' foreigners spoil the sauna water and spread AIDS. *The Three Wise Monkeys.*

47. Shafak, Elif. (2010, July). The politics of fiction. *TED.*

48. Allen, Erika. (2015, May 7). Something rotten in New York City nail salons. *The New York Times*. http://www.nytimes.com/times-insider/2015/05/07/something-rotten-in-the-state-of-nail-salons/

49. Demick, Barbara. (2004, August 4.) In S. Korea, a silver lining to being bi-racial. *Los Angeles Times*. http://articles.latimes.com/2004/aug/06/world/fg-amerasian6

50. (2015, May 23.) Pity the children. *The Economist*. http://www.economist.com/news/asia/21651873-once-among-biggest-sources- infants-international-adoption-south-korea-stemming, May 23rd 2015, 01:00

51. R.L.W. & D.H. (2015, March 4). The glass-ceiling index. *The Economist.* http://www.economist.com/blogs/graphicdetail/2015/03/daily-chart-1

52. OECD Employment Database 2014. https://www.oecd.org/gender/data/genderwagegap.htm

53. Jung-a, Song. (2013, June 11). Asian women face glass ceiling. Financial Times. (http://www.ft.com/cms/s/0/50242166-ce60-11e2-8313-00144feab7de.html#axzz4JOo3j1wI, June 12, 2013

54. Lee, B. J. (2013, July 30). Samsung's female executives shatter South Korea's glass ceiling. Newsweek. http://www.newsweek.com/samsungs-female-executives-shatter-south-koreas-glass-ceiling-65613

55. McNamara, Alix. (2016, June 6). The world's 100 most powerful women. Forbes Magazine. **http://www..com/power-women/#tab:overall**

56. Southerton, Don. (2009, April 17). Legal implications of harassment in the workplace. Korealegal.org. http://www.koreaexpertwitness.com/blog/commentary/legal-implications-of-harassment-in-the-korean-workplace/

57. Chamie, Joseph. (2014, March 6). Women more educated than men but still paid less. YaleGlobal. http://yaleglobal.yale.edu/content/women-more-educated-men-still-paid-less-men

58. (2014 March 28). Women in the workforce. The Economist. http://www.economist.com/blogs/banyan/2014/03/gender-gap-japan#comments

59. Seigel, Jordan I., Pyun, Lynn, & Cheon, B.Y. (2010, August 31). Multinational firms, labor market discrimination, and the capture of competitive advantage by exploiting the social divide. Harvard Business School Working Paper

60. Gladwell, Malcolm. (2006). The Tipping Point. New York. Little, Brown and Company.

61. Rosin, Hanna. (2010, Dec). New data on the rise of women. TED. http://www.ted.com/talks/hanna_rosin_new_data_on_the_rise_of_women?language=en

62. Chung, Connie. (Spring 1995). Korean society and women: Focusing on the family Yisei. http://www.hcs.harvard.edu/~yisei/issues/spring_95/yisei_95_30.html

63. Raymond, Joan. (2009, Jan 22). Men, women and IQ. Newsweek. http://www.newsweek.com/men-women-and-iq-87117

64. http://en.wikipedia.org/wiki/Married_Women's_Property_Act_1882

65. http://europa.eu/epic/countries/denmark/index_en.htm

66. Miller, Claire, Cain, (2015, May 15). Mounting evidence of advantages for mothers of working children. The New York Times. http://www.nytimes.com/2015/05/17/upshot/mounting-evidence-of-some-advantages-for-children-of-working-mothers.html

67. Sandburg, S. (2013) Lean In: Women, Work, and the Will to Lead. New York: Knopf http://www.ted.com/talks/sheryl_sandberg_why_we_have_too_few_women_leaders68

68. Ibid.

69. Commander Kim, (2013, Dec 24). Korean mothers scared to take maternity leave. KoreaBang. http://www.koreabang.com/2013/stories/korean-mothers-scared-to-take-maternity-leave.html

70. Kotkin, Joel. (2011, Oct. 27). Overpopulation isn't the problem: It's too few babies. Forbes. http://www.forbes.com/sites/joelkotkin/2011/10/27/overpopulation-isnt the-problem-its-too-few-babies/2/

71. Baer, Drake. (2016. Feb 1). South Korea's gender problem could lead to an existential crisis. *Tech Insider.* http://www.techinsider.io/why-south-korea-is-becoming-the-oldest-country-2016-1

72. Baer, Drake. (2016, Jan 21). The only way Japan can solve its devastating sex problem. *Tech Insider.* http://www.techinsider.io/how-japan-can-solve-its-sex-problem-2016-1?pundits_only=0&get_all_comments=1&no_reply_filter=1#comment-56a1c20ee15ce56b052bb579

73. Kang, Michelle. (2012, Dec 21). *Korean Joongang Daily* http://koreajoongangdaily.joins.com/news/article/article.aspx?aid=2964272

74. Alvarez, Gloria. (2014, Oct 18) representante de Guatemala (Movimiento Cívico Nacional Guatemala) - en Zaragoza, España. Organizado por Red Iberoamérica LIDER. www.iberoamericalider.org. https://www.youtube.com/watch?v=xkYEXS16dZA

75. Shaffir, Stav. (2015, Jan 21). True Zionism speech.https://www.youtube.com/watch?v=mfyFlK5bkPU

76. Zakaria, Fareed. (2012, Feb 8). A more peaceful world if women in charge? *CNN.* http://globalpublicsquare.blogs.cnn.com/2012/02/08/a-more-peaceful-world-if-women-in-charge/

77. Having a furry friend may enhance, extend human life. n.d. http://missouri-families.org/features/healtharticles/health119.htm

78.   Stone, Dan. (2013, March 1). 100 million sharks killed every year, study shows on eve of international conference on shark protection. *National Geographic.* http://voices.nationalgeographic.com/2013/03/01/100-million-sharks-killed-every-year-study-shows-on-eve-of-international-conference-on-shark-protection/

79.   Dog meat trade. n.d. http://www.hsi.org/issues/dog_meat/

80.   Korean activists, fighting for animals on the front lines. n.d. http://www.careanimalrights.org/

81.   Korea has kept the number one spot among countries in the Organization for Economic Co-operation and Development (OECD), which includes the United States, Australia, New Zealand, Europe, Israel, Chile, Mexico, Japan and Korea, for several years now.

82.   https://en.wikipedia.org/wiki/Happy_(2011_film)

83.   Waldinger, Robert. n.d. The study of adult development. http://hr1973.org/docs/Harvard35thReunion_Waldinger.pdf

84.   Waldinger, Robert. (2015, Dec 23.) What makes a good life? Lessons from the longest   study on happiness. *TED.*

85.   Widrich, Leo. (2012, August 8). What happens to our brains when we exercise and how it makes us happier. *Buffer Social.* https://blog.bufferapp.com/why-exercising-makes-us-happier

86.   Mercola, Joseph. (2015, January 23). The remarkable effects of exercise on cognition and brain cell regeneration. *Peak Fitness.* http://fitness.mercola.com/sites/fitness/archive/2015/01/23/brain-benefits-exercise.aspx

87. https://www.presidentschallenge.org/informed/digest/docs/199712digest.pdf

88. Huffington, Arianna. (2014, April 16). Arianna discusses 'Thrive' with Amy Chua. *The Huffington Post.* http://www.huffingtonpost.com/huff-tv/arianna-amy-chua_b_5159972.html

89. Kelly, Megyn. (2015, October 7). *Charlie Rose.* https://charlierose.com/videos/20413.

90. Hartley, Regina. (2015, November). Why the best hire might not have the best resume. *TED* https://www.ted.com/talks/regina_hartley_why_the_best_hire_might_not_have_the_perfect_resume/transcript?language=en

91. Lambert, Brent. (2011, June 11). The fascinating story of Einstein's childhood, his rebellious youth and his definition of God. *FEELguide.* http://www.feelguide.com/2011/06/11/the-fascinating-story-of-einsteins-childhood-his-rebellious-youth-and-his-definition-of-god/

92. Robinson, Ken. (2006, June). Do schools kill creativity? *TED.* http://www.ted.com/talks/ken_robinson_says_schools_kill_creativity/transcript?language=en

93. Corruption perceptions index 2015. *Transparency International.* http://www.transparency.org/cpi2015

94. Chico, Harlan. (2012, November 7.) In S. Korea, the best education means a sacrifice for the parents. *The Washington Post.* https://www.washingtonpost.com/world/asia_pacific/in-s-korea-the-best-education-means-a-sacrifice-for-parents/2012/11/05/6adb0564-256f-11e2-9313-3c7f59038d93_story.html, Nov. 3, 2012.

95.   Grant, Adam. (2016, February.) The surprising habits of original thinkers. *TED.* https://www.ted.com/talks/adam_grant_the_surprising_habits_of_original_thinkers?language=en

96.   Faroohar, Rama. (2010, August 16). The best countries in the world. *Newsweek.* http://www.newsweek.com/best-countries-world-71817

97.   Smudger. (2013, May 4). Avoiding conflict and the Korean in-laws. *South Korea Inside Out.* http://smudgem.blogspot.com/2013/05/avoiding-conflict-and-korean-in-laws.html

98.   Sutherland, Rory. (2011, December.) Perspective is everything. *TED.* http://www.ted.com/talks/rory_sutherland_perspective_is_everything?language=en

99.   Shafak, Elif. (2010, July). The politics of fiction. *TED.* https://www.ted.com/talks/elif_shafak_the_politics_of_fiction/transcript?language=en

100.   http://www.wikihow.com/Be-a-Nonconformist

101.   Longman, Jere. (2002, June 21). On SOCCER; South Koreans savior is found in Dutchman. *The New York Times.* http://www.nytimes.com/2002/06/21/sports/on-soccer-south-koreans-savior-is-found-in-dutchman.html

102.   Kocken, Michael. (2014, March 17). Seven reasons why Korean has the worst productivity. *Business Korea.* http://onehallyu.com/topic/277243-insider-perspective-seven-reasons-why-korea-has-the-worst-productivity-in-the-oecd/

103.   Fried, Jason. (2011, April). Why I run a flat company. *Inc.* http://www.inc.com/magazine/20110401/jason-fried-why-i-run-a-flat-company.html

104. Thatcher, Margaret. (2013). *Margaret Thatcher: the Autobiography*. New York, New York: Harper Perennial.

105. http://hua.umf.maine.edu/Reading_Revolutions/Confucius.html

106. Burkus, David. n.d. "The Peter Principle" and other reasons to think twice before accepting a new promotion. *Behance*. http://99u.com/articles/14856/the-peter-principle-and-other-reasons-to-think-twice-before-accepting-a-new-promotion

107. Bersin, Josh. (2013, March 20). How corporate learning drives competitive advantage. *Forbes*. http://www.forbes.com/sites/joshbersin/2013/03/20/how-corporate-learning-drives-competitive-advantage/#7dbac5d167fc

108. Xue, Faith. (2016, April 29). Career code: Allure's editor in chief on how to kill it in the workplace. *Byrdie*. http://www.byrdie.com/michelle-lee-allure-career-tips/

109. Phillips, Matt (2008, December 4). Malcolm Gladwell on culture, cockpit communication and plane crashes. *The Wall Street Journal*. http://blogs.wsj.com/middleseat/2008/12/04/malcolm-gladwell-on-culture-cockpit-communication-and-plane-crashes/

110. Kirk, Don. (2002, March 26). New standards mean Korean Air is coming off many shun lists. *The New York Times*. http://www.nytimes.com/2002/03/26/business/new-standards-mean-korean-air-is-coming-off-many-shun-lists.html

111. DeHart, Jonathan. (2013, July 16). Asiana Airlines crash: a cockpit culture problem? *The Diplomat*. http://thediplomat.com/2013/07/asiana-airlines-crash-a-cockpit-culture-problem/

112. Siler, Steve. (2015, November 25). Peter Schreyer talks Genesis and Hyundai Design, G90 to debut by year's end. *CAR and DRIVER.* http://blog. caranddriver.com/peter-schreyer-talks-genesis-and-hyundai-design-g90-to-debut-by-years-end/

113. Choi, Kyung-AE. (2013, March 5). Q&A Hyundai design chief. *The Wall Street Journal.* http://blogs.wsj.com/drivers-seat/2013/03/05/qa-hyundai-design-chief/

114. Koren, Leonard. (2008). *Wabi-sabi for artists, designers, poets & philosophers.* Point Reyes, CA: Imperfect Publishing.

Acknowledgements

Million thanks and love to my husband Carlos for many evenings and weekends that we couldn't spend time together to write this book.

I also want to thank Meredith Martin, Shirley Ho, Shirley Chan, Ogan Gurel, Jane Lee, Jagie Daya, Jinsoo Seo, Pat Lee, Enric Turull, Armin Moehrle, Chuck Rudnick, and Claudine Lorme for their inputs and encouragements in different stages of this writing journey.

Author Bio

Sun Segura is partner and managing director of the award-winning design firm, Segura Inc. and the innovative digital type foundry, T26 Inc. Both companies are highly acclaimed in the international design community. T26 was a major force at the dawn of the digital type industry and has inspired many designers around world through its originality and rule-breaking designs.

Segura has successfully managed both companies for over 20 years. She speaks four languages and is an avid tennis player. She lives in Chicago and Miami with her husband and dog.

65713556R00223

Made in the USA
Lexington, KY
21 July 2017